A TWIST IN THE TAIL

CHRISTOPHER BECKMAN

A Twist in the Tail

*How the Humble Anchovy Flavoured
Western Cuisine*

HURST & COMPANY, LONDON

First published in the United Kingdom in 2024 by
C. Hurst & Co. (Publishers) Ltd.,
New Wing, Somerset House, Strand, London WC2R 1LA
Copyright © Christopher Beckman, 2024
All rights reserved.

The right of Christopher Beckman to be identified as the author
of this publication is asserted by him in accordance with the
Copyright, Designs and Patents Act, 1988.

Maps © Ben Pease, Pease Press Cartography.

Distributed in the United States, Canada and Latin America by
Oxford University Press, 198 Madison Avenue, New York, NY 10016,
United States of America.

A Cataloguing-in-Publication data record for this book
is available from the British Library.

ISBN: 9781911723417

This book is printed using paper from registered sustainable
and managed sources.

www.hurstpublishers.com

Printed in Great Britain by Bell and Bain Ltd, Glasgow

CONTENTS

ACKNOWLEDGEMENTS

Much like anchovies are often the hidden ingredient that elevates a dish to new heights of flavor, there are many people who worked their magic behind the scenes to make this a better book. I must begin by thanking the individuals who were essential to this entire undertaking: Pauline Harley in France, Daniele Calvani and Isabel Barrado in Spain, Karima Moyer-Nocci and Ilaria Edoardi in Italy, and the great Rebecca Dowd in Australia. Each of them was instrumental: tracking down obscure references, wading through the carnage of the early drafts, and diligently performing triage. They know where all the bodies are buried. My deepest gratitude to each of you. As usual, any mistakes are entirely my own.

For helping move the manuscript one step closer to publication, my appreciation also extends to Mi Zhou, Nayanika Mathur, Haruko Okusu, Helen Stevens, and Dianne Jacobsen.

In Italy, the great Sergio Premoli opened many doors in the pursuit of the Italian anchovy, and the wonderful June Di Schino deserves a special thank you for bringing a number of anchovy recipes to my attention. I would also like to thank Monica Barone, Massimo Montanari, and Filippo Ribani (who uncovered a trove of early Renaissance anchovy references). And special

ACKNOWLEDGEMENTS

thanks to Michelangelo Balistreri at the Museo dell'Acciuga e delle Arti Marinare outside Palermo, who helped piece together the crucial role Sicilian salters played in Italian and Spanish anchovy history.

For the often-elusive Spanish anchovy, I am indebted to Lurdes Boix of the Museo de l'Anxova i de la Sal, who took the time to guide me through the museum and bring the anchovy fishery in Costa Brava to life. A special thank you to Nik Duserm in L'Escala, as well as the delightful Jorge Zorilla at Conservas Juanjo in Santoña, who walked me through every facet of salting anchovies. Elisa Pérez Costas guided me through the wholesale fish market in Vigo, Spain. ¡Un millón de gracias!

Chris Kaplonski, Kate Haigh, and Philip Robins all added pieces to the British anchovy puzzle, and I am grateful to each of them.

A very special thank you to the immensely talented Elena Di Capita for the exquisite Gyotaku print gracing the cover. Ben Pease crafted the maps, and it has been a pleasure from start to finish.

Un grand merci to Michael Dwyer at Hurst Publishers for his support and vision in getting this book into print. Everyone at Hurst improved this book, especially my brilliant editor Alice Clarke, as well as Lara Weisweiller-Wu, Kathleen May, Daisy Leitch, and Niamh Drennan. A huge shout out to Raminta Uselytė for spreading the word and David Gee for the fantastic cover design. The eagle eyes of Rose Bell and Lusana Taylor-Khan will always have my appreciation.

But most of all I would like to thank my wife, Perveen Ali, who, throughout the writing of this book, has had to make room in our marriage for anchovies and endure endless drafts of the manuscript taking up valuable real estate on our dining room table. Without her keen insights and thoughtful revisions, this manuscript would never have arrived, and it is to her this book is dedicated.

INTRODUCTION

TANGLED TASTES—DECIPHERING ANCHOVY
PREFERENCES

Our relationship with food is a funny thing. It all begins simply enough with breast milk, which serves as a source of life-sustaining nourishment. But things become more complicated when we migrate to solid foods, as our newfound senses get in on the act. Our sense of smell perceives the aroma of food, our sense of sight detects visual cues, and our sense of touch (fingers, lips, tongue) alerts us to temperatures and textures, all of which contribute to whether we find food sublimely delicious, merely sufficient, or shudder-inducingly repulsive. Our associations with food are also deeply rooted in culture, drawing on our life experiences, the people and places around us, and our position in society. Whether we love or hate certain foods—such as anchovies— speaks as much to our culturally conditioned understanding of the world as it does to our sense of taste.

In Europe and North America, for every person who craves anchovies and sings their praises, there is someone else who simply cannot stand them. As one exasperated blogger succinctly stated: "The mere thought of them makes me want to vomit."[1] This kind of deep-seated loathing stands in stark contrast to the way in which anchovies are widely embraced in East and Southeast Asia, whether they are consumed regularly as fish sauce, sun-dried, or fresh. The anchovy divide in the West extends beyond the individual to the collective; in some countries, entire segments of the population are anchovy-mad, while in others, anchovies completely fail to register on the culinary radar. What accounts for such a range of attitudes?

Throughout the history of western Europe, conflicted feelings about anchovies have often had less to do with their flavor than their status. Writing in the sixteenth century, the Italian doctor Giovanni Filippo Ingrassia captured the prevailing sentiment when he cautioned that anchovies could be eaten on occasion, "as long as you don't fill the whole meal with [them] as the poor usually do."[2] The message was clear: anchovies are best left for the destitute. Anchovies were also shunned for social reasons, with the more refined members of society casting them aside in favor of larger fish with more status.

And yet, for every criticism hurled their way, we return time and time again to anchovies for their unique way of enhancing the flavor of food. Unsure of what to do with a piece of meat? Roast it alongside an anchovy or two or serve it with an anchovy-infused sauce. Stuck for a seafood recipe? Enliven it with a touch of anchovy. Most vegetables and salads pair beautifully with anchovies as well, whether draped across the top or whisked into a dressing or sauce. Whether we like it or not, we are physiologically hardwired to respond to anchovies, and they can work their magic in practically every dish.

Shortly after my father passed away, I wrote to my stepmother, Sue Wilkins, who is a professional chef, confessing that I was in the throes of yet another prolonged anchovy binge. It seemed as though every meal I prepared could be improved with the addition of a few (or a lot of) anchovies. As the weeks passed, my cupboards filled up with more and more anchovies in a variety of forms: oil-packed, salted, smoked, stuffed in olives, marinated in vinegar, pressed into paste, or melted into a sauce. I just couldn't get enough.

"You know," my stepmother replied in one of her emails, "your father loved anchovies." *Really?* My heart skipped a beat. My father was somewhat of a private man, and I never knew that we shared a love of anchovies. It was both reassuring and heartening to learn that we had this curious connection. Was I the recipient of an "anchovy gene" from my father? If so, it certainly skipped my siblings; in fact, it is only recently that my sister reached a sort of *détente* with them, diplomatically recognizing their right to exist.

My father's love of anchovies shouldn't have surprised me, for he was a sort of lapsed gourmand who lazily rode the foodie bandwagon in his later years. Before he retired, he and my stepmother opened the restaurant Little City Antipasti Bar in North Beach, San Francisco. He ran the front of the house, and she was the Executive Chef out back. "I remember the first meal that your father ever cooked for me when we began dating," my stepmother wrote to me. *What does one cook for a professional chef on a first date?* "He made 'Roman Lamb' infused with anchovies from *The Gourmet Cookbook*," she reminisced. "He won me over with that dish."

Anchovies may not seal the deal with the love of your life like they did for my father, but they can certainly improve your next meal if given the chance. My own biased and highly unscientific investigations have revealed a fascinating paradox: if you prepare a meal and subtly season it with anchovies, but neglect to mention this to your dinner guests, the almost universal response is enthusiastic. People love the taste without knowing why, and the compliments flow like wine. But if you mention afterwards that the meal contained anchovies, invariably, a few of your guests will become decidedly cooler in their feelings about it. Even more disheartening, if you announce before dinner, say over drinks, that anchovies will be present, then a fair percentage of your guests will have mixed feelings about the dish *before they even try it!*

Another problem with anchovies in America is that until very recently, most canned anchovies were of horrendous quality. All too often, the anchovies offered for sale in American supermarkets are packed in the lowest-quality oil—rarely olive oil—and are often borderline rancid. To make matters worse, many Americans' first encounter with an anchovy is with the cheapest, slightly bitter variety that is sold in bulk to low-end restaurants, exposed to oxygen for weeks on end, and then unceremoniously dumped onto a pizza.

In many parts of the world, on the other hand, people treat anchovies with far more respect. They are packed in glass containers with good-quality olive oil, taste delightfully meaty with a clean flavor, and can be eaten straight out of the jar, as the great American food writer James Beard liked to do. In Italy, anchovies are widely consumed across all segments of society. Whether they are minced into a marinade, added to a vinaigrette, mashed into a paste, or simmered with garlic, olive oil, and chili flakes, anchovies are an indelible part of Italian cuisine. In Spain, *per capita* consumption of anchovies currently stands at a staggering 5.9 pounds per person annually (although that was not always the case, as we shall see).

Traditionally, Americans have boosted the flavor of their food with animal fats and butter. Who hasn't discovered the joys of rendered duck fat, for example? Like all animal fats, it brings tremendous flavor to food, imbuing dishes with a depth of umami that supplies instant gratification. But sadly, duck fat is terrible for you, as are animal fats more generally. Anchovies, however, deliver a burst of umami richness without the artery-clogging complications associated with animal fats. In fact, anchovies are good for you. They are loaded with amino acids, B vitamins, and omega-3 fatty acids, and their bones are an excellent source of calcium. Unlike stock cubes, which are loaded with salt and a whole slew of ingredients that tend to muddy the culinary waters, an anchovy fillet simply adds umami.

Umami is at the heart of what makes anchovies so special. Preserved anchovies—whether salted, packed in oil, or marinated—have some of the highest levels of umami known in the plant and animal kingdoms, and this explains their recurring role in western European cookery for the last 2,000 years.

For most of our history, just four tastes have been recognized: sweet, sour, bitter, and salty. These four tastes were first singled out in the fifth century BCE by the pre-Socratic Greek philosopher Democritus. Aristotle and Plato repeated the mantra of four tastes, and so it went—with a few notable exceptions—until an exceptionally astute Japanese chemist named Kikunae Ikeda, working temporarily in a German laboratory between 1899 and 1901, first hypothesized that there might be an unidentified additional taste.

In the course of his research, Ikeda noticed something peculiar: there appeared to be something in common, taste-wise, among seemingly unrelated foods such as asparagus, tomato, cheese, and cooked meats, and this went beyond the four tastes that were recognized at that time. Equally intriguing, Ikeda recalled that *dashi*, corresponding to the name of a traditional broth used ubiquitously in Japanese cuisine, was made from Kombu seaweed and dried fish flakes. It too did not align with any of the four officially recognized tastes. Might there be an unrecognized fifth taste?

Upon returning to Japan, Ikeda set about analyzing Kombu seaweed (*Laminaria japonica*) to tease out the chemical foundation for its unique flavor. After months of painstaking chemical reductions, his original pile of seaweed yielded a tiny amount of slightly brownish crystals with the molecular formula of $C_5H_9NO_4$: glutamic acid. As Ikeda continued to distill the glutamic acid, he found that by adding a single sodium molecule, he obtained its sodium salt, which exploded with flavor when sprinkled on food. This was the fifth taste Ikeda had been searching for. Ikeda named this new taste "umami," after the Japanese verb *umai*, meaning tasty or delicious (Fig. 0.1).

Fig. 0.1: Kikunae Ikeda (1864–1936) coined the term "umami" to describe the newly discovered elusive fifth taste. Unlike sweet, sour, bitter, and salty —which are all straightforward and need no explanation—umami is far more complex and difficult to define. Among the proposed candidates: savory, brothy, earthy, musty, protein-y, mouth-watering, and mushroom-like. (*Courtesy of the Umami Information Center.*)

INTRODUCTION

When we talk of umami, what we are really talking about is glutamate. Glutamate (or "glutamic acid") is one of the most prevalent amino acids in plants and animals, as shown in Table 1 below.

Table 1: Umami content of different foods. Anchovies, fish sauces, and dried mushrooms are all potential "umami bombs," as the common expression goes, with some of the highest proportion of free glutamates.[3]

Food category	Free glutamate (mg/100g)	Food category	Free glutamate (mg/100g)
Seafood		*Fungi*	
Anchovies (cured)	1,200	Shiitake (dried)	1,060
Sardines	337	Shiitake (fresh)	71
Scallops	44	Button mushrooms	42
Salmon	33	Truffle	9
Meat and poultry		*Cheese*	
Ham (air dried)	337	Parmigiano Reggiano	1,680
Chicken (raw)	44	Roquefort	1,280
Beef (raw)	33	Stilton	820
Pork (raw)	23	Gouda	460
		Camembert	390
		Cheddar	182
Vegetables		*Milk*	
Tomatoes (sun-dried)	648	Human breast milk	19
Tomatoes (fully ripened)	200	Goat's milk	4
Tomatoes (green)	20	Cow's milk	1
Green peas	106		
Garlic	99		
Spinach	48		
Green pepper	10		
Cucumber	1		

Fruits and nuts		Dried seaweed	
Walnuts	658	Kombu	
Avocado	18	(Saccharina	
Grapefruit	5	japonica)	3,200–1,400
Apple	4	Nori (Porphyra	
		yezoensis)	1,378
		Wakame (Undaria	
		Pinnatifida)	9
		Fish sauces	
		Japan/Vietnam/	
		Thailand	1,383–950
		Soy sauces	
		Korea/China/	
		Japan	1,264–782

However, we cannot taste the vast majority of these acids as they are in the wrong chemical shape to bind with the taste receptor cells that carpet our tongues. Bound glutamic acid is so called because it is bound to a protein molecule, and, as a result, is tasteless. The other naturally occurring form is called free glutamic acid ("L-glutamate," or just "glutamate" for short), which, as the name implies, is an "unattached" glutamate molecule, which is umami-rich.

It takes cooking, roasting, broiling, boiling, fermenting, ageing, and curing to break down the proteins attached to glutamic acid and releasing the free glutamates. The moment a plant or animal dies, its organic matter starts to break down and glutamate molecules begin the process of freeing themselves from the proteins. Only then does the glutamate react with the receptors on our tongue to initiate the magic of umami. This explains why some foods generate enormous amounts of umami (like cured anchovies or sun-dried tomatoes), while others (such as raw anchovies or cucumbers) do not. One striking example of this can be observed with Italian cured ham (prosciutto). Initially, raw ham has practically no free glutamate content, but with consistent ageing and the ensuing breakdown of proteins, the free glutamate content rises dramatically and eventually one arrives at umami-rich prosciutto.

If you've ever wondered why tomatoes are rarely combined with other fruits, it's owing to their extremely high levels of glutamate (one of the highest of all fruits and vegetables). Because of their exceptional free glutamate levels, tomatoes pair exceptionally well with other savory flavors such as cooked meats and fish, cheese, and mushrooms, all of which are also high in free glutamates. Dried seaweed and fish sauces are off the charts in umami, as are soy sauce and fermented beans. Fresh anchovies, like all fresh fish, are extremely low in glutamates, but as they are cured and aged, their proteins break down and their glutamates skyrocket. When a cured anchovy encounters the glutamate receptors on one's tongue, a cascade of electrical signals is sent to the brain triggering a release of neurotransmitters. These neurotransmitters create a unique pattern of neural activity at which point you say, "Damn—that was good."

A Twist in the Tail explores how anchovies have navigated the shifting currents of western European and American cuisine starting with the Roman era. Since that time, the popularity of anchovies has fluctuated wildly, going in and out of fashion. The anchovy has been both highly valued as a flavor enhancer, and disdained as a worthless little fish, often simultaneously. As we will see, this ambiguity speaks to how the status of a seemingly simple fish can become entangled with gastronomic trends, class, and larger questions of identity. Anchovies provide a unique lens through which to examine European and American culinary history.

A TWIST IN THE TAIL

Each country has developed its own relationship with anchovies. The ancient Romans were the earliest group in Europe to harvest and consume anchovies on a truly industrial scale. When it came to Roman cuisine, *garum* (a fish sauce often made with anchovies) was the name of the game. Yet some ancient authors (and their modern counterparts) were quite conflicted about it.

In France, anchovies were a cherished flavor enhancer used increasingly from the mid-seventeenth century to the beginning of the nineteenth century, when they reached their high point and seasoned practically everything. But then everything changed, and no fish fell out of favor as fast as the anchovy in France. This begs the question of what caused their downfall, and why they were largely abandoned.

Fortunately, anchovies are highly adaptable, and in Britain, they were reinvented several times to suit evolving food norms. Perhaps no country in Europe has utilized anchovies in such diverse ways over time. The most profound evolution started with increased trade from Southeast Asia, which set the stage for the incarnation of the British anchovy we know today.

In some countries, anchovies were flat-out rejected, as in the curious case of northern Spain. Even though modern Spaniards consume more anchovies than anyone else in Europe, for most of their history, anchovies suffered the wrath of elite disdain, which trickled down the social ladder, limiting their appeal across all classes of society. Not until Italian immigrants turned up on the Cantabrian coastline did things take a happy turn for the better.

Even in Italy, where anchovies have been consumed more consistently than in any other European country, they have not been without their detractors. The great Italian chef Bartolomeo Stefani, for instance, utilized anchovies in many of his recipes. However, even he could not resist making an occasional below-the-belt comment. His recipe for grilled sturgeon—considered the king of fish—includes a "Salsa bastarda" made with amber and anchovy. Why the derogatory title? Amber was a princeling among ingredients, but the anchovy contaminated its purity, thus rendering it illegitimate.

Americans had little time for anchovies, preferring their fish with more meat on their bones. Nonetheless, anchovies eventually found a home at two surprising ends of the social spectrum, high society and poor immigrants. How they eventually gained wider acceptance is a tale of changing culinary tastes.

While the consumption of anchovies around the world has varied enormously, nowhere else have they proved to be as contentious as they were in Europe and America. It is this ambiguous status that anchovies have occupied that makes them so fascinating—and so revealing. Despite the occasional hostility directed towards them, anchovies have nonetheless managed to remain in the gastronomic game due to their extraordinarily high levels of umami. Even though early Europeans had no concept of umami, one thing many understood was that anchovies made their food taste better. A lot better.

Roskilde

Baltic
Sea

North Sea

York

BRITANNIA

Lünberg

Elbe

London

Thames River

Rhine River

Irish Sea

Danube River

Atlantic
Ocean

Seine

Poissy

Metz

Etamps

River

Auxerre

Salzburg

Orléans

Avallon

Loire River

Dijon

GAUL

Cluny

Geneva

Lyon

Cremona

Parma

Venice

Bay of
Biscay

Po

River

Comacchio

Bobbio

Ravenna

Genoa

Marseille

Arles

Rhône

River

Pisa

ITALIA

Ligurian
Sea

Marseille

Rome

Tiber River

Adriatic
Sea

Douro River

Ebro River

Castro dei Vosci

Naples

Amalfi

Barcelona

Pompeii

HISPANIA

Valencia

Mallorca

Tyrrhenian
Sea

Tróia

Ibiza

Guadalquivir River

Mediterranean Sea

Palermo

Ionian
Sea

Baelo Claudia

Malaga

Neapolis

Lixus

MAURETANIA

N

0   100   200 miles

0 100 200 km

1

THE ROMAN AND MEDIEVAL ANCHOVY

FROM SOUGHT-AFTER SAUCES TO
A SCARCELY GLIMPSED FISH

Throughout the Roman Empire, the fish sauce garum—*often made with anchovies—was consumed in vast quantities, from the far reaches of the Red and Black Seas, across the Mediterranean world, to the shores of the Atlantic Ocean. As a result, anchovies were one of the most traded commodities, after the Mediterranean trinity of wine, wheat, and olive oil. Roman aristocrats, ordinary citizens, freedmen, and slaves all consumed* garum *on a near daily basis. But then a curious thing happened. By the end of the Roman Empire,* garum, *the condiment king that had been cherished for more than 500 years, slowly faded away and disappeared from the ancient western world. The story of why this happened reveals a tug-of-war between taste and status that played out thousands of years ago, and this is where our journey begins.*

Garum *flavors the ancient Roman world*

To start at the beginning would take us deep into prehistory, when written records did not exist. Archaeology is yet to fully piece together the relationship between anchovies and people from that time. One could begin with the Phoenicians, as they also consumed anchovies and may have been responsible for the initial spread of fish sauce throughout the Mediterranean basin. We could even start a little later in time with the ancient Greeks, as they made ample use of anchovies, which they called *garos* (γάϱος), from which the Roman word "*garum*" derives. But instead of these tempting possibilities, we begin with the ancient Romans, as it is during this period that anchovies made a major appearance on the gastronomic stage of Europe.

During the Roman Empire anchovies were highly sought after, and huge hauls could be brought in over a relatively short period of time. Summer was high season for anchovies, and fishermen used nets to entrap large schools where they spawned in the warm waters close to the shoreline. However, because of their high oil content, anchovies decayed rapidly once caught and removed from the sea. This presented the fishermen with a challenge if they wanted to profit from their bounty. One solution was to convert the catch of fresh anchovies into a preserved fish sauce with a long shelf life.

The production of Roman fish sauce was quite straightforward in its fundamentals, although the number of technical variations and fish species that could be added into the mix was nearly infinite. From Latin texts, we know of four basic types of Roman fish sauce: *garum*, *liquamen*, *muria*, and *allec*. With the possible exception of *muria*, the manufacture of these different fish sauces followed the same basic production technique. In a large terracotta jar or cement-lined vat, whole fish (especially if they were small, like sardines or anchovies) or parts of larger fish cut into pieces (including their blood, organs, and viscera) were alternated with layers of salt. Everything from the smallest minnows to the largest bluefin tuna could be used to produce *garum*. As the salt drew moisture out of the fish, the sauce maker collected the liquid and poured it back over the top several times to increase its potency and flavor (Fig. 1.1).

Garum and *liquamen* were often cured in direct sunlight, typically for around three months, but sometimes for a year or more. Eventually, as the fish decomposed and their proteins began to liquefy, a golden-hued, semi-viscous, fermented liquid would emerge. This *garum* was then transferred to large terracotta vessels called "amphorae" so that it could be shipped throughout the Empire. Ancient Hispania (now modern Spain) was a major producer of *garum*, with salting factories dotting the coastline. One of the largest fish-salting and *garum* factories was located at Tróia (off Setúbal in Portugal). Over twenty-five dedicated workshops are thought to have produced up to 35,000 litres of *garum* a year. Another enormous *garum* production center operated in Neapolis (Tunisia). Perhaps the largest in the ancient world was

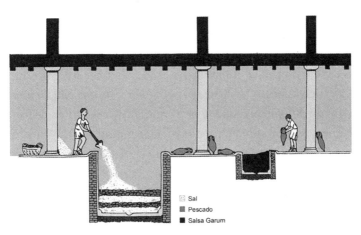

Sal
Pescado
Salsa Garum

Fig. 1.1: A contemporary illustration of industrial-scale *garum* production at Baelo Claudia in ancient Hispania (now southern Spain). On the left, a worker alternates layers of salt with fish to produce *garum*. On the right, a worker extracts fully fermented *garum* from a storage vat and transfers it to amphorae for transport. (*From* The Official Guide of the Archaeological Ensemble of Baelo Claudia, *p. 107. Used with permission.*)

located at Lixus (on the west coast of Morocco). As the cold waters off Lixus are particularly rich in sardines and anchovies, it is likely that these were the two main species of fish used in their version of *garum*.

The long-distance trade for *garum* flowed practically everywhere that Romans, or Roman outposts, were located. An amphora vessel used for *garum* was found near modern-day Salzburg, Austria, and numerous *garum* amphorae have been recovered in Switzerland, most likely transported via the River Rhône and across Lake Geneva. In Britain, archaeologists have recovered *garum* amphorae from sites in London and as far north as York and Hadrian's Wall. *Garum* amphorae have also been unearthed in the Near East. Lebanon, Palestine, Egypt, and the north coast of Africa have all yielded an abundance of such vessels, and literary sources indicate that all social classes in the Mediterranean basin consumed *garum* on a regular basis.

Curiously for such a popular Roman commodity, there is little modern agreement on just how to define *garum*, *liquamen*, *muria*, or *allec*. A contentious and long-running academic debate has centered on how different types of fish sauce were produced and which types of fish were used. Were *garum* and *liquamen* distinctly different products, or were they merely different names for the same or similar products? Depending on the time and place, both seem to hold true. Either way, until recently, modern scholars rarely mentioned anchovies in any of these discussions, as bigger and more prestigious fish dominated the conversation.

British researcher Sally Grainger has undertaken some of the most comprehensive studies of Roman fish sauce. By analyzing Latin texts in conjunction with extensive experimental archaeology recreating Roman fish sauces in a modern laboratory setting, Grainger arrives at the following definition: "*Garum* is a sauce made from the fresh blood and viscera of selected fish, mainly mackerel, fermented with salt." She then characterizes *liquamen* as being "made by dissolving whole small fish, as well as larger pieces of gutted fish (including the empty mackerel bodies used to make *garum*), into a liquor with salt." *Muria*, she says, is the liquor excreted by salted fish, a "less fishy" brine than *garum* or *liquamen*; and *allec* is defined as a by-product of fish sauce production—the leftover dregs at the bottom of the vessel—that could be used as a fish paste in its own right.[1] Thus, *garum* sits at the top of the fish sauce hierarchy, with *allec* at the bottom rung.

Perhaps. But perhaps not. The attempt to delineate and classify in such precise terms may be very scientific, but it leaves little room for the messy reality of variations and hybrids. Most likely, there were innumerable varieties of *garum* and *liquamen* that differed depending on the techniques and species of fish used to produce them. It is unlikely that any two fish sauces tasted the same, even if they shared the same name. French writer Maguelonne Toussaint-Samat summarized it best over three decades ago: "Each port had its own secret recipe for its own special brand of garum."[2]

Another problem with modern classification schemes is that they do not align well with what ancient authors say themselves, as their descriptions of *garum* veer all over the map. Some writers refer to *garum* as being made from the blood and viscera of mackerel, while others refer to tuna and other large fish. A few writers even cite smaller fish, like anchovies, as *garum*'s main ingredient. Another issue with using ancient authors to gain insight into fish sauces is that they did not understand the biochemical processes that produced *garum*: they believed *garum* was the result of putrefaction, rather than bacterial fermentation.

The conundrum that ancient authors wrestled with was how this supposedly rotten fish sauce also made food taste so much better, whether added to a simple vegetable stew served at the local greasy spoon or combined with a fine cut of lamb in a luxurious villa. This fundamental misunderstanding about *garum* left a slew of conflicted feelings in its wake. Artemidorus wrote that "garum is nothing but putrefaction," while Pliny the Elder, author of *Natural History*, the encyclopaedia of the ancient world, claimed that *garum* was the "secretion of putrefying matter."[3] The noted Stoic philosopher Seneca decried: "Do you not realize that garum Sociorum, that expensive bloody mass of decayed fish, consumes the stomach with its salted putrefaction?"[4] The poet Horace objected to *garum* in more prosaic terms: "It stinks."[5]

Everyone ate *garum* in the Roman world, but for elites, obsessed as they were with power, prestige, and decorum, *garum* acquired an ambiguous status. While Pliny the Elder claimed that it was produced through putrefaction, he also referred to it as an "exquisite liquid" that added "taste" to food.[6] In a similar manner, while Horace commented bluntly that *garum* "stinks," he also spoke of it as a "table delicacy."[7] Even Martial, who went so far as to compare the body odor of a woman named Thais to "an amphora of putrid garum," also referred to it as "noble" and devoted an entire epigram to it titled "The Proud Sauce."[8]

Despite some of the positive things written about *garum* in the past, it seems as though only *garum*'s negative aspects resonated with some modern authors. In his history of ancient Rome, the Italian historian Ugo Paoli's aversion to *garum* led him to remark, "Our stomachs would probably revolt at a dish prepared with garum."[9] Similarly, the usually reliable American food writer M. F. K. Fisher claims there is only one place to go after eating *garum*: straight to the "*vomitoria!*"[10] Even the grande dame of British classicists, the great Mary Beard, sneeringly describes *garum* as "that characteristically Roman concoction of decomposing marine life, euphemistically translated as 'fish sauce.'"[11]

Contemporary perceptions of *garum* have interfered with our understanding of it, reframing its earlier mass consumption as a gastronomic misstep, despite the fact that it is not so different from modern fish sauces consumed by over a billion people in

Asia every day. Compounding this problem, it is difficult to determine with certainty whether the comments of ancient authors were meant to be taken seriously or as satire. When the satirist Martial wrote, "Accept this exquisite *garum*, a precious gift made with the first blood spilled from a living mackerel," was he poking fun at the extravagant and sometimes absurd language used by Roman elites to describe their food and drink, or was he hinting at something else?[12]

Also, many modern authors tend to assume *garum* is made from mackerel, leaving anchovies and other smaller fish entirely out of the discussion. Archaeology, on the other hand, tells us a different story, one where anchovies and other small fish were major players in fish sauces *of all kinds*. To get an idea of just how prevalent they were, we turn to ancient Pompeii, a *garum* shop, and an extraordinary fish-sauce seller whose knack for marketing was far ahead of his time.

Scaurus and his rich fish sauce

At the foot of Mount Vesuvius in central Italy, near the mouth of the River Sarno on the Bay of Naples, lies the Roman town of Pompeii. In the early first century CE, Pompeii was a small provincial port town bustling with foreign traders. Pompeii was, in many respects, a typical Roman town with a small number of fabulously wealthy people and an enormous number of ordinary folks: tradesmen, artisans, the poor, and slaves. The proximity of the rich and poor defined ancient Pompeii; while the rich sipped the finest Falernian wine from a chalice, the poor were always nearby, often with a ceramic cup of cheap plonk in hand.

On the afternoon of August 24, 79 CE, Mount Vesuvius erupted in a series of cataclysmic blasts that over the next two days would blanket Pompeii and the surrounding region in hot ash. The pyroclastic surges that followed the initial eruption covered the town in a lethal brew of hot gas and pumice in depths up to 3 meters, sealing its fate and bringing untold misery and death to its inhabitants. But it also left the town in a remarkable state of preservation, as if frozen in time. Archaeologists love a good destruction layer, as the suddenness of such events can provide a snapshot into the lives and material culture of those who lived in the past. At Pompeii, one can reconstruct the city and its inhabitants with a remarkable degree of detail, something that is rarely possible at other sites.

By excavating the volcanic ash and pumice to reveal the city buried beneath, archaeologists and historians have been able to piece together the remarkable story of a freedman—a former slave—who amassed a small fortune. His name was Aulus Umbricius Scaurus, and he became rich producing, distributing, and selling fish sauce. Throughout Pompeii and the surrounding regions, 30 percent of the vessels for fish sauce that were recovered displayed Scaurus' tell-tale, hand-painted labels, which led one wag to dub him the "Ketchup King of Campania."[13] History journalist Heather Pringle calls him a "Campanian Tycoon," and one of his *garum* vessels was found as far away as the River Rhône in France, attesting to the international reach of his *garum* empire.[14]

Scaurus' newfound wealth elevated his extended *familia* out of poverty and into the ranks of Pompeii's elite. Such wealth also brought him a fine villa located on the western reaches of the town. Wealth in the Roman Empire, not unlike today, also brought civic standing, and no doubt paved the way for the election of Scaurus' son to the rank of magistrate. All his success and wealth, his villa, and the fine food and drink that came with it—a lifestyle of the rich and famous in modern parlance—was due to fish sauce. And thanks to the work of a number of archaeological specialists, we now know that much of the *garum* recovered in Pompeii was made from anchovies and other small fish.

Written sources indicated that Scaurus may have owned as many as six *garum* shops in Pompeii, run by members of his extended household. As an astute businessman, Scaurus made sure his name was prominent on his product, and some of his labels read "The best liquamen of A. Umbricius Scaurus," or "from the manufactory of Scaurus."[15] Other labels introduce a modified version of his name, such as "from the manufactory of Aulus Umbricius Abascantus," or "from the manufactory of Aulus Umbricius Agathopus."[16] Mary Beard suggests that these may have been slaves of Aulus Umbricius Scaurus, who "were now running workshops or other garum outlets that were still partly dependent on their old master."[17]

Given the scale of his business, it is plausible that slaves or former slaves handled much of the day-to-day operations, although there are indications that Scaurus' wife or daughter may have been involved as well. Serious business was always conducted in his villa, where greasing a palm or two ensured the smooth flow of business. But keeping an eye on his retail operations was probably part of his routine, as he checked in on current sales or inventory levels. Scaurus would have made his way about town on foot, and we can learn a thing or two about anchovies by imagining him strolling back to his villa from one of his *garum* shops.

As Scaurus set off down the street, the bustling city would have been alive with mercantile activity. A mosaic at the entrance to one house affirmed that commerce was foremost on the minds of many: "Profit is my joy."[18] Whenever money is involved, theft is not far behind, and a mosaic at the entrance of a different house served a more practical concern: "*Cave Canem*" (Beware of the dog). Passing a shop further down the street, Scaurus may have seen a hastily painted inscription next to a doorway: "A brass pot disappeared from this shop. If anyone brings it back, he'll be rewarded with 65 sesterces."[19] Technology aside, the lives and loves of Pompeii's inhabitants were remarkably similar to our own.

Sooner or later, Scaurus' walk would have brought him past the shop of one of his competitors in the fish sauce trade. While Scaurus may have been a *garum* kingpin, he did not have a monopoly, and we can be certain that this was not one of his own establishments, as not a single fish sauce amphora recovered within it mentions his brand name. First excavated in 1960, the anonymously owned "*garum* shop" was a converted private residence where archaeologists recovered almost a hundred fish sauce vessels, including the smaller-sized one called an *urceus* (plural *urcei*). Some of these were in active use at the time of the eruption, but many were stored upside down, and their labels, called *tituli picti*, indicate that they were in the process of being recycled. So well did the hot ash and pumice from the eruption of Mount Vesuvius seal these containers, that the excavators in 1960 noted that some still carried the distinct smell of fish sauce after nearly 2,000 years.

In 2019, the Italian archaeozoologist Alfredo Carannante published the first detailed analysis of fish bones recovered from one of the amphorae in the *garum* shop. The results of his research were not surprising for those who see small and locally caught fish as forming the backbone of the *garum* industry in Pompeii. Thousands of tiny fish bones were examined, from an estimated 515 individual fish. Carannante concludes that they were all one year of age and belonged to the same species of small fish that schools in the waters off Pompeii: picarels.

Modern fishermen catch picarels off Pompeii from August to mid-September, as the schools move in close to the shoreline. If the eruption of Mount Vesuvius occurred on August 24, then these picarels were probably caught during the first or second week of August. Why is this important? Carannante explains: "The garum composition in Pompeii reflects the strategies of the local human population exploiting its marine environment rather than gastronomic selection of specific species to produce certain recipes."[20] In other words, fish sauce manufacturers in Pompeii produced *garum* according to the availability of locally caught small fish, rather than trying to fulfill a recipe based exclusively on larger fish like mackerel and tuna.

Interestingly, picarels were not the most prevalent fish found in the *garum* shop. Anchovies were. While we cannot rule out that the owner of this *garum* shop might have had another facility that focused on larger and more expensive fish, the money-makers in this operation were clearly anchovies, followed by picarels. Just over a decade earlier, a joint team from the universities of Cadiz and Venice undertook a preliminary analysis of the remains found in the vessels of the *garum* shop. In the back garden, several large *dolia* were excavated and analyzed. *Dolia* are enormous earthenware vessels—some could hold over 1,000 litres—with wide rims and rounded bodies used for storing dry goods or fermenting wine. It appears that these *dolia* were converted for fish sauce production. Lining the inner walls and collected along the bottom of the *dolia* were the microscopic remains of anchovy vertebrae and scales. In the nearby courtyard, a further eight amphorae contained exclusively anchovy remains, three held the remains of picarels, and six more contained a mix of the two. A further six amphorae had carried a mix of all kinds of different fish, with anchovy bones being the most prominent, followed by a hodgepodge of sea bream, herring, shad, and a few other species, such as mackerel, tuna, and bonito.

Surprisingly, the excavation also revealed that some of the vessels contained fish sauces that were in *various stages of production*. Traditionally, it had been assumed that all fish sauce was manufactured along the coast in large operations, and that the *garum* shops in town were simply the retail outlets. But the presence of *garum* in various stages of production suggests that some operations were much smaller, even taking place in converted houses. Lots of folks were getting in on the act with their own versions of what we might call small-batch artisan *garum*.

The *garum* shop in Pompeii appears to have been a small operation that supplied the local population. But according to Pliny the Elder, Pompeii was one of the most important production centers for *garum* in the ancient world after Baetica, Mauretania, and Leptis Magna. If this was the case, and if anchovies were the dominant fish source in the Pompeii shops, should the hierarchy of quality fish sauce be reconsidered? Carannante appears to concur: "Maybe the anchovy and picarel *garum/liquamen* can be considered an elite item rather than a cheap common ingredient for everyday cuisine as often described."[21]

Carannante's conclusion takes us to the heart of the matter. Traditionally, *garum* was thought to refer to highbrow fish sauce made almost exclusively from mackerel and other large and pricey fish. Anchovies were considered second- or third-tier fish, and were either left out of the discussion, or dismissed as only featuring in lower-quality fish sauces. If *garum* was the most expensive kind of fish sauce manufactured, then how does one account for the fact that in Pompeii and the surrounding towns, *garum* labels have been found across all social classes, from elite residences down to the humblest abodes? Numerous working-class taverns also had ample supplies of amphorae with *garum* written on their labels, as did food shops and even a wine shop. In fact, as the American classicist Robert Curtis notes, "Of the nearly two hundred [fish sauce] vessels discovered so far in Pompeii and Herculaneum, approximately 118 were *garum* vessels, 52 *liquamen*, 21 *muria*, and 11 *allec*."[22] The same trend holds true for the city of Rome, and across the whole of Italy during this period. If *garum* was the most expensive fish sauce, made with only the finest fish, then we would expect to find it only in small numbers, with *allec* and *muria* being the most prevalent as these were consumed by the poor. But archaeology tells us the opposite, which reframes our understanding of *garum* and how all classes were consuming it.

Returning to Scaurus' stroll, we could imagine him passing several of Pompeii's 150 (at least) taverns, inns, or bars, though it is unlikely that the ever-present smell of *garum* would have lured him in for a bite to eat, as that would have been beneath his station. Scaurus would have eaten at home, with food prepared by his own cook. But perhaps in his younger days, prior to being favored by the gods, he might have been a regular. Modest houses in Pompeii lacked cooking facilities, and most inhabitants stepped out regularly for prepared food. Simple staples like bread, hard-boiled eggs, cheese, nuts, and fruit were probably kept on hand, but if you were hungry and wanted something hot, you headed down to the local tavern to get your fix.

So, what were people eating in taverns, inns, and bars in Pompeii? Based on the excavations of food remains, pulses represented a good portion of the locals' diet, lentils in particular. But foodstuffs do not get to the heart of what piqued their taste buds. For that, we should look to *Apicius*, the only surviving recipe compilation from ancient Rome. Lentils were a staple across the Italian Peninsula and were eaten very simply by most people, but *Apicius* presents us with a highly aromatic, flavor-forward version:

Another lentil dish "*aliter lenticulum*"

Cook (the lentils) when they have been skimmed, add in leek and green coriander. Pound coriander seed, pennyroyal, *laser* root, mint, and rue seed. Pour on vinegar, add honey, *liquamen*, wine, flavor with *defrutum*, add oil and stir. If it needs anything, add it. Thicken with starch, pour on green oil, sprinkle with pepper and serve.[23]

The first thing that stands out in this recipe is the *liquamen*, which happens to be the second most frequently listed ingredient in *Apicius* after black pepper. Over 350 of the 459 recipes in *Apicius* include fish sauce, and in that guise, our reliable workman anchovy would have found its way to many a genteel table.

If we truly want to understand what the Romans thought of fish sauces, then this statistic answers our question. Ancient Romans of all stripes loved fish sauces, and they used them on everything they ate. When *Apicius* was compiled in the late fourth century CE, *liquamen* was the preferred term over *garum*, but they should be thought of interchangeably, as only a high-quality fish sauce would have been included in an elite cookery book.

The lentil recipe found in *Apicius* also captures the complex flavors that characterized the Roman-era palate. A balance of sweet, sour, bitter, salty, and umami notes was the desired goal in all Roman cookery. In the lentil recipe, the directions call for skimming—or "descumming"—the pulses after they have cooked, indicating that dried rather than fresh pulses were used. The consistency of the final dish would probably have resembled that of a polenta-like gruel or thick soup.

Historian Florence Dupont writes that "Rome lived on vegetables," and the same could also be said for Pompeii.[24] Leeks, onions, cabbage, kale, and broccoli are all well represented in the plant remains excavated at Pompeii. As with any seaside town, fresh seafood was abundant. Indeed, paintings and mosaics depict the rich local catch: spiny lobsters, squid, eels, clams, and octopuses, as well as a wide range of fish. However, seafood was mostly destined for the tables of the truly wealthy, as it was too expensive to be served in restaurants and taverns. Given its high price tag, eating fresh fish conferred status, with large fish like bass, sea bream, and gilthead at the higher end of the spectrum and smaller fish like anchovies and picarels at the lower end. But one thing that stands out about the Roman Empire, especially in contrast to later periods of European history, is that all fish, whether large or small, had a certain degree of value.

As Scaurus continued down the street, he would have passed one of the grandest houses in Pompeii, now known as the "House of Marcus Fabius Rufus and the Golden Bracelet." A

"Golden Bracelet" was indeed found, but it is the *garum* amphorae recovered within the house that have the real story to tell. Cobbled together from several preexisting properties to form one grand estate, Rufus' home—adorned with fine sculptures, impressive paintings, and enormous mosaics—set the bar for refinement and taste. If ever there was a moment to uncover some high-end *garum* made from mackerel, this would have been it. What we find instead—surprise, surprise—is anchovies. Once again, contrary to the texts that speak of "noble" *garum* made with the first blood of a still-breathing mackerel, what we consistently find in Pompeii is *garum* made with anchovies and other small fish. This does not negate the claim in many Latin texts that some kinds of mackerel *garum* were considered the absolute best, much like an excellent vintage of Dom Pérignon champagne for us today. But how reliable are these texts as a guide to which sorts of *garum* were regularly consumed in Pompeii, even in the house of the phenomenally wealthy Marcus Fabius Rufus?

While Pompeii consistently yields amphorae with *garum* labels, the classicists Christopher Grocock and Sally Grainger adroitly point out that "[i]t is not unthinkable to imagine that many people were sold a fish sauce that was not quite what it said on the *tituli picti* label."[25] Given the lack of good manufacturing controls, untold numbers of amphorae might have contained anchovies and picarels and been labeled otherwise. Or, to quote Mary Beard, during the Roman Empire, "[t]rade was vulgar and traders untrustworthy."*[26] While deliberate mislabeling and recycling of fish sauce vessels help us appreciate the factors at play, might the sheer number of *garum* amphorae with anchovy resi-

---

* One cannot help but be reminded of the ongoing Italian olive oil scandal, in which producers regularly blend a range of lower-quality olive oils and then label them as "Extra Virgin," the highest grade.

due on their interiors indicate that something else was going on in Pompeii?

Some scholars have suggested that sauce makers might have regularly produced different classes of fish sauces (*garum, liquamen, muria, allec*) from *the same type of fish*, such as anchovies. In that case, might producers have manufactured a single batch of anchovy fish sauce, and then utilized the prized, clear liquid at the top for the highest grade *garum*, and so on down the line until they reached the dregs at the bottom which were sold as *allec*? This would help to explain why the labels of so many amphorae refer to *garum* (which traditionally was thought to refer to mackerel or tuna), yet the remains recovered within them are consistently anchovies. While we still lack enough detailed information, it appears that anchovies were the unsung heroes of Pompeii's fish sauce industry.

While the academic debate rages on, one thing is clear: fish sauce made Scaurus fabulously rich. As he arrived home to his multiplex villa, he would have had the option of using one of the three main entrances that opened onto the street. Each entrance led to its own *atrium* and *impluvium* (shallow water basin), but we will follow Scaurus in through the entrance at number 15 Vico dei Soprastanti. Upon entering the *atrium*, he would have glanced with pride at his grand mosaic surrounding the *impluvium*, which was unlike any other in Pompeii. Most mosaics feature geometric designs, ornamental elements, or decorative lines called "meanders," all of which would have confirmed the good taste and breeding of their owners. But Scaurus was a businessman *par excellence* who never missed an opportunity for self-promotion. Each corner of the meander band in his mosaic features an outline of an oversized terracotta *urceus* vessel of the type used to hold fish sauce (Fig. 1.2).

"Placing the mosaic vessels outside the meander," writes the classicist Robert Curtis, "was unusual and bound to attract

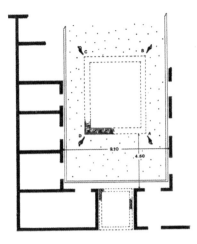

Fig. 1.2: Collected rainwater would have filled the center of Scaurus' *impluvium*, framed by a (badly damaged) mosaic meander border. At each of the four corners is an oversized *urceus* vessel, turning the floor of his atrium into an advertising billboard. (*Courtesy of Robert I. Curtis. Used with permission of the Archaeological Institute of America (Boston), from "A Personalized Floor Mosaic from Pompeii", published in the* American Journal of Archaeology *88 (1984); permission conveyed through Copyright Clearance Center, Inc.*)

attention."[27] Why would Scaurus break with the aesthetic traditions of good taste to which every other house in Pompeii conformed? Curtis argues convincingly that the larger-than-life-size *garum* vessels were designed so that visitors would inevitably read their inscriptions, unashamedly promoting Scaurus and his fish sauces.

Each mosaic in Scaurus' *impluvium* has a different label, requiring the viewer to walk around the entire water basin to read each one. The abbreviated inscription on mosaic (B) reads: G[ari] F[los] SCOM[bri] SCAURI EX OFFI[ci]NA SCAURI, which translates as "The flower of Scaurus' mackerel *garum* from the factory of Scaurus." The inscription on the second mosaic (C) reads: LIQUA[men] FLOS, which translates as the "Flower

29

of *liquamen*" (Fig. 1.3).[28] Although we do not know with certainty which fish Scaurus used in his *garum*, it is safe to say that his labels were selective in what they revealed, as most likely were many *garum* labels. A small *urceus* vessel was analyzed in the Museo Archeologico Nazionale di Napoli, with a label reading: "Flower of garum made with mackerel, a product of Scaurus from the workshop of Agathopodi."[29] Yet curiously, a preliminary analysis revealed almost exclusively anchovy bones, "with possibly a few elements of ... chub mackerel."[30]

Even repackaged as a mosaic, Scaurus' self-promotion was anything but thinly veiled, presenting a classic case of *nouveau riche* interior design. By contrast, old-guard Pompeiians displayed elegant mosaics in lavishly furnished villas, all conforming to the established standards of good taste. While Scaurus was accepted in some circles of the provincial town of Pompeii, the old guard would have looked down their noses at him, pegging him as a tawdry upstart and his home as a McMansion. It takes only a glance back at his inauspicious beginnings as a slave to understand why Scaurus would have wanted to flaunt his achievements and strove to imitate the material trappings of the elite, albeit in his own fashion.

Scaurus was exactly the kind of newly rich freedman that Roman satirists loved to lampoon in their writings. One of the most famous of these works is *The Satyricon*, written by Petronius in the first century CE. The chapter called "Trimalchio's Dinner" tells the story of a freedman and former slave of enormous wealth who hosts a dinner party. A central theme throughout the chapter is that nothing is as it seems, whether it is Trimalchio himself (who is rich, but a fool), or the food, which is disguised to resemble exotic flights of fancy. Trimalchio is portrayed as an uncouth, fat, balding man obsessed with his bowel movements and flatulence. Lording over the dinner table while picking his teeth with a silver toothpick, Trimalchio tries to impress his

Fig. 1.3: An archaeologist reveals some of the mosaics in Scaurus' *impluvium*, (A) The depiction of *garum* vessels (B) and (C) provides a glimpse into the mind and manners of a Pompeii entrepreneur who defied the odds. Photographs circa 1964. (*Special Collections, University of Maryland Libraries. Copyright (1964) University of Maryland.*)

guests (mostly freedmen themselves) with an extravagant dinner featuring dishes of absurd proportions. One of these over-the-top dishes is served with *garum*:

> As he [Trimalchio] said this, four slaves came forward with a solemn dance-step to the sound of music and took off the cover from the upper part of the tray. As soon as they had done this we saw, underneath the cover, capons and sows' breasts, and a hare with feathers stuck in its back so as to represent Pegasus. We observed also in the corner of the tray a figure of Marsyas [a Greek satyr and the son of Olympus], holding a wine-skin from which highly peppered *garum* sauce flowed out over the fish, which swam in it as though they were in a brook. The slaves began to applaud, and we all joined in vigorously, laughing as we fell to, over these choice dainties.[31]

The arrows of scorn are palpable. He is a figure to be loathed, as are his guests. At the end of the dinner party, Trimalchio boasts about having had a famous guest at his house, a certain Scaurus, that some scholars have linked to none other than our Ketchup King of Campania. Whether or not this was, in fact, our

Pompeiian parvenu, or some other, as certain scholars have argued, it indicates how someone like Scaurus would have been seen in his milieu.

It is easy to get caught up in debates surrounding historical identities and the composition and definition of fish sauces, but we should not forget that in the past, fish sauces were simply a seasoning that made food taste better. As a natural source of monosodium glutamate, they delighted the taste buds and excited the senses. Lest there be any remaining doubts about the ancients' love of *garum*, there is perhaps no better ode to this exceptional flavor enhancer than a letter recovered from an ancient dumpsite near the town of Oxyrhynchus in central Egypt. The papyrus note documents a mother trying to coerce her son to come home for the weekend. After some opening complaints about her failing health, she tempts him using the centuries-old tactic of home cooking—in this case, the promise of his favorite fish sauce. Every parent knows that you do not lure your children home with unpleasant-tasting food (however good for them it may be), but rather, you gently bribe them with their favorites, which in fourth century CE Roman Egypt included her son's favorite *garum*.

Top picks from Apicius *highlight the prevalence of* garum

As we first saw within our walk with Scaurus, the cookbook *Apicius* helps us to truly appreciate the Roman Empire's love affair with *garum*. Its recipe for "Another lentil dish" captures how the flavor enhancer is a versatile seasoning that adds complexity and depth to a wide range of dishes. With its origins tucked away in ancient Hellenistic kitchens, we may never know who first brought together the initial collection of recipes that bore its name. But regardless of how it came into being, its contribution to understanding Roman, medieval, and western

European gastronomy is invaluable. In his charming and eloquent introduction to *Apicius*, chef and author Joseph Dommers Vehling summarizes it best:

> The Apicius book is a living thing, capable of creating happiness. Some gastronomic writers have pointed out that the man who discovers a new dish does more for humanity than the man who discovers a new star, because the discovery of a new dish affects the happiness of mankind more pleasantly than the addition of a new planet to an already overcrowded chart of the universe.[32]

Apicius probably began life as an informal collection of Greek recipes meant for a high-status household. As Greek power waned and the Roman Empire rose, someone translated the book into Latin, and new recipes were added to the evolving collection. Based on the style of the Latin used, Christopher Grocock and Sally Grainger argue that most of its recipes date to no later than around 250–300 CE. Along with luxury dishes like boar, lamb, and sea urchins are recipes for much simpler fare, such as vegetables, grains, and pulses.

Early research attributed authorship of *Apicius* to the first-century CE Roman gourmand Marcus Gavius Apicius, but more recent scholarship argues against this. Writing in the second century CE, the Roman poet Juvenal said that "Apicius" signified a gourmand, one preoccupied with food. Grocock and Grainger draw upon this definition and argue that the term "Apicius" simply denotes "good food." All we really know with certainty is that it is currently the oldest known complete cookbook in the world.*

Just how it reached us, however, is far from certain. At some time around the sixth century CE, the *ad hoc* collection of reci-

---

* The earliest known collection of recipes comes from three small clay tablets from ancient Mesopotamia (modern Iraq), and dates from roughly 1700 BCE. Thirty-five Akkadian recipes are attested, but their fragmentary nature makes qualifying them as a cookbook problematic.

pes was compiled into book form, but that version was lost. Whose guiding hand structured *Apicius*, where, when, and why are all unknown. In fact, we only know of *Apicius* through two later ninth-century CE copies that were derived from the missing sixth-century parent. One copy is thought to have been used as a copying exercise for scribes, as it was written in various hands, while the other opened with richly ornate pages, crafted for a wealthy patron. Grocock and Grainger posit one such candidate as Charles the Bald—grandson of Charlemagne—the noted bibliophile who ruled the western part of the Carolingian Empire, from northern Italy to the Netherlands, between 843 and 877 CE.

Strangely, the *Apicius* trail goes cold for the next 500 years. It is as if someone tucked away the manuscript in a monastery or palace library and then promptly forgot all about it. No new copies were made or any mention of the book recorded until its fateful rediscovery by Enoch d'Ascoli, which will be recounted later in this book. After being rediscovered and brought back to Rome from Germany, a slew of manuscripts were hand-copied in the fifteenth century. Starting in 1458 and continuing for the next forty years, a new round of scribal activity resulted in seventeen new copies being scattered across Europe. It was almost as if the once obscure cookbook suddenly became a medieval bestseller, and everyone wanted a copy for their library (medieval manuscripts were far too valuable to be kept in a kitchen, and besides, most cooks could not read) (Fig. 1.4).

Apicius contains a total of 459 recipes divided into ten chapters including "Meat dishes," "Greens," "Fowl," "Pulses," "Luxury dishes," "Quadrupeds," and "Seafood." One of the remarkable things about the cookbook is that it reveals the conceptual framework that guided Roman cuisine. The ingredient combinations depict a palate that reveled in mixing savory flavors (roasted meats, grilled fish, *liquamen*) with sweet flavors

Fig. 1.4: Themes of abundance and pleasure were evocatively illustrated in this close-up of the frontispiece to Martin Lister's 1709 edition of *Apicius*. The attribution of the cookbook to "Apicius Coelius" was a medieval scribal error.

(honey, dates, sweetened wines), acids (vinegars), and bitter flavors (astringent herbs) to arrive at a complex, multilayered cuisine that contained, as seen in the recipe for lentils, all five tastes: sweet, sour, bitter, salty, and umami. Given the Roman penchant for complex and contrasting flavors, care needs to be taken when judging the recipes in *Apicius* against our western sensibilities, which often strive to capture the essence of a single (or a few) select ingredients in a dish.

Sadly, some modern authors, perhaps nudged along by Hollywood's "sword-and-sandal" epics, have interpreted the more theatrical and exotic aspects of *Apicius* to mean that Romans simply could not stand anything in its natural state and that all meals were a performance geared towards affirming status and power. Peacock brains, flamingo tongues, dormice, and lamb testicles are often cited as examples of such extravagance. Mary Beard points out that Hollywood loves nothing more than staging an indulgent Roman banquet scene, ideally followed by an orgy, or, failing that, the perennial favorite, a half-naked "barbarian" slave (i.e. a Christian) fighting a fetishized and leather-clad Roman. But the Roman banquet as portrayed in CinemaScope does not mirror what people ate on a daily basis, or even what they ate when they attended an actual banquet. Roman writers were often no more objective about food than their Hollywood counterparts. All too often, they would use food to demonize their enemies, criticize society, or nostalgically link themselves to a somewhat simpler, though mythical, past.

By and large, well-to-do Romans ate all kinds of simply prepared foods, such as roasted meats, vegetables, pulses, bread, and fruit, seasoned with whichever ingredients they had on hand. As the foundational seasoning, fish sauce was central to cookery, but there was nothing to suggest that dishes were heavily doused in it. While Petronius described a veritable flood of the stuff in "Trimalchio's Dinner," it is more likely that they used it widely but sparingly, perhaps a few drops added to some black-eyed peas to enliven them, or a splash used to perk up some roasted meat.

So beloved was the combination of *liquamen* and meat that out of the seventy meat recipes in the chapter "Quadrupeds," only six do not contain *liquamen*. Lamb was often stewed with a little *liquamen* in a pot or basted with it while roasting on a grill. The fish sauce intensified the lamb with no residual fishy taste. Even today, savvy Italians will rub their Easter lamb with anchovies and garlic the night before the big feast at the end of Lent.

Another ingredient that Romans were simply mad about was the herb *laser*, also known as *silphion*. Many of the recipes in *Apicius* that feature *laser* combine it with *liquamen*. It is hard to describe exactly how this would have tasted, as *laser* became extinct in the third century CE (legend has it that the last stalk was served to Nero). However, we know that the *liquamen* provided a salty and umami-rich complement to the bitter pungency of *laser*. Along with pepper, these two ingredients formed the foundation of flavor that defined many dishes in Roman cuisine. Take, for example, the following recipe from *Apicius* for fried fish with a herb sauce:

Herb sauce for fried fish *"ius diabotanon in pisce frixo"*

Prepare, wash and fry whatever fish you like. Pound pepper, cumin, coriander seed, *laser* root, oregano, rue, pound again; pour on vinegar, add date, honey, *defrutum*, oil, flavor with *liquamen*. Put into a pan, bring to heat; when it is simmering, pour it over the fried fish, sprinkle with pepper and serve.[33]

With the addition of dates, honey, and *defrutum* (a syrup made from grape juice) it would be easy to assume that this was an overly sweet sauce that escaped a modern-day child's menu. However, all three sweeteners were probably used quite sparingly, and the vinegar further helped to tame them. The goal in Roman cookery was always the same: a well-rounded dish that hit a number of different notes.

One seafood recipe found in *Apicius* took its name from the small town of Baiae, a fashionable, seaside resort located on the Bay of Naples. Given its proximity to Pompeii, it is likely that our fish-sauce seller Scaurus would have been familiar with both the town and the recipe named after it. Vehling notes that Horace liked the town, but Seneca and his ilk warned against it, shunning its all-night beach parties and houses of ill repute. Vehling sees this recipe as a precursor of the French-style bouillabaisse from Marseille and titles his interpretation of the recipe "Baian seafood stew." Grocock and Grainger interpret the recipe as more of a relish, perhaps a mezze-like side dish to be eaten with a little bread.

While *Apicius* contains a number of elite recipes for seafood, meats, and even exotic ingredients such as sows' teats and flamingo, what most people ate in the Roman Empire on a daily basis were vegetables and pulses, usually accompanied by bread or farro gruel. Cabbage was a staple around the Mediterranean world, and it was eaten in a variety of ways, boiled, stewed, pickled, and fermented. However it was prepared, it was often accompanied by *liquamen* as an essential flavor enhancer.

Surprising by western standards, the Roman love of *liquamen* even extended to fruits, and *Apicius* includes several recipes that are a testament to Roman culinary ingenuity, such as the following recipe for melons:

Long and round sweet melons *"pepones et melones"*

Pepper, pennyroyal, honey or passum, *liquamen*, vinegar. Sometimes silphium is added.[34]

While the pairing of a fish sauce with fruit might at first glance appear off-putting, the modern descendant of this recipe is not hard to find in the contemporary Italian recipe of *"prosciutto e melone."* Prosciutto is extremely high in umami and is slightly pungent, much like *liquamen*.

By adding *liquamen* to so many of their dishes, the ancient Romans had intuitively figured out something that modern science has only recently caught up with: we are hardwired to respond to the taste of umami. It is the electrical-chemical response triggered by the taste of umami that drove the ancient Romans to season so many of their dishes with *garum*. So why don't people in the West season their food with *garum* today, as they did in the past?

Garum *consumption declines as three key factors align*

Several factors contributed to *garum*'s slow decline in the western Roman Empire. First, and perhaps most significantly, the Italian archaeologist Claudio Giardino explains that when the Roman Empire entered its long and slow demise, salt—so essential to the creation of *garum*—became an increasingly valuable commodity as local authorities started to heavily tax it. What was once a cheap and plentiful resource increased in value until it was no longer financially feasible to utilize it for creating *garum*. An enormous amount of salt was required to produce a litre of *garum*, whereas just a pinch could be directly sprinkled onto food instead.

Second, in the fourth and fifth centuries CE, transportation systems broke down. Successive waves of "barbarian" migrations from the north weakened the Empire, and pirates raged across the Mediterranean Sea, making the shipment of *garum* exceedingly difficult when boats were attacked. Unlike dried spices or salt, which could be squirreled away in any nook of a boat's hold, *garum* required oddly shaped ceramic amphorae for transport. Ceramic pots required careful and extensive packing to withstand the relentless battering in a sailboat's hold.

The third factor in *garum*'s demise related to the changing foodways of the early Middle Ages. As *garum* (like all foods) could serve both as a symbol of identity among members of a group and as a marker that differentiated groups, it became symbolically charged. *Garum* was intrinsically linked to the Roman Empire, and for precisely this reason, it would also have been viewed as a marker of Roman culture by the northern tribes who started to exert their influence in the fifth century CE. The rejection of *garum*, like the rejection of the Roman Empire, became a way of aligning oneself with the new political powers that were sweeping down from the north and overrunning the western Mediterranean world.

With the different foodways that each culture embraced, the increasing value of salt, diminished trade, and the decline of the western Roman Empire, it is not difficult to see how *garum*—a once essential seasoning—fell out of favor. But despite its declining role, *garum* was still occasionally consumed. Through the records of a eighth-century tax treaty called the "Liutprand Capitulary," we learn that *garum* was sporadically consumed by elites in northern Italy. But in a twist entirely appropriate to our story, the origin of this *garum* was not the traditional coastal towns of the Italian Peninsula, but rather the distant shores of the eastern Mediterranean, perhaps by way of Constantinople. It seems that for elites of the period, the "Dark Ages" (at least gastronomically) might not have been so dark after all, thanks to the importation of golden-hued *garum*.

The last gasps of garum: *Comacchio and Anthimus*

The Italian archaeologist Sauro Gelichi had long been intrigued by Comacchio, a small town on the Adriatic coast of northern Italy near Venice. Comacchio attracted little interest in historical and archaeological circles, but Gelichi was curious as to why it was mentioned in the Lombard King Liutprand's Capitulary in the eighth century. Gelichi hypothesized that its trade must have been far greater and more valuable than suspected. Commencing excavations in 2007, Gelichi and his team were rewarded with some of the richest archaeological finds along northern Italy's 1,000 kilometers of Adriatic coastline. Buried just a few feet beneath the modern city of Comacchio, hundreds of thousands of broken amphora fragments lay untouched since antiquity, indicating that the town operated as a key trading hub that linked the Byzantine east with the Germanic west.

Gelichi and his team carefully examined the broken amphorae rims, handles, necks, bodies, and bases, as well as the types of clay used in their manufacture, and compared them to their eastern counterparts from Constantinople to Syria. They were able to piece together trade routes and identify the types of goods that were being exchanged. Oil, wine, spices, textiles, herbs, and incense were all shipped from ports in the eastern Mediterranean to Comacchio, where they were transferred to flat-bottomed river boats for transit up the Po River in northern Italy.

Part of the luxury cargo being transferred at Comacchio was an old Roman favorite: *garum*. This raised the question: who was consuming *garum* from distant lands in the eastern Mediterranean? As Gelichi and his team posit, some of it may have been intended for local elites from Comacchio whose political and cultural ties were still linked to the Byzantine Empire (where *garum* was still consumed regularly). But the sheer number of broken amphorae shards recovered in Comacchio forced the excavators to turn their attention upriver. Italian historians Alberto Capatti and Massimo Montanari similarly conclude that the elite Lombards (eponym for the northern Italian province of Lombardy) further along the Po River valley were the likely candidates: "In the eighth century," they write, "*garum* was sold along the banks of the Po by merchants from Comacchio, and Lombard rulers would request a payment of *garum* at the river port of Parma."[35] Italian archaeologist Alfredo Carannante and his colleagues reinforce this destination for *garum*, noting that the Lombard King Liutprand paid an officer of his army "a salary of a golden *solidus* (a Roman era coin of roughly 4.5 grams of gold), a litre of oil, a litre of *garum*, and two ounces of pepper."[36]

The Lombards originally hailed from southern Scandinavia, as Paul the Deacon wrote in his eighth-century *History of the Lombards*. From his account, we learn that the Lombards had been on a multigenerational march down through Europe, passing through northern Germany in the first century CE, then Austria and Slovakia, before finally, in the sixth century CE, sweeping around the eastern end of the Alps to settle in the fertile Po River valley of northern Italy. Along the way, intermarriage and political alliances brought several European tribes into the fold, including the Saxons, Bulgars, and Ostrogoths, among others. By the time they rolled into northern Italy, they were a formidable force that easily conquered the formerly Byzantine countryside.

So why would the Lombards, a meat-loving tribe from the far north, take such a shine to *garum*? Apart from an occasional monk in a monastery or a well-off aristocrat, Italians were no longer consuming much of it. *Garum* was a distinctly Mediterranean seasoning linked to a style of cooking and repertoire of dishes that were decidedly Roman in character and no longer widely in fashion.

The acceptance or rejection of a new food by a colonizing group is highly variable, but in the case of the Lombards, one possible explanation points to their desire to legitimize themselves as the rightful rulers of the land through assimilation. As part of this project, the Lombards adopted Roman names and titles, not only to sanction their presence on what was essentially local Italians' land, but also as a means of linking themselves to Rome's illustrious past. As the rightful heirs to the Roman Empire (at least in their minds), the consumption of *garum* may have symbolized this relationship in gastronomic terms. They wanted not only to control the territory, but to attain *romanità*— the essence of being Roman—and how better to do that than to eat like a Roman? *Garum* may also have served as a social marker, distancing the Lombard elites from the locals, many of whom were now too poor to afford the costly import.

While Lombard elites and their military officers of the Po River valley were occasionally consuming *garum*, they were not alone. *Garum* was also being traded to local monasteries. Archives from the monastery at Bobbio in the Apennine Mountains indicate that the monks were receiving intermittent shipments of it. As a costly import akin to exotic spices and fine wine, *garum* may seem to have been out of place on the austere grounds of a monastery. However, there was always a certain amount of tension in medieval monasteries between the early church's heavenly ideals and the earthlier desires of its monks. Those who dedicated themselves to a contemplative life of prayer were often the sons of well-to-do families, thus unprepared for (nor interested in) a life of material deprivation, especially when it came to the all-important daily meal. Despite the best efforts of church authorities to encourage self-abnegation, medieval monks, no less than their later counterparts, relished good food, and this meant meat fragranced with *garum* and spices, ideally enjoyed with a tipple or two of wine.

So widespread was the desire for flavorful food and good hooch in monastic circles that it forced Saint Benedict in 516 CE to plead for compromise: "Although we read that wine is never for monks, it is hard to persuade modern monks of this. At least we must all agree that we are not to drink to satiety, but with moderation."[37] Most likely, church authorities would have liked to restrict *garum* and exotic spices, along with meat ("The whole life of a monk ought to be a continual Lent," as Saint Benedict's Rule makes clear), but the practical realities of running a monastery in often remote locales under harsh conditions meant turning a blind eye to these all-too-human little luxuries.[38]

The shift in consumption of *garum* draws our attention to the changing world of food in the early medieval period when the traditions of the Roman south converged with those of the Germanic and Frankish north. It was around this time that western gastronomy pivoted from its Roman traditions (built upon earlier Greek foundations) to its medieval incarnation, which would hold sway for the next several hundred years. Roman cuisine had traditionally been defined by the blending of distinctly different flavors—sweet, sour, bitter, salty, and umami—to arrive at a harmonious whole. This potpourri of flavors was grounded in the wheat–wine–oil triad that defined Roman alimentary values.

"A perfect dish," write Alberto Capatti and Massimo Montanari, "was thought to be one in which *all* flavours were simultaneously present" (original emphasis).[39] This contrasted with the foods of the Germanic and Frankish north, which commonly featured roasted meats, beer, butter, and lard.

Food oppositions are one way to understand some of the differences between the northern European and Roman cultures: meat versus vegetables; beer versus wine; oats and rye versus wheat. While northern European traditions emphasized a culture of self-sufficiency (both oats and rye could be produced locally), Roman agricultural traditions leaned towards the cultivation of wheat, which was mostly grown abroad and transported over great distances to feed the cities of the Roman Empire. The Roman gastronomic ideal relied upon the Mediterranean staples of bread, wine, olive oil, and *garum*, all culturally charged products requiring human invention and processing, as culinary historian Karima Moyer-Nocchi points out. The diet of the northern tribes, on the other hand, was more reliant on foraged foods, hunting, and dairy, favoring beer over wine. Obviously, there were many exceptions to these kinds of oppositions, and the vast majority of people most likely made do with whatever was at hand, be it northern or southern in outlook.

The intersection of these two conflicting alimentary value systems is captured in the first medical treatise of the medieval period, Anthimus' *De observatione ciborum* ("On the Observance of Foods"), written in the sixth century CE. Our knowledge of this Byzantine Greek's origins and education is scant, but we do know that as a young man he was involved in a failed plot against the Emperor Zeno in Constantinople. After conviction at trial, he was exiled to the court of King Theodoric at the Ostrogoth capital of Ravenna, about 30 kilometers south of Comacchio. Although trained as a physician, he was clearly a man of many talents. Theodoric made him ambassador to the king of the

Franks, whose name, confusingly, was Theuderic. It is not clear whether Anthimus traveled to Theuderic's court at Metz (in northeastern France), or even whether his treatise was written prior to or after his departure. What is certain is that his work is invaluable, as it captures a moment in time in the early medieval period when Roman and northern European gastronomic traditions rubbed up against each other.

Composed in the form of a letter, Anthimus' medical treatise was meant to inform the Frankish king of the benefits and dangers of different kinds of foods. It illustrates how gastronomy was shifting and that new tastes, recipes, and ingredients (cloves!) were emerging in Europe. But in the midst of his discussion about healthy foods and how best to prepare them, Anthimus drops a bomb that stops us dead in our tracks. In a section discussing boiled versus roasted pork, he proclaims: "We ban the use of fish sauce from every culinary rôle."[40] And just like that, the once treasured seasoning became an outcast.

Why would a Byzantine physician from Constantinople (where *garum* was still avidly consumed), exiled to Ravenna on the Adriatic coast (where *garum* was occasionally consumed), compose a medical treatise for a Frankish king in northern Europe forbidding *garum*? Perhaps the simplest explanation for such a curious decree relates to how highly charged *garum* had become in the early medieval period. Just as consuming *garum* may have served as a convenient symbol of gastronomic identity for the Lombards who lived south of the Alps by linking them to Roman traditions, its rejection by the Franks living north of the Alps differentiated them from the Roman and Byzantine worlds, thereby reaffirming their distinct Frankish identity. As an astute observer, Anthimus may have recognized which way the gastronomic winds were blowing and crafted his medical treatise, with its rejection of *garum*, accordingly.

Garum's days were numbered, and the few mentions of it in the written record are rife with disdain. Echoing out of the past comes an all-too-familiar complaint about *garum*, courtesy of Liutprand of Cremona, who in 968 CE was sent to the court of the Byzantine Emperor Nicephorus II Phocas. The diplomatic mission quickly turned into a clash of cultures, with Liutprand being snubbed at every turn. Not only was his entourage denied entry, but the wine was sub-par, and the meals dragged on for hours. Perhaps most egregious of all, the food was in the *"Apicius"* tradition. Liutprand wasted no time in complaining back to his boss that the barbaric court "stank" of that disgusting fish sauce, *garum*.

The uncertain status of anchovies in the early medieval period

While *garum* was navigating its way through the changing gastronomic landscape of western Europe in the Middle Ages (a process that would see it eventually disappear by the late medieval period), the trajectory of salted anchovies was far less clear, and even locating them in the written record is challenging. The tale of a French king and his Lenten almsgiving, or "charity" as it is known today, illustrates the anchovy problem in all its medieval complexity. Were anchovies widely available and consumed, as some have argued, or were they rarely eaten, as their omission from historical documents seems to suggest?

To address this question, we begin with the Frankish king, Robert the Wise or Pious (972–1031), both sobriquets being somewhat inconsistent with his three marriages (a messy affair that led to his excommunication) and his turbulent relationship with his three sons, who loathed and eventually killed him. Despite his chaotic family life, Robert considered himself a devout ruler, and he regularly engaged in prayer, fasting, and almsgiving—the three pillars of medieval Christianity. Almsgiving was very much a medieval *quid pro quo* arrangement whereby the more you gave, the more divine favor you hoped to receive. This was particularly important for Robert as he appears to have been thoroughly despised, surrounded by enemies, and constantly on the cusp of warfare.

In their book *Alice o acciuga?*,* Fulvio Basteris and Aldo Rodino refer to King Robert the Wise to support their argument that anchovies were widely available and consumed at that time. In doing so, they draw upon Robert's biography, written by the Benedictine monk Helgaud (Friar Helgaud de Fleury). According to Helgaud, Robert engaged in extensive almsgiving during Lent in numerous different cities, including "Paris ... Senlis, Orléans, Dijon, Auxerre, Avallon, [and] Étampes."[41] Detailing his generosity, Basteris and Rodino write that "during Lent he [Robert] would have bread, wine, and *salt-cured anchovies* distributed to hundreds of beggars wherever he happened to be" (emphasis added).[42] While this interpretation is certainly appealing, as it brings anchovies back onto the medieval stage, how confident are we that they were in fact anchovies and not some other salted fish?

The idea that salted anchovies were widely available throughout France during this period presents several challenges. For one thing, it is not clear from which translation of Helgaud' biography Basteris and Rodino were working. Perhaps they were using an Italian translation that was particularly broad-minded in how it interpreted the Latin terms for fish? This was quite different from the more conservative French version, which translated all three Latin terms (*piscis*, *piscem*, and *piscium*) into the French term *du poisson*. This refers to "fish" in a generic sense, rather

---

* The title *Alice o acciuga?* playfully refers to the two most common names by which anchovies are known in modern Italy, illustrating the challenges of utilizing common names when it comes to identifying specific species of fish.

than the more specific "salt-cured anchovies." Equally problematic, as Pauline Claire Harlay pointed out to me, is that all the cities Helgaud mentions are in north-central France where salted herring—not salted anchovies—were the most prevalent salted fish available, followed by sardines. It was only in the south of France, especially along the Mediterranean coastline, that salted anchovies were available in sufficient quantities for King Robert to dole them out to beggars and the poor.

The imprecision surrounding medieval fish terms complicates our understanding of anchovies at this time. The lack of historical sources on the fish trade during the early medieval period does not help either. A reoccurring problem throughout history is that the same fish can be known by many different names. For example, the Spanish use *bocarte, boquerónes,* and *anchoa* to refer to anchovies. At times, these terms are synonymous and interchangeable, but when used in restricted local circumstances, they may take on more specific meanings. By the same token, just as one type of fish can be known by different names, so too can several different kinds of fish be known by the same name. This goes a long way towards explaining the elusive medieval anchovy.

One example of this conundrum comes courtesy of an accounting book from the monastery of Cluny in France. Written at the beginning of the 1300s, the ledger documents how funds were allocated for food, with eggs and cheese requiring the most funds, followed by an unspecified type of cooking oil. An entry for 109,000 salted fish purchased in a three-month period catches our attention. Crucially, the Académie de Mâcon translates the Latin term used in the accounting book, *allecia,* to the French *harengs* (herring), with the critical caveat that this term should not be understood as referencing herring specifically, but rather, in a more general sense, "all kinds of small salted fish, such as anchovies."[43] In the French manuscript *Lexicon manuale ad scriptores mediae et infimae Latinitatis,* Abbé Migne makes a similar point for the word *halex*, which, he notes, refers equally to herring, sardines, and anchovies.[44]

This etymology illustrates the risks in using written sources as a guide to understanding anchovy consumption in the early and high medieval periods. While salted anchovies may have been in greater circulation than these sources suggested, we should not overstep and take this to mean that they were widely available and consumed. Too many factors worked against anchovies in the first half of the medieval period. It would have taken higher-quality salt, improved brining techniques (to prolong the shelf life of salted fish), and better distribution networks for salted anchovies to have become more visible and widely known in the medieval era.

Despite the limited scope of salted anchovies in this period, the poorest of the poor were probably still eating *fresh anchovies* all along the Mediterranean coast, much as they had always done. But the fate of anchovies was about to change. Over the next several hundred years, anchovies found their way onto the fishmonger's table and back into the pages of history.

Herring heralds a new era for salted fish

Our first glimpse of the monumental changes that were in store for anchovies occurred in England around the year 1000 CE. To understand this "northern" piece of the medieval anchovy puzzle, we turn to English middens (garbage dumps). By carefully analyzing fish bones from middens across England, British archaeologist James Barrett and his colleagues were able to pinpoint a drastic change in consumption patterns from primarily freshwater and migratory species of fish, such as carp, salmon, and eel, to fish caught in the sea, such as herring and cod. Freshwater fish bones predominate in middens from the seventh to the tenth centuries, but sometime around the first millennium CE, a surge in herring and cod bones signal that a fundamental shift was underway.

Barrett and his colleagues term this unique moment the "fish event horizon," pointing to expanding pan-European trade in preserved fish from the sea. Even though anchovies were not directly a part of the "fish event horizon" in England, changing consumption patterns and a corresponding increase in trade laid the foundations for anchovies' eventual rise at the end of the medieval period and the beginning of the early modern era.[45]

The most significant catalyst for the "fish event horizon" was urbanization. As the gravitational pull of England's budding cities attracted more and more of the rural population, freshwater sources of fish were unable to meet the increased demand. The dietary needs of these urban populations in northern Europe, coupled with the church's increasing number of mandated meat-free days for Catholics, stimulated trade in fish from the sea. The traders and merchants who filled this need would find their fullest expression in the creation of the Hanseatic League, a loose confederation of merchant guilds scattered across the coastal cities of the Baltic and North Seas. As the process of urbanization quickened, and salted fish became increasingly lucrative, Hanse merchants were perfectly positioned to capitalize on the expanding trade.

Over time, the Hanse merchants improved the processing, packing, and barreling of herring, and this meant that cheaply sourced fish protein could be shipped long distances. This had a tremendous impact on western European foodways. The French historian Cécile Le Cornec notes that in the 1100s, 65 percent of the fish eaten in France came from freshwater sources.[46] But less than a hundred years later, that figure had dropped to 20 percent, as salted fish from the sea came to dominate the market. This figure continued to drop in the coming centuries, with a similar trend occurring throughout the rest of Europe. At its peak in the late fifteenth century, salted herring traded by the Hanse reached as far as Russia in the east, Ireland in the west, and Spain and Italy in the south (Fig. 1.5).

One drawback to having all this herring in circulation in northern Europe was that even though it was a vital food source, consuming it was often a somewhat joyless affair. Salted herring was not a beloved fish, but rather a medieval necessity. While we may think fondly of the salted or smoked fish we savor over Sunday brunch, early forms of preserved herring were barely palatable and cringe-inducingly salty. The real benefit of salted and smoked herring was that it could last in the cupboard for at

Fig. 1.5: A block print depicting the herring fishery at Scania (southern Sweden), circa 1550, by Olaus Magnus. The overwhelming abundance of Scania's herring run is depicted symbolically on the right side of the illustration by the halberd—a medieval weapon topped by an axe blade with a "thorn" on its backside—which stands upright in the sea after being planted in a densely packed school of herring. (*The History Collection/ Alamy Stock Photo.*)

least a year, offering a sort of insurance policy for the dreaded "lean" days when meat was forbidden. Nonetheless, this new reliance on salted herring nudged the door open to their distant cousins, salted anchovies.

Salted fish surface slowly in southern Europe

While northern Europe was developing a mania for salted fish, driven not so much by a love of salted herring as the protein it provided during Lent and meatless days (and the profits it generated), southern Europe was slower to develop a commercial salted fish industry of its own. In contrast to the north, where salted fish acted as a catalyst to trade, neither salted nor fresh fish played a significant role in trade in the Mediterranean world around the turn of the millennium. This is surprising, because when we think of the so-called Mediterranean diet, one of the first things that comes to mind is fish. But given there was little demand for salted fish (and even less money to be made from it), traders focused their efforts on more profitable goods such as luxury items and grains. It took time for salted fish to become a consistent commodity in the Mediterranean world, but once it did, it took the region by storm. Just where many of these preserved fish came from, and how anchovies fared in all this, is a tale of economics, conquest, and changing foodways.

From the Strait of Gibraltar to the shores of the Levant, one of the ways the Mediterranean world defined itself was in relation to the sea. And yet, surprisingly, the Mediterranean Sea itself was a distinctly fish-poor body of water. With its warm, clear, and nutrient-deficient waters, the Mediterranean paled in productivity compared to the cold and nutrient-dense waters of the Atlantic Ocean, which teemed with millions upon millions of herring in the North Sea; countless cod off Norway, Iceland, and

Newfoundland; vast schools of sardines off the west coast of Spain; and anchovies along the Atlantic coasts of France, Spain, Portugal, and Morocco. This, in turn, helps to explain why medieval Mediterranean fisheries were generally much smaller, with limited production. To be sure, mackerel, sardines, anchovies—*inter alia*—did have productive zones in the Mediterranean, all of which supported local fisheries. But the fish-poor state of the Mediterranean had been recognized as far back as the Roman era. Even the great Roman statesman Seneca complained that the waters off Rome were overfished and barren.

Preserved fish were not consumed with the same frequency as fresh fish in the early to high medieval period (outside of fasting days and Lent), and references to them are scant. However, by the early 1200s, trade was gaining momentum throughout the Mediterranean basin, and this had implications for anchovies. Some of the increased activity was linked to transporting Crusaders to the Holy Land, but with the increasing profits to be made from trade, merchants in coastal cities such as Barcelona, Marseille, Genoa, Pisa, Naples, Amalfi, and Venice rushed to outfit cargo ships. Tucked away in the holds along with the usual luxury items were dried fruit, oil, timber, metals, linen, leather, and sometimes even slaves. Amidst all this cargo was the odd barrel of salted fish, including salted anchovies. Although salted tuna, mackerel, sardines, and dried octopus were more profitable and comprised the bulk of the preserved fish trade, anchovies were now on the move in the Mediterranean.

Another factor that drove trade was the opening of the Strait of Gibraltar. For several centuries, Muslim rulers in southern Iberia had shut down the only sea passage to the Atlantic Ocean, making trade through the critical passageway nearly impossible. But with Christian advances against the Muslim states in southern Iberia in the thirteenth century, the Strait of Gibraltar became navigable once again, and traders ventured out into the Atlantic to find new markets.

Some of the first beneficiaries of the new sea route to the Atlantic were traders who exploited the rich fishing grounds off Galicia, in western Iberia, and Portugal, both of which began supplying preserved fish to the Mediterranean world. In the past, these productive fisheries only supplied inland areas adjacent to the coastline, but by the 1300s, large amounts of salted sardines, as well as dried hake, octopus, and conger eel, were being shipped to eager markets in Mallorca, Valencia, and Barcelona. Occasionally, barrels of anchovies made the journey as well.

While many of these salted fish from the Atlantic were being consumed locally in the cities and towns of eastern Iberia and the Balearic Islands, some were being sold for the next leg of the journey to points further east. Traders from Genoa and Pisa became familiar sights in the ports of Barcelona and Valencia, buying all the preserved fish they could get their hands on. One document from the late 1300s records that salted anchovies were purchased in Barcelona and shipped onwards to Genoa. From the docks of Genoa, some of these salted anchovies were likely sold to small-time traders, who carried them over the Apennine Mountains to inland towns in northern Italy. By the early 1400s, Galician sardines and Portuguese anchovies were arriving regularly in southern Italy.

But the real game-changer for preserved fish in the Mediterranean arose with the trade of salted herring from northern Europe. In 1277, the first Genoese traders from the Italian Peninsula were recorded passing through the Strait of Gibralter *en route* to markets in Flanders and England. The Mallorcans were hot on their heels, as were traders from Catalonia and Venice. On their outbound leg, they carried the luxury goods that were sought after in the north, along with dried fruit, saffron, and oil. On the return, their holds were filled to the brim with lead, tin, wool, and cloth. By the later 1300s, they brought back an increasing number of salted herring as well. Dried cod would follow. As the food historian Rachel Laudan writes, "Fish-rich northern Europe began supplying the fish-poor Mediterranean."[47]

Within a couple of generations, salted herring from northern Europe were plentiful in the Mediterranean region, forever altering their foodways. Encouraged by the Christian church, as preserved fish facilitated fasting, salted herring started flooding into ports around the Mediterranean world. The British historian Richard Hoffmann, in "Frontier Foods for Late Medieval Consumers" (2001), notes that by 1340, northern salted herring was well known on the Castilian plains of central Spain. A generation later, a merchant's manual in Italy explains how tidy profits could be made by importing salted herring from Flanders to Tuscany.

As salted herring became more available across the Mediterranean in the late medieval period, this helped pave the way for other preserved fish, even low-ranked ones at the time like anchovies. One illustration of the growing role of anchovies in Italy comes from the charming correspondence of Ser Lapo Mazzei—"Ser" being the Latin equivalent of "sir"—a notary and official in the city of Florence in 1404. In his wide-ranging and chatty correspondence with his mentor, Francesco di Marco Datini, we learn his thoughts about anchovies and their rather paltry position in the food hierarchies of the day.

Over the course of several letters, Ser Lapo protests that his mentor has been supplying him with overly generous gifts, such as partridges. Although he was clearly delighted with them, decorum required him to state that they were above his station. Such cloying modesty and obsequiousness may appear rather heavy-handed to modern sensibilities, but it was well within the norms of the day when addressing a hierarchical superior in the late Middle Ages. This helps to explain why, when replying to Francesco, Ser Lapo complains that such gifts are simply too much for a modest man such as himself: "I like coarse foods," he writes, "those that make me strong enough to sustain the work

I must do to maintain my family. This year I would like to have, as I once had, a little barrel of salted anchovies."[48]

Ser Lapo's endearing letter perfectly captures the ambiguous status that anchovies occupied in the late medieval period. On the one hand, they were deemed a low-ranked fish only suitable for a junior official still navigating the complex corridors of medieval power. On the other hand, we can detect a genuine warmth and affection for them. This contradiction reminds us of ancient Romans bragging about the finest *garum* costing a small fortune, unaware that they were actually eating (in Pompeii at least) *garum* made from anchovies. The enigmatic standing of the humble anchovy carried forth in the following centuries in France, the gastronomic powerhouse that reshaped elite cookery in Europe.

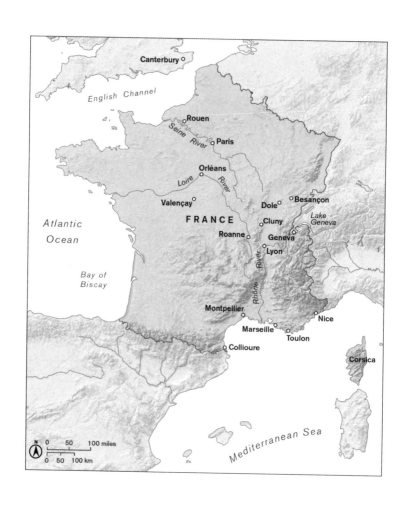

Canterbury

English Channel

Rouen

Seine River

Paris

Orléans

Loire River

Valençay

FRANCE

Dole

Besançon

Cluny

Lake Geneva

Roanne

Geneva

Atlantic Ocean

Lyon

Rhône River

Bay of Biscay

Montpellier

Nice

Marseille

Toulon

Collioure

Corsica

N

0   50   100 miles

0   50   100 km

Mediterranean Sea

2

THE FRENCH ANCHOVY

A GLORIOUS RISE AND SAD DEMISE

The story of anchovies in French cuisine is a complicated affair. After a long slog through the early and high Middle Ages, when anchovy mentions in the culinary world were few and far between, our flavorful fish finally found its way onto the pages of early cookery manuscripts. French cookbooks take us on a captivating journey through the evolution of haute cuisine. *Through their recipes, we see how anchovies rose to lofty heights of sophistication but soon found themselves swimming against the current with the development of the famous "mother sauces." At the same time, in other French gastronomic traditions, anchovies had always been hiding in plain sight; you just had to look harder to find them.*

Anchovies appear in print: Le Viandier de Taillevent

In the late medieval period, around 1300, many recipe collections were in circulation in France's royal and aristocratic circles. Several of these *ad hoc* collections were compiled into manuscript form by an unknown hand in the decades that followed. Then, perhaps around mid-century, Guillaume Tirel added a treasure trove of new recipes, and the resulting collection became the first true *haute cuisine* cookbook in France: *Le Viandier de Taillevent.** Rising through the ranks of medieval kitchen drudgery to become "Master Chef" to several French kings, Guillaume Tirel is one of the towering figures of French culinary history. So great were his talents that he was given a noble burial and depicted on his tomb in knightly armour with a heraldic shield featuring three stew pots—the ultimate tribute to his culinary greatness. In 1486, *Le Viandier de Taillevent*, or *Le Viandier* as it is commonly referred to, was published in printed form, and it became *the* culinary classic that would define French aristocratic cooking for the next 250 years.

Le Viandier is a rich resource for understanding aristocratic taste in the Middle Ages. Cookbooks from this time were not cutting-edge publications. They mostly contained tried-and-true recipes handed down for generations, with an occasional nod to more innovative trends and techniques. Bookending the culinary continuum were the high feast dishes: generously spiced meats and exotic birds like peacock and swan. Such dishes were the very height of late medieval cuisine—the stuff of feudal legends—served to lords and counts attired in silk tunics and the finest furs. At the other end of the continuum, and in accordance with the Christian dietary calendar, fish, the sin-free substitute for meat, played a central role in satisfying appetites on days of abstinence.

In line with historical precedents, the fish in *Le Viandier* are organized hierarchically, starting with the most esteemed and desired—those from freshwater lakes and rivers. Next on the list are what Tirel called "round sea-fish" (e.g. porpoise), followed by

---

* "Taillevent" is literally "wind-slicer," owing to his legendary carving skills.

"flat sea-fish" (e.g. sole), with cuttlefish, crustaceans, and bivalves tacked on willy-nilly at the end. As a classification scheme, it left much to be desired, but it did hand down a record of the hierarchical principles that guided Tirel and other chefs in the late medieval period. Anchovies, not surprisingly, are listed almost at the very end, just in front of smelt, which are even smaller and more insignificant. Oddly, sturgeon are ranked last, though this was most likely a scribal error.

Given this ranking system, we are fortunate that Tirel even bothered to include an anchovy recipe. But he did. This single recipe in *Le Viandier* is quite straightforward, and when accompanied by one of Tirel's sauces it would undoubtedly have been delicious:

Anchovies (*Abies/Alles de mer*)
Cut into strips, roasted; eaten with mustard sauce or in wine sauce.[1]

Sauces were essential to late medieval cookery, and the logic behind pairing a mustard or wine sauce with anchovies was right in line with the prevailing humoral theories of the day. As fish were considered both humid and cool (because they came from water), the trick was to cook and pair them with sauces that would counteract this with warmth and dryness. This achieved the humoral balance believed to aid digestion and increase overall health, and helps to explain why so many fish, including anchovies, were roasted over a fire (which was drying) and then served with a sauce that was also thought to be drying, such as mustard or wine.

Medical theories aside, not only did sauces make everything taste better, but the spices within them made everyone who consumed them feel just a tad bit better about themselves. As spices cost a small fortune, when they were stirred into a sauce it now tasted of wealth and power. Colorants could also elevate any sauce to new heights of exclusivity. Enhancing the color of a sauce was amusing and visually intoxicating, no less so in the late medieval period than in modern molecular gastronomy today. Color was also used to denote the status of individual guests, often in amusing ways. One such dish in *Le Viandier, Coqz heaumez*—"Helmeted cocks"—features a roasted piglet placed on a serving tray with an egg-glazed roasted cock riding on top of it, complete with a fabricated helmet and lance. The lance "should be covered with gold- or silver-leaf for lords ... or with white, red, or green tin-leaf," depending upon the status of the invitees.[2] A piglet charging into battle with a cock on top would surely have elicited knowing smiles and titters of laughter from the ladies, who knew all too well the myth of the knight in shining armor.

The brilliance of the banquet: Du fait de cuisine

Banquets were the theatres in which social status was staged and performed. The successful execution of these gastronomic productions formed a central preoccupation of the second of our three late medieval cookery books. Amiczo Chiquart's *Du fait de cuisine* (1420), often translated into English as "On Cookery," is a sort of tribute to the power and prestige of his patron Victor Amadeus, Duke of Savoy. The banquets that Chiquart concocted for the duke were fabled affairs, both for the types of dishes served and their quantities. "One banquet," notes culinary historian Ken Albala, "calls for 100 head of cattle, 130 sheep, 120 pigs and 200 piglets, 200 lamb, 100 calves, 2,000 hens, and 12,000 eggs."[3] Despite the sheer abundance of food, the number of dishes served to an individual was strictly limited and directly proportional to his or her social standing. While the specific numbers varied throughout Europe, cardinals and the highest-ranking nobility typically received the most choices of food on offer, while the aristocracy received somewhat less, and those further down the social hierarchy received even less. Behind the scenes, servants may have benefited from the trickle-down system and consumed the leftovers. At the very least, they would have been served some porridge, bread, and a glass or two of cheap plonk. From the king all the way down to the stable boy, everyone's worth could be calculated by the food and drink that went down their gullets.

While the style of Chiquart's food sat firmly within the French sphere of influence, it nonetheless drew upon Mediterranean and Italian elements that lent many of his dishes an international air. This was particularly evident in the fish recipes in *Du fait de cuisine*, which were served with sauces from all across Europe: turbot with a green sauce, sardines with a mustard sauce, and salmon and ray with the most popular sauce of the age—the camel-colored, cinnamon-scented cameline—and so on. Fresh anchovies were also served with a sauce, albeit one that was drawn from two distinctly different culinary traditions. Part of the sauce can be traced to the common cookery of the Mediterranean, utilizing ingredients that could be found in any household, whether high or humble. The second part of the sauce is absolutely aristocratic, as the "warm" and "dry" embrace of the spices anchors it firmly in the courtly traditions of the late medieval period:

Anchovies with parsley, onions, vinegar and spice mix on top.

(*Les anchoyes au percy, oygnions et vin aigre, et la poudre par-dessus.*)[4]

This may be one of the earliest written anchovy recipes to feature parsley, onions, and vinegar, though one can imagine that the poor had probably been eating anchovies this way for hundreds, if not thousands, of years. Chiquart's spin on this was to take things one step further with the addition of *la poudre par-dessus* (the spice mix). Although Chiquart did not list the ingredients for *his* version of spice powder, D. Eleanor Scully and Terence Scully note that it typically comprised the "big four" spices of the day: ginger, cinnamon, cloves, and grain of paradise (aka melegueta pepper, which has a faintly ginger-like flavor).*[5]

A "how to" guide for the bourgeoisie: Le Ménagier de Paris

Our final anchovy recipe from this period comes courtesy of *Le Ménagier de Paris* (1393), a sort of household management guide that reminds us that "how to" books addressing cookery, domesticity, and/or entertaining never go out of style, whether they are from the late medieval period, the Victorian period with the likes of Mrs. Beeton, or anything by Martha Stewart in twenty-first-century America. Intriguing domestic and gastronomic details abound in *Le Ménagier de Paris*, ranging from the expected morality of a new wife, to de-salting fish, to ensuring that cow's milk has not been diluted with water. The emphasis on practical information made *Le Ménagier de Paris* a far more useful and complete cookery book for the common reader, whereas *Le Viandier* or *Du fait de cuisine* were intended for professional peers. In *Le Ménagier de Paris*, the author speaks in the voice of a wise, seasoned elder instructing his young bride on her domestic duties. To this end, the author goes into minutiae that most professional chefs would deem far beneath their station.

---

* It is worth noting that spice powders may have been significantly more subtle than their ingredient lists would suggest. This primarily relates to the degraded state of medieval spices. Some estimates indicate that spices may have taken up to a year (or more) to reach France from their sources in the East, and their aroma and color would have been severely degraded after these epic journeys. Medieval spices pale in comparison with our modern counterparts, which are harvested at the peak of their pungency, vacuum sealed, and delivered fresh via modern transport.

Who was the anonymous author of *Le Ménagier de Paris*, the man who went so far as to note that he may soon die, and that his new bride would require a new husband? Although not nobility (had he been, we can be sure he would have mentioned it), the author may very well have been part of the emerging upper-bourgeois class on which the king was increasingly coming to rely for matters of state. Clearly, he was well-connected, as he name-drops a dinner party that he attended hosted by Monsieur de Lagny for none other than the *Monseigneur de Paris*, the Procurator and King's Counsel. Ken Albala has theorized that he may have been an "elderly businessman, or perhaps Lawyer," while others have speculated that he may have worked in Paris's *parlement*.[6] The distinguished British sociologist Stephen Mennell sums up the thoughts of many when he writes: "Quite why a man of that background had such a knowledge of cookery has never been satisfactorily explained."[7]

What we do know is that this anonymous author lived on the Île-de-la-Cité in central Paris and aimed to emulate the lifestyles of the rich and famous in fourteenth-century France. Perhaps for this reason, his section on cookery contains a fair number of recipes that were copied straight from the pages of *Le Viandier*, including several for big-game meats and their accompanying sauces. But as his manuscript was intended as a practical guide for his new bride, it also includes all the vegetables that everyone was actually eating, but that never made it into top-tier manuscripts such as *Le Viandier* and *Du fait de cuisine*. His meatless recipes, such as a herb omelette with dark leafy greens or a mushroom tart, would find a welcome reception in any contemporary kitchen.

Le Ménagier de Paris contains two recipes with anchovies, which the author called "*ales*." One of these—anchovies with mustard sauce—was lifted straight from *Le Viandier*. The author also included the first written recipe in French for a floured and fried anchovy, which he noted could be served with either a jance or garlic sauce. If cameline was the most popular sauce in the late medieval period, then jance was an excellent candidate for runner-up. As cinnamon was to cameline sauce, ginger was to jance sauce. A key difference between the two—as they shared many spices in common—was that cameline sauce was served uncooked at room temperature, whereas jance was heated and served hot.

The inclusion of a couple of anchovy recipes in the medieval *Le Ménagier de Paris* is not surprising, as it covers the range of dishes that an upper-bourgeois household should have in its repertoire—from fancy dinner parties to far humbler meals between a husband and wife, including the simple vegetables they regularly ate, often grown in their own garden. In such a setting, a small barrel of salted anchovies may have been among the foodstuffs stored in their basement or larder. Like pickled vegetables, a barrel of salted anchovies could last for a season or two and could always be counted on for weekly fasting days.

If anchovies were at the very bottom of the fish hierarchy, then why did the two most preeminent cookery books in France at the time, *Le Viandier* and *Du fait de cuisine*, filled with recipes destined for the very highest ranks of French society, include recipes with anchovies at all? Italian culinary historian Massimo Montanari presents one argument to explain how low-ranked ingredients, such as anchovies, garlic, and root vegetables, might have found themselves on the tables of royalty. It all had to do with the idea of *ennoblement*: the act of elevating a lowly food to a higher gastronomic realm. According to Montanari, ennoblement works in two different ways. The first is by taking a humble ingredient and changing its social destination. Garlic, for example, is "artificially made elegant" when placed inside the cavity of a duck.[8] In this case, ennoblement is operating by proximity: garlic is elevated by its presence next to a high-ranked food. This helps to explain why garlic sauces, which were traditionally perceived as peasant cooking, are also often found in elite manuscripts.

The second part of Montanari's theory also comes to the aid of anchovies. When a lowly foodstuff is paired with costly ingredients, such as spices, it acquires a patrician touch and is elevated to a higher status. Montanari draws an example from a medieval Italian manuscript, in which turnips are magically transformed from a base root vegetable to something of exceptional character by the addition of costly spices. Cabbages, leeks, and onions could also be ennobled. Once properly spiced, "any food is worthy of a lordly table."[9] Applied to anchovies, this may help us to decipher the culinary code that allowed royalty and the aristocracy to eat an otherwise shunned fish. When doused with a fancy sauce laden with spices, anchovies rose above their lowly status as one of the smallest fish in the sea.

From the ranks of royalty to the plates of peasants

While anchovies were penetrating aristocratic circles, they were also making inroads at the other end of the social spectrum. One region in eastern France that witnessed an increase in anchovy consumption among the poor at this time was Franche-Comté. Traditionally, this region received the bulk of its seafood supply from the North Sea, with salted herring and dried cod (stockfish) widely available in the market towns of Besançon and Dole. But at the start of the sixteenth century, new trade routes opened between Franche-Comté, Provence, and Italy. Swept up in this mercantile whirlwind were anchovies. At one of the largest trade fairs in Lyon, at the intersection of these three regions, the great French historian Fernand Braudel tells us that barrels of salted anchovies were a principal commodity, with vendors ranging from the humblest peddlers to prominent merchants.[10]

Utilizing municipal archives, church documents, and toll books, we can chart the advance of anchovies into the Franche-Comté region. In the city of Besançon, the governors published a "Decree on sea-water fish" in the early 1500s, which informed traders of the dreaded *gabelle* (salt tax) that would be levied on fish. The rate of this tax was highly variable in France, but in the Franche-Comté region it was so inflated that it often comprised up to two thirds of the price of salted fish. Among the fish that the decree mentioned were sole, cuttlefish, salmon, plaice, skip-jack tuna, porpoise, mackerel, sardines, and anchovies (*hanchoy*). From lists like these, we can see how anchovies arrived in eastern France, something rarely documented just one century earlier.

The perennial problem with fish of any kind was spoilage, and this led to detailed city ordinances concerning their sales. Some ordinances indicated where fish could be sold (nowhere near butter or dairy), who could sell them (usually fishmongers, but in some cases, surprisingly, butchers), and on which days (only on market days and never on Sundays). Spoiled fish were a particular concern, as rot, decomposition, and contagion were thought to be linked to the plague, a recurring event associated with food shortages and death. Maintaining sufficient food supplies was one of the city elders' most important jobs, and they were vigilant in penalizing crafty merchants who attempted to sell tainted products.

Assuming a barrel of salted anchovies passed the freshness test, how were the poor eating them? Most likely, they were consumed much as the English diarist and naval administrator Samuel Pepys would do in mid-seventeenth century London, accompanied by a little bread and some watered-down wine. Preserved fish (in whatever form), bread, and watered-down wine were commonly consumed for breaking one's fast (breakfast) throughout Europe—a quick and tasty way to begin the day. Prior to eating, the anchovies would have been rinsed in an acidic liquid such as wine, vinegar, or verjuice to remove as much of the salt as possible. The body would be split open, the spine removed, and the fillets eaten as a salty whet, much like one would eat a salted herring. For the poor of Franche-Comté, there is nothing to indicate that they were adding salted anchovies to their one-pot stews, as others were doing in the south of Italy. Rather, salted anchovies, like salted herrings, were eaten on their own, typically accompanied by bread.

While the food of the poor remained relatively static during the transition from the late medieval period to the Renaissance, anchovies were starting to be perceived in a better light. But this change in perception evolved slowly and required several hundred years to bear fruit. One man who inadvertently helped nudge anchovies into wider acceptance was the renowned Renaissance humanist François Rabelais.

François Rabelais: the influence of giants on the tiniest of fish

Although anchovies are only mentioned once in all five books of Rabelais' masterpiece, *Gargantua and Pantagruel* (circa 1532–64), the context in which they were mentioned is fundamental to our story. Indeed, it was precisely during the 1500s that French cuisine was starting to take its first tentative steps away from its medieval roots. Over time, these incremental steps would come to embody much of what was considered "French" in France's gastronomic repertoire. The single anchovy mention in Rabelais' works is a sort of innocent bystander in all this, but one that relates to his larger project of subverting the medieval hierarchies (social, religious, and gastronomic) that had held sway for the previous millennium. Turning social and linguistic conventions on their heads, Rabelais' stories conceptually transformed many of France's low-ranked foods—such as anchovies—into objects of delight, opening up new possibilities for our humble fish.

Who was Rabelais? His curriculum vitae spoke to a fully engaged mind firing on all cylinders: a friar in the Franciscan order, a physician with a *doctorat* from the Université de Montpellier, a scholar versed in law and ancient Greek and Latin, a humanist, and a wordsmith *par excellence*; in short, the very definition of a Renaissance man. Despite his formal training as a cleric, his obsession with humanism consumed him, and it was inevitable that Rabelais would eventually run afoul of the Catholic church. Indeed, he would almost certainly have been burnt at the stake if not for his friendship with King François I and the distinguished French diplomat Guillaume de Bellay, whom he served as a personal physician. Even with such powerful patrons, Rabelais was forced to flee France on several occasions, as the Collège de la Sorbonne in Paris in 1543 censured his works as "obscene."

Obscene they are, but in the best possible way. Rabelais never tired of taunting the church: "the habit maketh not the Monk," he wrote, hinting that the true meaning of his work required courage to uncover. "That is why," Rabelais wrote, "you must open this book and scrupulously weigh what is treated within," explaining that the medicine it contained was not as "frivolous" as the book's title suggested.[11] Central to this undertaking were food, drink, and flatulence, but these "frivolities" masked his critique of French society and the church. As much as the church, royalty, and aristocracy tried to present a unified understanding of the world that ranked everyone and everything in hierarchical terms, Rabelais set out to dissect this narrative and challenge their conclusions.

The first book in Rabelais' series was published in 1532 and was followed by four more volumes. Collectively, the books tell the tale of two giants, Gargantua and his son Pantagruel, chronicling their adventures at a time when the world was rapidly changing, and Renaissance humanism and the Protestant

Reformation were undermining the old Catholic order. Nothing was as it seemed in the topsy-turvy world of Rabelais, and everything was larger than life, from Gargantua and Pantagruel themselves to their voracious appetites (Fig. 2.1).

Rabelais placed such an emphasis on food and the act of eating that in his prologue, he advised readers that they should not *read* his books so much as *consume* them. Food and consumption were intrinsic to his undertaking, as reflected in the main characters' names: Gargantua ("throat") and Pantagruel ("the ever-

Fig. 2.1: Even as a child, Pantagruel had an enormous appetite, suckling 4,600 cows at every meal. The outsized appetites of its protagonists coupled with its rich language and bawdy humor found enthusiastic audiences across generations. Publishers continually brought out new editions, such as the 1854 version that featured illustrations by Gustave Doré. (*Courtesy of the Bibliothèque nationale de France.*)

thirsty one"). Even the introduction of Gargantua's father, Grandgousier ("big gullet"), was closely linked to food and drink:

> In his day Grandgousier was a jolly good fellow who loved to drink neat as well as any man then in the world. And he enjoyed eating salty things. To that end he normally kept an ample store of Westphalian and Bayonne hams, plenty of smoked tongue, an abundance of eels in season, beef cured in salt and mustard, supplies of mullet-caviar, a provision of sausages ... but always from Bigorre, Longaulnay, La Brène and Rouergue.[12]

One of the significant points in this passage is that salted foods are far from stigmatized; in fact, they are exalted. Fresh meat and fish may still be first choice, but one could now also "enjoy" eating salted foods. Up to this point, salted foods—like anchovies—were sometimes viewed suspiciously, unless ennobled by a sauce or spices. But in Rabelais' passage, salted ham, beef, and sausage are all celebrated, and by specifying which towns the different salted meats came from, Rabelais acknowledged their provenance. This recognition of the geographical diversity of French food was an important step in the formation of a national cuisine, illustrating how France was coming to understand itself in gastronomic terms.

In Book IV, Pantagruel—now all grown up—sets off on a sea voyage to East Asia to consult the legendary Oracle of Bacbuc, a narrative that Rabelais modeled after Homer's *Odyssey* and the story of Jason and the Argonauts. After a series of bizarre episodes—a flying pig defecates hot mustard during one battle—Pantagruel and his companions come upon a final island where some of the inhabitants are called Gastrolaters (worshippers of the belly). Their God, Master Gaster (Latin for stomach) is worshiped and idolized above all others. As Pantagruel enters Master Gaster's court:

> The Gastrolaters were ... huddled together in groups and bands, some merry, elegant and cuddly, others sad, grave, severe and sour:

all lazy doing nothing, never working, "a useless load and burden on the world," as Hesiod put it ... They all held Gaster to be their great God; they worshipped him as a God; sacrificed to him as to their God Almighty. They had no other God before him ...[13]

No wonder the Catholic church was so desperate to lop off Rabelais' head; the Gastrolaters were allegorical stand-ins for the great mass of useless monks filling France's monasteries. All they wanted was food and drink. For Rabelais, these foolish monks were a waste of resources and a "burden on the world." And nothing about their obsession was new or specific to the time of Rabelais, as monks often had been preoccupied with their bellies since the very foundations of the Catholic church. This was why Saint Benedict in the sixth century CE gave up in despair at forbidding alcohol, as it was entirely hopeless. At best, he implored monks to drink modestly. The appetites of monks could no more be controlled in the sixth century than in the sixteenth century.

A loud bell thundered through the court, Rabelais continued, and all the Gastrolaters lined up as if for battle. As they marched in formation towards Master Gaster, they were followed by "fat serving-lads" carrying an endless procession of dishes. Savory breads, salted venison, salmagundis (a salad of mixed ingredients, including meat and fish), smoked ox tongues, legs of lamb in garlic sauce, capons, and ducks in onion sauce *à la française* were among the dishes presented to Master Gaster. Pantagruel is aghast at the wanton display of gluttony. But there was more: on their fasting days, the Gastrolaters had a separate Lenten menu containing every known seafood in France:

> For their *entrées* they offer him: caviar, pickled mullet-caviar, fresh butter, pease-pudding, spinach, fresh herrings, soused herrings, sardines, *anchovies*, marinated tuna, cabbage in olive-oil, buttered beans, hundreds of kinds of salads: of cress, hops, bishop's-bollocks, rampion, Judas-ears [a variety of fungus growing out from ancient elder-

trees], asparagus, woodbine and many others, salted salmon, salted eels, oysters in the shell [emphasis added].[14]

Just what Rabelais was getting at with his encyclopaedic list of Lenten dishes is hotly debated. Scholars are divided and theories abound. On the one hand, the entire episode may have been a parody to illustrate the hypocrisy of gluttonous Catholics during Lent, a time when the faithful are supposed to fast as a means of mortifying the flesh. On the other hand, as Ken Albala and Robin Imhof note, it might simply have been "a rhapsodic paean to the pleasures of the palate."[15] Arguments can be made for both, and they are not necessarily mutually exclusive. Pauline Claire Harlay suggests that whatever the case, these food lists were vehicles that introduced southern cultural elements into the northern French aristocratic literary landscape.[16]

The practice of incorporating new regional foods into the larger French gastronomic discourse was of considerable interest to writers at that time, as not only were new culinary words being introduced into written Middle French, but a new appreciation for the gastronomy of France was spreading in aristocratic circles. Rabelais' mention of anchovies (spelled "anchoye" in the original text) helped to legitimize a southern provincial product as a bona fide French commodity. The French naturalist Pierre Belon captured the enthusiasm that accompanied this development in his *L'Histoire de la nature des oyseaux* (1555), in which he wrote that "neither the Spanish, Portuguese, Flemish, Italians, Hungarians, Germans, nor any other subjects of the Roman Church have such magnificence in their preparation of food as the French."[17] This French national pride in all things gastronomic contributed to creating the space for regional products and new culinary practices and ingredients to flourish. In the copper pots of aristocratic kitchens, where pan-European medieval-style cookery had dominated for a millennium, new seasonings and flavor combinations were being cooked up.

Timothy Tomasik observes that Rabelais became aware of these wider gastronomic changes in France through a series of cookbooks published in Lyon and known collectively by the surname of the publisher: Sergent. The initial cookbook of this series was *Petit Traicté auquel verrez la manière de faire cuisine* in 1536, and, as Tomasik notes, it was "the first 16th-century cookbook entirely divorced from medieval culinary texts."[18] Six years later, Sergent published *Le Livre fort excellent de cuysine*, which combined recipes from the preceding work along with a host of new ones. Tomasik asserts that some of Rabelais' terminology and recipe titles indicate that he was in a dialogue with these works:

> In the Sergent family of cookbooks, many fish dishes are prepared with butter. This is a striking innovation in regards to medieval practices, where fish is almost never prepared as such ... Butter never appears in [Rabelais'] meat-day menu, and yet it appears at least three times in the meatless-day menu. By including so many references to butter in the meatless-day menu, Rabelais was simply ratifying an association between fish and butter that had already been established by contemporary cookbooks.[19]

This was a crucial development, as butter would change everything for anchovies in France. The new French fashion of pairing fish with melted butter helped launch anchovies into aristocratic French cuisine, as did evolving ideas about humoral theory.

Medicine: the shift which favored our flavor-filled fish

In her article "The Origin of the Modern Western Diet," Rachel Laudan compares traditional court banquets in the mid-sixteenth and mid-seventeenth centuries and identifies profound differences between them. The medieval banquet would have been filled with food that could best be described as a distant relative of what we know today, with disconcerting flavor combinations and dishes with unfamiliar names. At a medieval supper, one would have likely been served a *blancmange*, a pudding-like puree of rice, chicken, and almond milk seasoned with a full farrago of medieval spices. Roasted meats would probably have been served with the ubiquitous cameline sauce, and guests would have quenched their thirst with *hypocras*, a spiced mulled wine. "Fast forward 100 years," Laudan writes, "and the food would be reassuringly familiar. On the table in the late 1600s might be beef bouillon, oysters, anchovies, and a roast turkey with gravy."[20]

Food preferences are stubbornly resistant, even more so than religious beliefs, according to some anthropologists. So what prompted this "revolution in taste," to use the words of Susan Pinkard, which came to define elite and diplomatic dining around the world for centuries to come?[21]

It turns out that the catalyst for the culinary revolution—which would open the door for anchovies to enter aristocratic cuisine in a major way—was a rather esoteric factor: medicine. Starting in the early sixteenth century, physicians could no longer reconcile Galen's humoral theory that good health relied on the four humors being in balance, which had held sway for the last 1,300 years, with the advances being made in human physiology. The tension between the two reached a tipping point as physicians surreptitiously acquired cadavers from local authorities in order to dissect them and conduct experiments. One such physician was Andreas Vesalius (1514–1564), a professor of medicine at the University of Padua in Italy. "His great work," writes Pinkard, "*De humani corporis fabrica* (*On the Fabric of the Human Body*), published in 1542 with magnificent illustrations inspired by Leonardo da Vinci, contradicted Galen on several points and raised damning questions about the general soundness of his methods."[22]

Another early critic of the Galenic paradigm was an itinerant physician from Switzerland named Paracelsus (1493–1541), né

Theophrastus von Hohenheim. Laudan notes that Paracelsus' "abrasive" character and unorthodox beliefs lent him a terrible reputation, with which few were willing to be publicly associated.[23] But his ideas carried weight behind closed doors. Advocating direct observation of the human body, Paracelsus constructed a new paradigm that challenged Galen's four-humor theory by asserting that digestion was initiated by fermentation. "Because fermentation included gentle heat and the production of vapors," writes Laudan, "it seemed to resemble (or was possibly the same as) putrefaction, distillation, and the interaction of acids and salts."[24]

These new beliefs allowed for the human body to be conceptualized in a completely new fashion. No longer did cooks (with physicians hovering over their shoulders) need to utilize spices as correctives to balance out competing humors. Rather, they were free to focus their efforts on a more pressing concern: pleasing their employers with the tastiest dishes possible. Among the first victims were spices, which could now be used far more judiciously. Heavily spiced medieval sauces were soon replaced by butter, cream, and marrow, all of which were reduced to further concentrate their flavors. Instead of heavy, textured sauces thickened with breadcrumbs, the new sauces were thickened with flour, a technique that is now called making a *roux*. And sugar—which had traditionally been used liberally as a humoral corrective across the entire culinary landscape—slowly found itself relegated to desserts, where it (mostly) remains to this day.

Fermentation was now thought to be key. Just as fermentation resulted in various grains magically becoming bread and alcohol (and grapes becoming wine), so too did the body ferment foods through the digestive process. Fermentation gained such currency that old food hierarchies found new ingredients in their midst. As Laudan observes, "chefs welcomed oysters, anchovies, green vegetables, mushrooms and fruits because they fermented so readily and thus did not need complicated preparation in the kitchen to be pre-digested."[25] That modern chemistry contradicts all of this is irrelevant: in the sixteenth century, fermentation moved the conversation forward and made perfect sense to its supporters. Thus, anchovies were not only part of new approaches to flavor, but also played into new ideas about health.

New ideas about food were also emerging in religious circles. In 1522, for instance, in what is known as the "Affair of the sausages," the Zurich-based pastor Ulrich Zwingli, along with several co-conspirators, challenged the Catholic church by eating two smoked sausages during Lent. Zwingli argued that there was no rule in the Bible that prohibited meat during Lent. Regardless of what one ate, he argued, everyone still had equal access to the heavenly afterlife. Not so, argued the Catholic church: Zwingli was promptly arrested and thrown into jail, but his sausages helped spark the Reformation in Switzerland. Fish was another beneficiary of these changing ideas that linked religion and food. Pinkard explains that through the defiant acts of reformers, fish no longer carried "such a heavy burden of association with self-denial and penitence."[26]

Anchovies reach uncharted waters: Le Cuisinier françois

Anchovies' long-awaited coming-out party occurred in 1651 with the publication of François Pierre de La Varenne's *Le Cuisinier françois*. Almost single-handedly, La Varenne launched anchovies as a key flavoring agent for aristocratic cuisine. The Sergent series of cookbooks had laid the groundwork for modern French cuisine, establishing the combination of fish and butter. But it was not until the arrival of *Le Cuisinier françois* that anchovies became a key flavoring agent in refined cooking.

Sauces were central to La Varenne's success. His recipe for "Pike with sauce," found in the English translation of his book,

The French Cook (1673), demonstrates his new approach. Once the pike is poached:

> ... take off the skin and take a drop of your short broth [consisting of the water and vinegar the Pike was cooked in], put it in a dish with half the yolk of an Egg well allayed, some very fresh Butter, and Nutmeg; let the sauce be well thickened [reduce it], and well seasoned with salt, Chibols [chives] and [lemon] peel, and if you will, put in it Anchovies; but take heed it become not oily, and serve your Pike hot.[27]

By combining butter, anchovies, fresh chives, and a dash of the poaching water, a rich, yet lightly briny sauce was concocted. This complemented the natural flavor of the pike, unlike traditional medieval and Renaissance sauces that sought to adjust the pike's humoral dampness through the addition of "dry" spices. The objective was to allow the taste of the principal ingredient to shine through as the protagonist, its flavor intensified by the supporting actor: the humble anchovy.

La Varenne's pike recipe was a dramatic departure from its medieval counterparts. One need only compare it with a pike recipe from *Le Viandier de Taillevent* to notice how tastes were changing. *Le Viandier de Taillevent* seasoned the poached pike with a cameline sauce, which was predominantly flavored by cinnamon as well as ground ginger, grains of paradise, cloves, and nutmeg. Even if the spices were used judiciously, this uncooked sauce poured over a pike would have been a formidable presence.

Spices aside, La Varenne's real innovation was butter; as T. Sarah Peterson writes, he utilized it in a staggering 39 percent of his sauces.[28]

Although La Varenne's embrace of butter charted a new way forward for French cookery, his cooking was not a total break from the past, something later cooks were quick to complain about. His recipe for turbot, for example, features anchovies, ginger, nutmeg, and that old medieval standby, saffron. Nutmeg is featured in almost every fish recipe (La Varenne clearly adored it), and when it is absent, mace often replaces it. While La Varenne may have had one foot in the past when it came to spices, his use of parsley, chives, and a bunch of fresh herbs (what we now call a *bouquet garni*) represented a radical departure from the medieval flavors that had held sway since the Roman Empire.

Anchovies soar to new heights: Le Cuisinier roïal et bourgeois

Our next illustrious cook to embrace anchovies was François Massialot, one of the founding fathers of French cuisine. In 1691, his ground-breaking work, *Le Cuisinier roïal et bourgeois* (released in English in 1702 as *The Court and Country Cook*), was published to great acclaim. What started with the Sergent family of cookbooks and gained momentum with La Varenne, flowered with Massialot. He established a series of foundational master recipes that brought everything to new heights of flavor and refinement. Anchovies appeared in forty-two of his recipes, flavoring a wide range of meats (deer, veal, pig, mutton), all kinds of fowl and seafood, and, above all, sauces (Fig. 2.2).

At the heart of Massialot's new style of cookery were his bouillons, *jus, coulis,* intensely reduced sauces, and *ragoûts* (stews), all of which helped to create the opening for anchovies to enter French cuisine in a big way. A *jus* consisted of the concentrated clear juices extracted from meat, fowl, or fish after hours of roasting over a fire. A *coulis* resembled a *jus,* but included finely ground pieces of meat, fowl, or fish, lending it a thicker texture. Massialot also understood how to capitalize on the flavorsome possibilities of an anchovy, and by introducing them into a *jus* or *coulis* he effectively turbo-charged the umami of a dish.

Massialot's pike recipe sheds light on the way in which tastes were evolving, especially when it came to flavoring fish. After a

Fig. 2.2: Massialot was the *chef de cuisine* to Philip I, brother of King Louis XIV. With his exuberant bow tie and saucy silk stockings beneath his ermine cape embroidered with gold *fleur de lys*, Philip I cut quite the dashing figure. He loved nothing more than attending court in women's clothes and excelled at dinner parties, often attired in the dress of a poor shepherdess. Painting attributed to Claude Lefebvre or Pierre Mignard, circa seventeenth century. (*Courtesy of Mairie de Bordeaux, Musée des Beaux-Arts, photo: F. Deval. Maidun Collection/Alamy Stock Photo.*)

light poaching to firm up its flesh, the pike is gently simmered in a stewpan with white wine, capers, anchovies, fresh garden herbs, mushrooms, and truffles. Taking care to cook at a low simmer—lest the pike overcook and fall apart—the final step requires "a lump of good butter" and a small amount of grated Parmesan cheese.[29] No spices, no mysterious cooking techniques, and no physician required.

By including anchovies in a range of dishes across the culinary spectrum, Massialot deemed them a must-have ingredient in every cook's arsenal.

Garnishing with fish: The Modern Cook

Vincent La Chapelle benefited from Massialot's anchovy insights. La Chapelle was a Frenchman who practiced his craft in England as a cook to the high and mighty, including the Earl of Chesterfield. In 1733, he published the first of his three-volume opus, *The Modern Cook.* In his introduction, La Chapelle observed that similarly to art, all cookery was subject to change. Despite the fact that nearly one third of his recipes were lifted directly from Massialot (especially those with anchovies), La Chapelle's work marked another huge step away from the medieval past and towards a future filled with lighter fare and a new emphasis on vegetables. Mushrooms, artichokes, celery, and asparagus all assumed a new prominence in his innovative cookery style. This was the moment that anchovies had been waiting for, and La Chapelle included them in an astonishing 104 recipes.

Despite these impressive numbers, La Chapelle was quite parsimonious about the quantities of anchovies he used, often calling for only a fillet or two. His anchovy sauce is a deceptive powerhouse of flavor: "Wash well two or three Anchovies, take out the Bones, cut the Anchovies small, put them in a Stew-pan, with a thin Cullis of Veal and Ham, seasoned with Pepper and Salt; let it be hot and relishing."[30] Although the anchovies provide one half of the fire power of this sauce, the contribution of the veal and ham *coulis* should not be underestimated, as it requires "no less than a whole leg of Veal ... and the nut of a ham to make it good."[31] When this intensely reduced *coulis* was added to the anchovy sauce, the result was a umami bomb that astounded aristocrats all across Britain and the continent.

In La Chapelle's recipe for "Chickens with anchovies roasted," anchovies are used in two different ways: both in the sauce and the garnish. Like almost all his meat or fowl recipes, this one begins with spit-roasting the chickens over a fire, an unsurpassed cooking technique that has never gone out of style. For the sauce, two anchovies are combined "with some good cullis" and the juice of one lemon.[32] To plate, the chicken pieces are placed on a bed of sauce, and sliced anchovies draped across them. In this dish, anchovies are not only the hidden secret ingredient, but also are presented in full view as a tantalizing garnish to whet the appetite.

A lighter touch: François Marin

Another cookery book that championed the new modern style of cookery was *Les Dons de Comus, ou, les délices de la table* (1742) by François Marin. One thing that set this cookery book apart from those that preceded it—a quality which the author was at pains to make clear in his introduction—was that Marin did not consider it a cookery book. Nor did he aim to teach one how to cook. Rather, his work was intended as a guide to fine-tune one's cooking in accordance with *the new modern taste*. As befitting such a philosophical approach, Marin did not provide recipes, offering instead lists of dishes and ingredients that might be used to compose a modern meal.

But despite all the talk of "new" and "modern" by Marin, La Chapelle, and others, much of this "new" and "modern" cuisine was in fact merely a refinement of the older-style cookery of Massialot and La Varenne, which was in itself a refinement of late medieval cookery. "This should serve as a reminder," writes

Stephen Mennell, "that even in a time of supposedly rapid culinary change, the break with the past is never very abrupt."[33] Indeed, almost a hundred years earlier, Nicolas de Bonnefons had already persuasively argued for what he called "*le goût naturel*" (the natural taste): "A cabbage soup should taste entirely of cabbage, a leek soup of leeks, a turnip soup of turnips, and so on ... What I say about soup I mean to apply generally as a law for everything eaten."[34]

The increased focus on *le goût naturel* and the intrinsic flavors of seasonal ingredients helped to set French cuisine on its unique trajectory. Gone were all the curious birds and marine animals with which medieval *haute cuisine* was so obsessed: peacocks, storks, swans, cormorants, porpoise, and whale had no place in the modern style of cookery, which emphasized lightness and a concern with how dishes were presented. Although many spices from the past were still used, they were now applied far more selectively, leaving a smaller footprint on the final dish. Even the manner of constructing a meal underwent changes, and a veritable bloom of small dishes, such as *hors d'oeuvres*, *entrées*, and *entremets*, became *de rigueur* in the dining rooms of the rich and famous. It was small dishes like these that would ensure that the humble anchovy played an outsized role in the century to come.

One of Marin's more interesting sauce recipes containing anchovies is *ravigote*, which comes from the verb "to invigorate." This flavorful sauce certainly lives up to its name. The recipe begins by mincing tarragon, chervil, salad burnet (a herb with a faintly cucumber-like flavor), mint, chives, capers, anchovies, garlic, and shallots. This mixture is then combined with oil, mustard, ham essence, salt, pepper, and vinegar. The addition of anchovies and ham essence would up the umami factor nicely in this fragrant herb vinaigrette. Chicken, veal, beef, and vegetables are all candidates to be served with this cold *ravigote* sauce.

THE FRENCH ANCHOVY

Anchovies reach their peak: Menon

One cookery book author embraced anchovies unlike anyone who came before him, publishing the most recipes featuring anchovies in the culinary history of France. To this day, we know him only by his pseudonym, "Menon," but whoever he was, and whoever he cooked for, Menon astutely capitalized on the innate possibilities of the anchovy. His eight cookery books (comprising fifteen volumes) included hundreds of recipes with anchovies, and it was with Menon that anchovies hit their high-water mark in French cuisine.

In *La Science du maître d'hôtel cuisinier, avec des observations sur la connaissance et proprietés des alimens* (1749), seventy-eight recipes include anchovies. In his English-language cookery book, *The Art of Modern Cookery Displayed* (1767), eighty-five recipes include them. Beef, veal, lamb, pork, rabbit, fowl, and even sausages were all amplified by the addition of anchovies. Menon had a keen sense of how anchovies enhanced the taste of fish and seafood, not as a foil but as a complement to slightly deepen the taste of the sea. He was also a master of micro-dosing; in his "duck with a duck sauce," just a single anchovy is added. This light touch is particularly evident in his vegetable dishes, where he uses a minimal amount of anchovy to give nature a subtle boost.

Menon also embraced the briny taste of anchovies by themselves, elevating them to be the star attraction in his recipe for *Rôtie (Toast) à la Minime*:

Rôtie (Toast) *á la Minime*;
An Order of Friars so called
Cut pretty large Pieces of Bread-crumbs, and fry
them in Oil; put them in the Table-dish, when
properly drained; and mix chopped Parsley, Shallots,
Capers, Pepper, and a pounded Anchovy, with some
Good Oil; pour this over the Toast; and garnish round
With Fillets of Anchovies soaked.[35]

With this simple recipe, Menon set in motion one of the most pleasurable (and profitable) alliances in anchovy history: anchovies and toast. Menon uses anchovies two ways in his version of anchovy toast. First, chopped shallots, parsley, capers, pepper, and an anchovy are minced together and spread on a piece of oiled toast. Next, the *hors d'oeuvre* is topped with anchovy fillets, displayed as the main attraction, much like in La Chapelle's chicken recipe. This recipe served as a sort of forerunner to what John Osborn would market to great success in England some fifty years later as "Gentleman's Relish," a savory snack enjoyed with fortified wine. Anchovy toast in myriad forms would find a huge following in the years to come.

Not only were anchovies being utilized in new ways during Menon's time, but the readership of cookbooks was also broadening. For centuries, the audience for cookery books had been primarily the inner circle of cooks for royalty and the aristocracy. But that was about to change. Our first glimpse of this change surfaces in Menon's second book, *La Cuisinière bourgeoise* (1746). This was the most successful cookery book published in the eighteenth century, with an unprecedented sixty-five editions. *La Cuisinière bourgeoise* reached the widest audience of any cookery book published at the time in France. But it was not just any audience that brought Menon lasting fame and changed the face of French cookery. It was an audience of women.

While royalty and the aristocracy hired nothing less than the finest male cooks in the land, who had a small armada of assistants at their disposal with a multitude of pots and pans, the majority of the aspiring bourgeoisie filled their kitchens with female cooks who were paid far less, almost always worked alone, and had fewer grandiose ingredients to work with. Targeting women was an astute move by Menon. Even though he never mentioned a woman in the pages of his cookery book, his intended audience was apparent from the feminine term *cuisinière* in the book's title. For the first time in France a cookery book was directed to a female audience, and it changed how cookery was understood throughout the land. Menon's work may have been inspired by the success of the 1727 English work *The Compleat Housewife*, by Eliza Smith, which foresaw women as a sizeable market target.

Although Menon's book contained simplified recipes with less costly ingredients, his cookery was still beyond the reach of 90 percent of the French population. For most of the urban and rural poor, the culinary changes associated with *la nouvelle cuisine* were almost imperceptible, far removed from their one-pot and bread lifestyle. While very little data exists on the diets of the poor in the early modern period, what we do know is sobering. One study indicates that most people in France during this period spent "70 to 80 percent of their income on food."[36] Another study reveals that between 50 and 90 percent of the rural population was unable to procure sufficient calories on a daily basis.[37] They consumed the same subsistence diet as their ancestors, comprising local grains, roots, and cruciferous vegetables day after day. The toll of long working hours, unhygienic living conditions, lack of medical care, and a poor diet meant that the average life expectancy was around thirty-five years of age. The only bright spots in this bleak scenario were Catholic holidays and harvest festivals, when cakes and pastries provided rare moments of sugar-coated levity in an otherwise drab and monotonous diet.

Crème-de-la-Carême: the demise of the anchovy in France

In the spring of 1792, with the French Revolution in full swing, the city of Paris was convulsed with violence and political intrigue. The Bastille had been stormed in July 1789, and within several months, the French monarchy would be abolished, with King Louis XVI and Queen Marie-Antoinette dispatched by guillotine on the Place de la Révolution in 1793.* More than 1,200 people were beheaded in Paris's largest public square at the foot of the Champs-Élysées, including some of the leading figures on both sides of the revolution. Beheadings became an everyday event, and as the more famous (or infamous) heads rolled, they were mounted on pikes and paraded through the cheering streets of Paris.

It was in this context that a boy of ten wandered the streets in search of food and shelter. Like many young boys fending for themselves in the city, hunger was his constant companion, and he drifted through small alleyways scavenging for anything edible. Donkey carts piled with cabbages, turnips, and carrots were always a tempting target. As the carts jostled over rough cobblestones, a turnip or carrot would occasionally tumble out, which an observant lad could pocket on the sly.

The boy stepped into a *boulangerie* (every block had at least one or two), but as usual, there was no bread on the shelves. Food shortages were becoming a regular feature of the revolution, and the boy had known hunger his whole life. He lived with his family in a small shack on Rue de Bac; his father was an impoverished workman who struggled to make ends meet. Years later, the boy would write that he had twenty-five siblings, while others put the figure at ten or fifteen. Whatever the count, there was not enough food for them all.

Not quite old enough to procure an apprenticeship, but with an appetite growing day by day, the boy was shown the door. He

---

* It was later renamed Place de la Concorde to reframe the horror and bloodshed of the Reign of Terror and symbolize the shift towards a more stable and peaceful era. "Concord" refers to a state of harmony and peaceful coexistence among individuals or groups.

wound up near a cheap tavern, where the owner beckoned him over and took him on as a kitchen boy. It was here, in a simple tavern, the name of which has long since been lost, that he began his apprenticeship with food. His name was Antonin, but history remembers him as "Carême."

There must have been something truly remarkable about Carême—some combination of drive, talent, and charisma—for when we next hear of him, he had managed to secure an apprenticeship with one of the most prestigious *pâtissiers* in Paris: Bailly. His apprenticeship at Bailly exposed him to an entirely different class of customer, a clientele far removed from the rough-and-tumble world of the tavern. For these wealthy Parisians, the current rage and "must-have" symbols of sophistication were elaborate pastry constructions known as *pièces montées* (set pieces); in effect, edible centerpieces on dining-room tables.

Carême became obsessed with every facet of *pièces montées*, from their design to their construction. While perfecting his spun-sugar masterpieces, he met one of Bailly's most important clients, who would unlock the doors of Parisian high society and set him on his path to culinary glory. Charles Maurice de Talleyrand-Périgord was the foreign minister of France, but, equally important for Carême, he was a man of enormous appetites who used food as an essential weapon in his diplomatic arsenal. Destiny held that these two, the renowned gastronome and the culinary genius, would recognize in each other an essential trait that was necessary to fulfill their greatness: ambition. Carême soon left Bailly to work in another kitchen, with the proviso that he could freelance on the side for important clients like Talleyrand, who soon became his benefactor. As Talleyrand spread the word about Carême's talents, the young chef found himself in demand all over Paris—including from Napoleon's sister, Pauline Borghèse—for whom he would provide *pièces montées* of unsurpassed quality and originality.

With the French Revolution receding into the past, and Napoleon undertaking a series of campaigns that menaced much of Europe, Talleyrand's diplomatic services became essential to the power-mad emperor. Napoleon urged Talleyrand to purchase the Château de Valençay in the Loire Valley to serve as a peaceful venue to host delicate negotiations, lubricated with the finest food and drink in France (Fig. 2.3). Talleyrand turned to Carême, and at the tender age of twenty-one, the young *pâtissier* and chef found in his patron a level of ambition that matched his own. They fed off each other's egos and together concocted a tribute to their mutual greatness: a different menu for every night of the year, with no repeats. It was an absurd proposition filled with bravado, but one that neither could resist. Such a feat had never been attempted

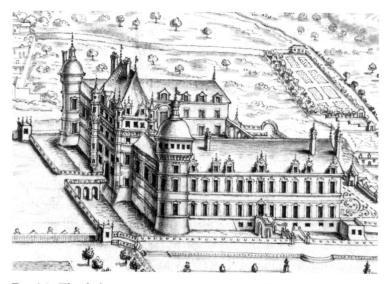

Fig. 2.3: The diplomatic campaign accompanying Napoleon's forays into much of Europe required a relentless schedule of entertaining at the chateau, with up to four diplomatic dinners per week. As Ian Kelly noted, "It was not unusual for him [Carême] to work over 50 days at a stretch without a single day off."[38] (*Courtesy of the Bibliothèque nationale de France.*)

before, and if they were to succeed, it would provide bragging rights that would echo throughout the salons of Paris.

Carême recorded all the menus served at the chateau and included many of them in his cookbook *Le Maître d'hôtel français* (1822). One such menu demonstrates the sheer scale of what they aimed to achieve:

MENU

18th August, Sunday. 10 to 12 covers.

TWO SOUPS

Macaroni soup à la Napolitaine

Consommé à la jardinière

TWO FISH RELEVÉS

Grilled seabass with anchovy butter

Fresh cod purée

TWO GROSSES PIÈCES

Beef à l'étendard

Turkey poult à la Macédoine

FOUR ENTRÉES

Little Shepherd's pies à l'Anglaise

Little aspics à la moderne

Rack of veal with Béchamel sauce

Fricassée of chicken à la Périgueux

TWO ROASTS

Capons with watercress

Pressed ducklings Rouen-style

TWO RELEVÉS

Brioche with dried currants and cream

Mille-feuille à la moderne

FOUR ENTREMETS

A TWIST IN THE TAIL

Cucumbers with teasels à l'Espagnole
Poached eggs with Béchamel sauce
Orange blossom jelly
Caramel custard cooked in a bain-marie[39]

Carême's menu is rather international in scope, which speaks to both the growing cosmopolitan nature of gastronomy in Europe *and* France's response to it. His English-style miniature shepherd's pie (served as a sort of *hors d'oeuvre*), the new-fangled macaroni soup from Naples (a starter), and the Macedonian-style turkey, all illustrate how Carême's grandiose cookery incorporated fashionable dishes from beyond France's borders. Domestically, certain regions were elevated and acknowledged by the name of their city of origin.

By way of example, Carême's pressed ducklings Rouen-style would soon become an iconic dish of lasting fame in France and around the world. This dish is still served to this day in one of the most famous restaurants in Paris, La Tour d'Argent. After removing the duck breast, the carcass is placed in a press, and tremendous pressure is applied, resulting in a stream of blood and marrow which forms the basis of the blood-wine sauce that is served over the duck breast. By naming many of his specifically French dishes after the regions or towns in which they originated, Carême helped to unify modern French cuisine, stitching the disparate regions of France together into a cohesive nation state. What Rabelais started, Carême brought to fruition.

Carême's menu also includes two dishes served with a béchamel sauce—one of his key contributions to modern French *haute cuisine*. To make his béchamel sauce, one begins by making a *velouté*, which is the time-bandit and money thief of this recipe. "*Velouté*" is the French word for "velvet" (which described the consistency of this sauce). Along with béchamel, it is one of the five mother sauces in *la cuisine classique*. Following Carême's instructions for the *velouté*, one places two slices of ham, a nut of veal, and a fowl in a pan. Things quickly become complicated when Carême calls for simmering it all in beef stock. How complicated? Carême helpfully notes that you should start the beef stock "first thing in the morning," as the basic simmer required five hours, not counting various steps involving vegetables. And how much beef for the beef stock? Carême suggests a "beef rump," which butchers typically sold in a 5-kilogram (10-pound) chunk. The *velouté* also requires an equal amount of fowl consommé, which also needs five hours of simmering, not counting prepping the birds or the vegetables, to say nothing of passing it all through a sieve to achieve the right consistency. In total, one is looking at a minimum of eight hours of concurrent simmering and reducing before the actual béchamel sauce can even be started.

So, where does all this costly meat and fowl and endless simmering and reducing get us? To umami (even if the term "umami" was completely unknown at that time). The reduction of roasted meats and fowl down to their essence creates an intoxicating undercurrent of protein-rich flavor so intense that when it strikes the glutamate receptors that carpet the tongue, an electrical signal is sent to the brain, provoking squeals of gastronomic ecstasy. Umami is one of the keys to understanding the popularity of Carême's acclaimed mother sauces.

There is only one small problem, though: Carême's béchamel sauce was totally impractical for the home cooks of his day, as it took forever to accomplish and cost a small fortune to make. It was recipes like these that eventually drove some English cooks (mostly women of modest means) mad, and made them rail against this kind of wasteful cooking. To squander 10 pounds of beef, numerous fowl, ham, and even some veal just to make a "French" sauce was considered absurd. For the frugal English, this epitomized everything that was wrong with French cuisine (and France).

And the fate of our humble anchovy? *Pas bien.*

Carême's umami-rich sauces marked the beginning of the end for anchovies in French cuisine. Carême sidelined anchovies from the main event, restricting them to guest appearances in *hors d'oeuvres* or the occasional flavored butter. In his cookery book *Le Maître d'hôtel français* (1822), fifteen of the fish dishes are served with anchovy butter (the mildest way to flavor with an anchovy), eight are served with an anchovy butter sauce (slightly more flavorful), and five are served with a traditional anchovy sauce (fully robust). As for meat and fowl, only three recipes in

Fig. 2.4: The frontispiece (cropped) to *L'Art de cuisine française* (1833), with a portrait of Carême engraved by Blanchard. Eventually comprising five volumes, this series was his masterpiece, an encyclopaedic work establishing himself as the foremost authority on French *haute cuisine* and the most famous chef in the world. (*Heritage Image Partnership Ltd/Alamy Stock Photo.*)

the entire cookbook include anchovies, all of which feature beef served with anchovy butter.

While Carême's mother sauces provided part of the explanation for the demise of anchovies in French cuisine, another factor was also at play. In post-revolutionary France, French *haute cuisine* was still trying to disentangle itself from its medieval roots. Carême followed suit, reducing the use of spices and replacing them with fresh herbs, such as tarragon, thyme, chervil, and parsley. In the process of tempering the last vestiges of medieval seasoning, Carême also cast out anchovies, locking them into a new, much more constrained role. From this point forward, anchovies were considered too brash, too loud. Although anchovies still featured in regional cooking from the south, they never regained their prominence in French *haute cuisine*.

By the early nineteenth century, France came to symbolize gastronomic greatness quite unlike any other country in the West. While the English may have been partial to English food, and Germans to German food, in France, the idea of culinary exceptionalism took root as national pride. The French responded to Carême's belief that French cuisine was on a par with the other fine arts, such as painting, sculpture, and architecture. As his countrymen came to see French cuisine as the best, so too did the rest of Europe. Before long, French cuisine was perceived around the world as the very embodiment of refinement and sophistication, but anchovies were no longer a central flavor enhancer and were largely left off the menu (Fig. 2.4).

The nail in the anchovy tin: Georges Auguste Escoffier

By the turn of the twentieth century, the most celebrated chef in the world, and the man whose very name had become synonymous with French *haute cuisine*, was Georges Auguste Escoffier. Among his many accomplishments, Escoffier codified French cookery, compressing it into a series of rules that cooks could master. He engineered the modern commercial kitchen and defined how food ought to be prepared within it. He also wrote the definitive French cookbook, *Le Guide culinaire* (1903), an encyclopaedic tome which is still revered as a foundational text. Such was his fame that everyone, from the renowned stage actress Sarah Bernhardt to the Prince of Wales, demanded to dine on Escoffier's food. The well-heeled clamored for a table at one of his restaurants, first at the Savoy in London, then at the Ritz in Paris, and finally at the Carlton Hotel in central London.

Escoffier took his culinary cues from Carême, as did every cook worth his salt in France. Emulating the great master meant drawing on his celebrated *cuisine classique*, an ornate and complex style of cookery. But reproducing Carême's cooking presented several problems. Firstly, despite all the modifications that Carême had made to *haute cuisine*, his cooking was still rooted in an earlier era. His dishes were often characterized by excessive spices and competing flavors. Secondly, Carême's recipes were difficult to execute in the tiny rooms that passed for commercial kitchens in Paris. While Carême did most of his cooking for private families in spacious, well-equipped kitchens, Escoffier found himself working in stifling, hot, cramped, smoke-filled basements. He lacked the space, manpower, and pantry to recreate Carême's elaborate and time-consuming recipes.

The solution to both problems was to simplify the great master's recipes. Escoffier's own personal style emerged, with a subtle approach to flavoring that dramatically limited spices and drew more heavily upon butter and cream. By relieving Carême's recipes of their intricacies, Escoffier introduced a no-nonsense approach to *haute cuisine*. According to the great French chef Michel Roux Jr., simplification became a sort of mantra for

Escoffier, a rallying cry that he repeated over and over throughout the years: *"Faites simple!"*

Escoffier's approach to béchamel sauce is a perfect example. He eliminated all the meat from Carême's indulgent version, but for a half-pound of veal (which was the star attraction in much of his cooking). To this, he added 8 ounces of butter and a mind-boggling 4.5 quarts of milk. A minced onion, salt, pepper, nutmeg, cloves, and a sprig of thyme rounded out the sauce. This béchamel sauce went on to conquer the world. *Faites simple.*

While Escoffier could never have too much dairy in his dishes, anchovies were almost non-existent. Less than 1 percent of the recipes in *Le Guide culinaire* contain anchovies, a scant 24 in a collection of over 3,000. Out of 223 vegetable recipes in his cookbook, only 2 include anchovies, and one of those is the regional Provençal dish of stuffed tomatoes. Such statistics point to the end of an era.

The only place Escoffier consistently used anchovies was in *hors d'oeuvres*, a trend that kicked off with Carême. Anchovy *allumettes* (an anchovy fillet on puff pastry), anchovy medallions (boiled potato disks with an anchovy fillet and egg), and rolled anchovies (pitted olives stuffed with butter and encircled by an anchovy) were all indicative of the new culinary real estate that anchovies came to occupy. Kerb appeal became increasingly important: whether wrapped around, folded over, or draped across, anchovy fillets were always plainly visible in Escoffier's *hors d'oeuvres*. This highly visual and decorative role for anchovies carried over to main dishes, such as Escoffier's cold salmon, where they were used to create a lattice pattern on the salmon after it was cooked. This stood in contrast to the behind-the-scenes approach traditionally used by chefs such as La Chapelle, Marin, and Menon.

A TWIST IN THE TAIL

Michelin stars outshine the humble anchovy

Anchovies in France took a big hit with Escoffier, then were dealt a fatal blow by a French tyre company. It all started innocently enough with two ambitious brothers and their desire to sell more automobile tyres. What they needed was a marketing gimmick to encourage more car owners to travel around France, thereby leaving more rubber on the road. In 1900, Édouard and André Michelin published their first road guide for motorists, exhorting the wonders of the French countryside with maps, hotels, and the all-critical list of garages where they could have a flat tyre repaired or, even better, buy a new one. In 1931, the Michelin Guide expanded to include a restaurant rating system that awarded stars based on the quality of the cooking and service. Over the course of the following decades, the Michelin Guides became runaway bestsellers, transforming how the public came to perceive fine dining. By simply bestowing a 1-, 2-, or 3-star rating, the guides revolutionized how we critique restaurants. Critics could write a 1,000-word essay filled with insight and nuance, but all the public wanted to know was how many stars a restaurant had.

Despite its success, the Michelin star system had unintended consequences in its early days. As Sakhi Nair points out, "Stars were only awarded to those restaurants that adhered to the rules of orthodox French cuisine."[40] As stars translated directly into profits, this placed tremendous pressure on chefs not to deviate too far from the principles laid down by Escoffier. There was little financial incentive to evolve, only to refine. Legions of chefs reproduced Escoffier night after night, decade after decade. Customers reinforced this trend by demanding that their "Lobster Thermidor" or "Duck à l'orange" taste the same whether it was prepared in Paris, Miami Beach, or Rio de Janeiro.

THE FRENCH ANCHOVY

A point of difference: Fernand Point and nouvelle cuisine

If Escoffier was the Catholic Pope of French *haute cuisine*, then Fernand Point was the dissident who planted the seeds for the reformation. While everyone else was painstakingly reproducing Escoffier, Point struck out in a different direction. Nathan Myhrvold, author of *Modernist Cuisine*, notes that Point "developed his own experimental cuisine," allowing the ingredients themselves to guide him.[41] "Mr. Point's menu was hand-written every day by his wife," writes *The New York Times* food and wine critic, Florence Fabricant, "and it depended on what the chef found in the market, a new approach at the time."[42] Several of France's future greats, chefs like Paul Bocuse, the Troisgros brothers, and Alain Chapel, worked as apprentices in Point's kitchen. Each of them would be instrumental in the creation of *la nouvelle cuisine*, the culinary movement that first rocked France, and then the world.

The label *la nouvelle cuisine* was a bit of a misnomer as it did not denote a consistent cooking style or technique but was rather an expression of freedom. The driving force behind it was clear enough: the desire to craft new kinds of cooking unencumbered by the old rules. Frustration had been building up for decades, and by the 1960s, a group of French chefs had had enough. Slowly at first, and then with increasing momentum, chefs brought a new sensibility into the kitchen, with an emphasis on simply prepared, healthy, seasonal ingredients. Ironically, this had been the declared aim of chefs ever since the time of La Varenne. The era of overcooked fatty foods doused with rich sauces that left you cemented to your seat had overstayed its welcome. *La nouvelle cuisine* allowed chefs to invent their own rules, incorporating flavors and techniques from around the world.

The influence of *la nouvelle cuisine* was apparent the moment one was seated in a restaurant. Traditionally, restaurants serving *la cuisine classique* were known for their elaborate menus, featuring hundreds of individual items. It was not uncommon to find chicken prepared in a dozen different ways. But maintaining such an extensive repertoire required the kitchen to utilize partially precooked dishes and to have a storeroom full of canned and prepackaged goods to ensure that every item was available year-round. Seasonality was often sacrificed at the altar of an extensive menu.

One of the central tenets of *la nouvelle cuisine* was to reveal the underlying essence of an ingredient or dish, as opposed to covering it up with a rich, meat-based sauce with its own distinct personality. The great French chef Daniel Boulud cites an early recipe that he considered instrumental to the development of *la nouvelle cuisine*. "The celebrated Troisgros brothers," he writes, "created thousands of dishes for their Michelin-three-star restaurant in Roanne, France, but this dish, Salmon and Sorrel Sauce ... more than any dish created by any other chef, marked the passage from the classic cooking of Escoffier to *la nouvelle cuisine*."[43]

What made this such an epoch-defining dish was a combination of technique, presentation, and a discerning use of ingredients. Traditionally, salmon was either poached or sautéed in a small lagoon of butter. Once plated, it was topped with a rich and decadent sauce. The Troisgros brothers' recipe tossed all that out of the window. Instead, the salmon was flash-cooked in a hot, dry, non-stick pan, with no butter or oil whatsoever. In keeping with one of the basic tenets of *la nouvelle cuisine*, it was only briefly seared—two minutes on the skin side followed by ten seconds on the flesh side—leaving the salmon succulent and tender. The next step was equally important: the sauce was plated first, with the fish placed on top. "It may not sound like much now," Boulud writes, "but it changed the way food was experienced."[44] The ingredients for the sauce were simplicity itself: a touch of butter, two mushrooms, a shallot, a little white wine and cream, and 2 ounces of sorrel. *Faites simple*, as Escoffier liked to say.

Despite the success of recipes like "Salmon with sorrel sauce," the public (as well as many chefs) were nonetheless baffled by *la nouvelle cuisine*. This prompted the journalist Henri Gault to create some guiding principles to define its parameters. In 1973, Gault published his manifesto, "The Ten Commandments of Nouvelle Cuisine." An abridged version reads as follows:

1. Thou shalt not overcook.
2. Thou shalt use fresh, quality products.
3. Thou shalt lighten thy menu.
4. Thou shalt not be systematically modernist.
5. Thou shalt nevertheless seek out what the new techniques can bring you.
6. Thou shalt avoid pickles, cured game meats, fermented foods, etc.
7. Thou shalt eliminate rich sauces.
8. Thou shalt not ignore dietetics.
9. Thou shalt not doctor up thy presentations.
10. Thou shalt be inventive.[45]

"The Ten Commandments" made it hard for the anchovy to prosper. Where things went particularly awry was with Commandment 6, which advocated avoiding marinades, cured game, and—most concerning for the beleaguered French anchovy—fermented foods. In one fell swoop, these umami-rich foods were singled out as problematic, and for many, anchovies epitomized fermented foods. Just when France was moving beyond *la cuisine classique* and embracing the possibilities of *la nouvelle cuisine*, the door once again started to close for anchovies. Writing in *The New York Times*, Amanda Hesser notes that between the 1960s and the turn of the twenty-first century, anchovies "were largely discredited."[46] Even the Caesar salad found itself being served without anchovies.

If one wanted to locate anchovies in *la nouvelle cuisine*, one could find them resting delicately in anchovy butter. Paul Bocuse, one of the most well-known French chefs in the world, featured anchovy butter in four recipes in his cookbook, *Paul Bocuse's French Cooking* (1977). Bocuse's cooking was characterized by his light touch, hence the choice of anchovy butter. Of the remaining six recipes that included anchovies, three were Provençal in origin, while the "Eel stew Burgundy style" was a refined version of a recipe that harkened back to an earlier era. Despite his stature as one of the greats of modern French cooking, Bocuse chose to keep anchovies at arm's length; respected, but almost exclusively relegated to butter.

Forever a fashionable fish: anchovies in Provençal cuisine

Despite *la haute cuisine* and *la nouvelle cuisine* limiting the role of anchovies in France, they were not totally invisible during this period. In the far south of the country along the Mediterranean coast, Provençal cuisine had been quietly celebrating them for hundreds of years. In the land of lavender and well-crafted rosé wine, affection for the humble anchovy never wavered, even as far back as the beginning of the nineteenth century.

The cookbook *Le Cuisinier méridional d'après la méthode Provençale et Languedocienne* ("The Southern Cook Based on the Method in Provence and Languedoc"), published in 1835, was a treasure trove of anchovy recipes, some of which challenged our most fundamental notions of what constituted a dish from Provence. For instance, when we think of a cold salad from Provence that includes anchovies, a Niçoise salad comes to mind. But curiously, no Niçoise salad is listed in this collection. Instead, we are presented with a *Turbot en salade*, in which turbot is substituted for tuna. Aside from the choice of fish, it is the same salad: on a bed of lettuce one adds hard-boiled eggs, anchovy fillets, pickles, capers, and white onion rings that have been simmered in consommé and then cooled (note the lack of potatoes). Turbot or tuna? Perhaps the substitution of turbot was intended to upscale the dish. Or could it be that at this early date, all kinds of fish were used in cold salads that featured anchovy fillets (as was the case in Italy), and that only over time did a version associated with tuna and the city of Nice emerge, proving to be the most popular?

The cookbook also provides a snapshot of how new ingredients were reshaping traditional recipes. When we think of the gastronomy of southern France, we often think of ripe tomatoes, zucchini, and potatoes, all of which are emblematic of Provençal cookery. But we should not conceptualize contemporary Provençal cookery as representative of the past. The chef and historian Clifford Wright writes that throughout the Middle Ages and well into the eighteenth century, the staples in southern France (like most of Europe) were cabbage and root vegetables. Even seafood, such as anchovies and sardines, was out of reach for all but the wealthiest, and most of the catch was salted and shipped to inland markets where it commanded higher prices.

What were well-represented in *Le Cuisinier méridional* are tomatoes, which within a couple of decades would become deeply entrenched in Provençal cookery as one of its most defining flavor profiles. Surprisingly, the pairing of tomatoes and anchovies—brothers in arms that brighten any dish—did not appear in a single recipe, although this was something that Italians just down the coast had become acquainted with a century prior.

One glaring omission from *Le Cuisinier méridional*—perhaps because it was too rustic—was *pissaladière*, the famous southern French tart that combines anchovies, olives, and caramelized onions baked on flat bread. With no cheese or tomatoes to temper its robust flavors, one contemporary has described it as a pizza with all the ingredients little kids cannot stand. While *pissaladière* is often thought of as a quintessentially southern French dish, an enduring symbol of Provence, its actual history, like tomatoes, zucchini, and potatoes, reveals a more complicated past. *Pissaladière* is not so French after all.

Like most of the small coastal towns in the region, Nice drew its culinary cues from the powerful Republic of Genoa in Italy, and this, in turn, provides one of several clues as to the origin of *pissaladière*. Linguists pointed out that the word *"pissaladière"* originated in the Ligurian region of Italy, of which Genoa is the capital. Further, many pointed to a dish in Genoa—a piece of flat bread brushed with a sort of *garum*-like fish paste—as the origin of *pissaladière*. Over time, the tradition of utilizing the least valuable parts of a salted fish (head, tail, innards) was adopted in Nice. This eventually evolved into the more decorative creation we know today, with anchovy fillets artfully arranged in a lattice or crisscross pattern on a bed of richly caramelized onions and interspersed with local Niçoise olives (Fig. 2.5).

Jumping forward about a century, in Jean-Noël Escudier's cookbook, *La Véritable Cuisine Provençal et Niçoise* (1964), anchovies are mentioned in a rousing ninety-two recipes. Some of Escudier's recipes lean heavily upon anchovies and broadcast their presence, while in others they are practically undetectable, unbeknownst to anyone but the chef. If one seeks an anchovy *hors d'oeuvre*, a number of candidates suggest themselves: pâté *à la Provençal*, *anchoïade*, anchovies with tomatoes, or Toulon-style bell peppers with anchovies. Anchovies are equally well-represented in the sauces, and in addition to the usual suspects—many made without butter or cream—Escudier's book presents more exotic fare, such as an anchovy and truffle sauce and a rather intriguing anchovy and almond sauce from the Var region. Meat, fowl, and fish all benefit from the warm embrace

Fig. 2.5: *Pissaladière* had its humble origins as fermented fish slop spread on bread, but with the addition of anchovy fillets, it attained a new level of respectability. (*MBI/Alamy Stock Photo.*)

of anchovies; they are an added plus in pasta dishes, make an ideal companion for vegetables, and bring a little sass to Provençal-style salads.

Escudier's basic *anchoïade* recipe calls for a mixture of anchovies, olive oil, a touch of vinegar, a pinch of pepper, and a crushed clove of garlic. For those looking to live a little more daringly, Escudier presents a second *anchoïade* recipe courtesy of the Provençal gastronome Count Austin de Croze. The recipe calls for twenty-four anchovy fillets; twelve packed in oil from Collioure, the small French fishing village on the border of Spanish Catalonia famous for its anchovies, and twelve preserved in salt. To these, one adds twelve almonds, three dried figs, two cloves of garlic, a small onion, herbs de Provence, a little fennel, red pepper, olive oil, and a spoonful of decadence (i.e. orange blossom water). Who said *anchoïade* doesn't do fancy?

A fish with two tales: anchovies in northern and southern France

When we talk about the French anchovy, then, we are actually talking about two different anchovies, each circulating in its own milieu. Day in and day out, the humble Provençal anchovy has unassumingly enhanced the cuisine of the south. The other anchovy—the one that made its way north to the City of Light—has been on a 400-year roller coaster ride. After a mediocre career in the Middle Ages, when it often needed costly spices to "ennoble" it, the *haute cuisine* anchovy rose to the very pinnacle of fine dining around the world, only to fall from favor and hit rock bottom in the twentieth century.

Nowadays, French cuisine has hit its stride once again: it is lighter and more flavorful (even playful), and the debates between traditional French food and innovation are *du passé*. Modern French chefs are free to take what they want from tradition, as they craft dishes limited only by the reach of their imagination. Paris is currently gaining more Michelin stars than ever—in 2020, it trailed only Tokyo on the list of cities with the most—and the quality of food and wine has never been better. Even "The Ten Commandments" have been revised: in the new version, fermented foods are welcomed with open arms. Fortunately, increasingly so are anchovies.

Atlantic
Ocean

North Sea

o Glasgow

Newcastle upon Tyne

o York
o Leeds

Manchester o

Nottingham o

B R I T A I N

Great
Yarmouth

Worcester o

Gloucester o

Oxford o

London

Thames
Reading
River

Canterbury

Irish Sea

Lewes

Dorchester o

English Channel

N   0   25   50 miles
    0   25   50 km

3

THE BRITISH ANCHOVY

CURTAILED BY THE CONVENIENCE OF CONDIMENTS

In the thousand years following the fall of Rome, anchovies faded from the gastronomic landscape of the British Isles. But with the increased trade that commenced at the end of the sixteenth century, salted anchovies started to appear on the stage of British cuisine. The consumption of anchovies in elite circles gained momentum in the seventeenth and eighteenth centuries when culinary traditions from France washed up on British shores. And then the story took a wildly unexpected turn with bottles of quick-fix umami that contributed to a bona fide anchovy efflorescence in wider British society. Not since the ancient Romans colonized England and brought with them their treasured garum *had anchovies featured so prominently in the British Isles.*

Swimming against the tide: a rough start for anchovies in England

England's earliest cookery book is a collection of recipes originally compiled in the court of King Richard II in the fourteenth century, named *The Forme of Cury*. While its foreign-sounding title might conjure up images of dishes from the Indian subcontinent, it essentially means "A Method of Cookery." Some have argued that it may have been compiled as a counterpart to recipe collections that were in circulation on the continent, such as *Le Viandier de Taillevent* in France or the *Libro della cocina* on the Italian Peninsula. But unlike those collections, which both contain a number of recipes that include anchovies, *The Forme of Cury* contains none.

The lack of anchovies in *The Forme of Cury* should not surprise us, as anchovies appear only fleetingly in the waters surrounding the British Isles. It takes a unique combination of water temperature and currents to create the right conditions for anchovies to thrive so far north. Even when anchovies were present in the past, they were often misidentified as sprat or baby herrings, which is why they were never recorded when the catch was brought into port. While Britain was a seafaring nation, and seafood composed a significant proportion of its diet, for the most part, anchovies were not included until they were imported from the Mediterranean Sea.

Even the word *anchovy* itself was probably not well known until near the end of the sixteenth century. The first written mention of the word was recorded in 1596–7, and it came to us from a surprising source: William Shakespeare. Our revered Bard introduced a host of new words into the English language, including *bandit*, *lacklustre*, and *lonely*, among many others. But it is the word *anchovy* that interests us, and to set the stage for its first appearance in print in England, we turn to Shakespeare's *Henry IV, Part 1*. The play was set in the tumultuous period of the early fifteenth century, when civil war was looming on the horizon. King Henry IV's son, Henry Prince of Wales, aka Prince Hal, was a bitter disappointment to his father, a dynamic that speaks to the timelessness of certain father/son relationships. Tired of the tedium at court, Prince Henry loved nothing more than carousing with ne'er-do-wells and hustlers. As we pick up the action in Act II, Scene iv, we find him drinking with his motley crew in a tavern as he orders one of his cronies to search the pockets of Falstaff, who is passed out in a chair:

PRINCE HENRY

Hark, how hard he fetches breath. Search his pockets.

He searcheth his pockets, and findeth certain papers.

What hast thou found?

PETO

Nothing but papers, my lord.

PRINCE HENRY

Let's see what they be: read them.

PETO

[Reads]

Item, A capon, ... 2s. 2d. [a castrated male chicken, 2 shillings and 2 pence]

Item, Sauce, ... 4d.

Item, Sack, two gallons, 5s. 8d. [a fortified wine from Spain]

Item, Anchovies and sack after supper, 2s. 6d.

Item, Bread, ob.

PRINCE HENRY

O monstrous! but one half-penny-worth of bread to

this intolerable deal of sack! What there is else,

keep close; we'll read it at more advantage: there

let him sleep till day.[1]

From these crumpled receipts, intended as a culinary character description of Prince Henry's wayward friend Falstaff, Shakespeare consigned the word "anchovies" to the English language. How it got there is a more complicated and speculative matter. It may have derived from one of the Portuguese and

Iberian words for anchovies, *anchova*. In turn, the word may have arrived in Portugal via Genoa or Corsica. In either case, the word *anchova* has been linked to the Latin *apua* (going back to the Greek, meaning "small fry"), or even, possibly, the Basque *anchu* (meaning "dried fish").[2] At any rate, we can assume that anchovies were associated with some of society's less desirable elements, as the scene where the action plays out is the seedy Boar's Head Tavern in Eastcheap, the preferred hangout for pickpockets, riff-raff, and drunkards. Not exactly the most auspicious start for anchovies on the British Isles.

While anchovies may have had some unsavory associations in Shakespeare's *Henry IV, Part 1*, a tad over twenty years later they were mentioned by another playwright, only this time, they were noted solely for their minuscule size. In Thomas Dekker's *The Noble Spanish Soldier* (1622), the threat of civil war once again looms large. The Spanish king has reneged on his promise to marry Onaelia, despite having taken advantage of her innocence, leading to the birth of a son. In Act IV, Scene i, Balthazar, a rather hot-headed lad prone to salty language, confronts the Duke of Medina and the Cardinal about a sinister plot to murder the king:

BALTHAZAR

Sirra, you salsa-perilla, rascal, toads-guts, you whorson pockey

French spawn of a butsten-bellyed spider. Do you hear, Monsieur?

MEDINA

Why do you bark and snap at my Narcissus, as if I were de French dog?

BALTHAZAR

You cur of Cerberus litter,

Strikes him

You'll poison the honest Lady? Do but once toot into her chamber-pot, and I'll make thee look worse than a witch does upon a close stool.

THE BRITISH ANCHOVY

CARDINAL

You shall not dare to touch him, stood he here

Single before thee.

BALTHAZAR

I'll cut the rat into anchovies.[3]

For the anchovy metaphor to land on the mark in a split second—as is necessary for effective theatrical timing—the public must, by this point in time, have been as aware that reducing someone to anchovies was the equivalent of our modern expression, "I'll make mincemeat of you."

The rough start for anchovies in the English language continued with the first written mention of them as a food source. In 1620, Tobias Venner published *Via recta ad vitam longam*, a medical treatise that gave health and dietary advice. There was much to like about Venner, as he was an educated man (Doctor of Medicine from Oxford) who promoted a holistic, cutting-edge approach to health. While still adhering to humoral theory, he departed from traditional explanations that emphasized diet almost exclusively, and focused equally on sleep, exercise, excretion, environment, and one's psychological state as factors contributing to optimum health. From this promising beginning, which modern medicine has embraced, his unfavorable theories about preserved fish were a regrettable stumble:

> Anchovas, the famous meat of Drunkards, and of them that desire to have their drinke oblectate the pallat, do nourish nothing at all, but a naughty cholerick blood ... Wherefore they may be convenient for the phlegmatick, so they drink little after them; but in my opinion, the speciall good property that they have, if it be good, is to commend a cup of wine to the pallat, and are therefore chiefly profitable for Vintners.[4]

Strike three against anchovies. Not only were they too salty and bad for your health, but the only benefit they bestowed was to vintners, who profited handsomely by quenching your thirst. Venner's theories were not inconsequential, as his books were aimed at a general, educated audience and enjoyed a wide readership. However, perhaps we can take his advice on salted fish with a grain of salt, as he also advocated the medicinal use of tobacco.

Pepys and his appetite for socializing and salted fish

Despite such dire warnings, anchovies did not entirely disappear from the British palate, and the tradition of consuming anchovies as a salty whet remained alive and well in many quarters. A salty whet—a savory morsel, much like a potato chip—was meant to "whet" your appetite and was often consumed with alcohol. It was as a tasty bite-sized treat that one of the most endearing characters of the mid-seventeenth century—and a bona fide foodie to boot—preferred to eat. His name was Samuel Pepys.

Samuel Pepys (pronounced "peeps"), or Sam, as many affectionately refer to him, came from a modest though not impoverished background. At the age of ten, he was sent away to live with a childless uncle in London who enrolled him in grammar school. Through hard work and family connections, he eventually secured a place at Cambridge University, acutely aware of the social gulf separating him from his well-to-do classmates. Through the intervention of his cousin Sir Edward Montagu (who would become Pepys' lifelong benefactor), a few years after graduation he joined the Navy Board overseeing contracts, a position that would prove to be highly lucrative. Over the next nine years, Pepys kept an extraordinary diary detailing his rise from a penniless clerk to a man who amassed a small fortune and was given audience by King Charles II himself. His diaries also provide a window into a rapidly changing and tumultuous period of British history, over 350 years ago.

Importantly for our purposes, Pepys was a sort of seventeenth-century foodie, and through his diaries, we get a first-hand look at what a rapidly rising naval officer ate in the 1660s. As befitted an Englishman of appetites, our man Pepys never seemed to tire of popping into a tavern for a quick bite to eat. As Kate Colquhoun writes, "Pepys grazed his way through the day at taverns."[5] Much of Pepys' grazing was on anchovies. In the first year of his diary, 1660, he recorded eating them eight times, a significant number of mentions. He had them as a snack in taverns with a spot of drink or while conducting business, as well as at home, often with breakfast or when entertaining guests. In a typical diary entry mentioning anchovies, he wrote about running into old friends on Tower Hill, following which he "took them home and did give them good wine, ale, and anchovies, and staid with them till night, and so adieu."[6] Most likely, these were salted anchovies eaten as a salty whet. Imported from Italy, often from the port of Genoa, anchovies were packed in alternating layers of anchovies and salt in small wooden casks. In England, the anchovies would then have been sold individually to the public at fish markets. Prior to eating, they were rinsed in water or vinegar to remove the excess salt, and then served whole: head, tail, bones, and all (Fig. 3.1).

Thanks to all the funds flowing his way courtesy of his new job, Pepys could now afford to throw dinners parties in a style he could only have dreamed of a few years earlier. Celebrating a successful operation to remove his kidney stones—a risky undertaking that not all survived—Pepys organized a dinner party at his house. He wrote:

> Very merry at, before, and after dinner, and the more for that my dinner was great, and most neatly dressed by our own only maid. We had a fricasee of rabbits and chickens, a leg of mutton boiled, three

Fig. 3.1: Samuel Pepys, age thirty-three, painted in 1666. Pepys loved his lute, and often played it on his rooftop late at night. In his hand he holds some sheet music. (© *National Portrait Gallery, London.*)

> carps in a dish, a great dish of a side of lamb, a dish of roasted pigeons, a dish of four lobsters, three tarts, a lamprey pie (a most rare pie), a dish of anchovies, good wine of several sorts, and all things mighty noble and to my great content.[7]

The celebratory feast was generously laid. Given the conspicuous lack of vegetables, such a diet may have accounted for his malady, but it was not untypical for those of his social standing, particularly when entertaining. Among the delicacies and popular dishes on the menu, anchovies were not merely an ingredient, but a dish in their own right, worthy of recording.

Despite his occasional wenching and the rows it caused with his wife, Elizabeth, Pepys revealed a genuine warmth for her. In yet another diary entry, we can see she was an indispensable ally at another dinner party for his family:

Home from my office to my Lord's lodgings [Pepys' house] where my wife had got ready a very fine dinner—viz. a dish of marrow bones; a leg of mutton; a loin of veal; a dish of fowl, three pullets [juvenile hens], and two dozen of larks all in a dish; a great tart, a neat's tongue [cow's tongue], a dish of anchovies; a dish of prawns and cheese.[8]

Once again, no mention of vegetables, but anchovies were duly noted, as well as some rather revealing insights into the all-too-human dynamics of the evening:

My company was my father, my uncle Fenner, his two sons, Mr. Pierce, and all their wives, and my brother Tom. We were as merry as I could frame myself to be in the company, W. Joyce talking after the old rate [meaning "as usual"] and drinking hard, vexed his father and mother and wife. And I did perceive that Mrs. Pierce her coming so gallant [referring to a flashy dress or appearance], that it put the two young women quite out of courage. When it became dark they all went away but Mr. Pierce, and W. Joyce, and their wives and Tom, and drank a bottle of wine afterwards, so that Will did heartily vex his father and mother by staying. At which I and my wife were much pleased.[9]

All the dynamics of a family gathering were at play: the minor grievances, the slightly domineering guest, and the cousin who drank and talked too much and annoyed everyone, as usual. All of which raises the question, why would Pepys invite this lot to a dinner when they clearly annoy the daylights out of him? Because, for better or worse, they were family, and as is often the case, families must be *endured*. It is perhaps for this reason that the postprandial discussion between Pepys and his wife left him feeling so pleased. One is reminded of the quote by Alice Roosevelt Longworth: "If you don't have anything good to say about someone ... come and sit by me."[10]

Whatever one thinks of Pepys and his interactions with the world around him, one thing is certain: the man loved his anchovies. Whether sitting in his chambers "drinking wine and eating anchovies an hour or two" or shooting the breeze at the Dog Tavern, where he treated Mr. Michell and his wife to "a dish of anchovies and olives," anchovies were part of Pepys' life, consumed much like salted nuts are in our own times.[11]

But occasionally Pepys overindulged on anchovies. One summer evening, Major Hart popped by his house, and the two of them got to talking and drinking and eating anchovies. The conversation must have been juicy as it appears that Pepys lost track of how many anchovies he had eaten. If not properly rinsed with vinegar and desalted, anchovies encrusted with salt are a recipe for disaster. As he noted later in his diary, all the anchovies "made me so dry that I was ill with them all night, and was fain to have the girle [his maid] rise and fetch me some drink."[12] As one who suffered from gout, salted anchovies would have only compounded his problems; but who among us has not enjoyed a little too much of a good thing, knowing full well that we will pay a price for it later?

Cooks catch on to the punchy potential of anchovies

When it came to a love of anchovies, Pepys was very much a man of his time. Starting around the 1650s, a veritable burst of cookery books was published in England after a thirty-year void, and anchovies were suddenly teeming. They went from being a somewhat maligned fish favored by drunkards, to a key flavoring agent of mid-century elite cuisine. Over the following two decades, a survey of cookery books illustrates the dramatic rise of anchovies in English cuisine—in 1653, *A True Gentlewoman's Delight* includes just three recipes containing anchovies, but by 1673, William Rabisha's *The Whole Body of Cookery Dissected* includes a staggering forty-four.

Anchovies were no longer simply a salty whet suitable for taverns, as in Shakespeare's day, but found their way into highbrow kitchens. What might account for the sudden profusion of elite English recipes that included anchovies? Employing Occam's razor, the simplest explanation is that the new affection for anchovies was the result of the recent publication of La Varenne's *Le Cuisinier françois* in 1651. Exactly two years after publication in France, the English translation of this book was released. Correlation, but not necessarily causation. Shortly thereafter, there was a burst of anchovies in British cookery books as the new flavor profiles from France came to dominate elite cookery in Britain.

Robert May's *The Accomplisht Cook* (1660) presented some recipes that epitomize the new style, while others remain firmly tethered to the past. For example, his recipe for "Pike with sauce" was straight out of La Varenne. To a little broth in which the pike has been boiled as a base, he adds butter, nutmeg, an egg yolk, anchovies, lemon, and white wine. This is the essence of the new French style as it allows a pike to taste like pike, intensified by the anchovy. But for all that he borrowed from La Varenne, May still had one foot firmly planted in the past. His "Pigeon" pie is nothing short of a medieval circus: pigeons, veal sweetbreads, sheep's tongues, mutton, larks, cockscombs, oysters, calves' udders, marrow bones, chestnuts, egg yolks, dates, cream, butter, artichokes, asparagus, orange juice, lemon juice, claret wine, and a shelfful of spices.

Rabisha's *The Whole Body of Cookery Dissected* of 1673 illustrates how the upper crust now enjoyed anchovies in everything, from gravies to fish, fowl, and, most prominently, meat. Many of Rabisha's recipes draw on medieval traditions, being still in the thick of a transitional moment in English cookery. The recipe "To stew a carp," for instance, captures both styles perfectly. After cleaning the fish and draining its blood, white wine is boiled with onion, garlic, ginger, nutmeg, herbs, and "three or four anchovies." So far, the recipe is exhibiting good French contemporary ingredients. When the broth boils, the carp is added and poached for fifteen minutes. Harking back to recipes from the past, however, the reserved blood is then added to the broth for a hit of old-fashioned flavor.

While Rabisha was busy addressing the needs of aristocrats, Hannah Woolley, in *The Queen-like Closet* of 1670, directed her attention to the overlooked middling class that sought to emulate elite cuisine on a more restrained budget. Astutely recognizing her audience, her title page read: *The Queen-like Closet; or, Rich Cabinet stored with all manner of rare receipts for preserving, candying and cookery. Very pleasant and beneficial to all ingenious persons of the female sex.* Woolley's brilliance was to simplify the complicated and costly recipes found in male-authored (and highly French-influenced) cookbooks and present them in a straightforward fashion directed towards women. "From her first book in the early 1670s," writes Kate Colquhoun, "Woolley addressed both those women who were rising up the social scale and had to learn it all from scratch and those who were tumbling down it."[13] Woolley included thirty-five recipes containing anchovies in her book, which helped to launch them on their way in Britain.

"To Pickle Sprats like Anchovies" typifies Woolley's recipes geared towards a limited budget. It also hints at the growing appreciation for anchovies in Britain. Sprats, like sardines and herring, are in the same family (*Clupeidae*) but are individual species. All three thrive in Britain's chilly waters. Anchovies, by contrast, are in a different family (*Engraulidae*), and generally prefer more temperate waters. By substituting sprats for anchovies, Woolley provided a low-cost alternative to imported anchovies from the Mediterranean. Following traditional salting techniques, the sprats are laid out in a barrel in alternating rows with salt, bay leaves, and lemon rinds. Making note that the barrel should be filled until it is airtight, the reader is then advised to "set it in a cool Cellar, and once a week turn it upside down; in three months you may eat them."[14] Here, the objective is to achieve a result that is "just as good" as what people of means could afford to have on their tables, at a fraction of the cost.

Pickling was another inexpensive way to enhance a variety of different dishes. Although Woolley's recipe for pickled mushrooms contains a number of spices, not all of them need to be included for a successful pickle. Mushrooms were relatively affordable and accessible, making them an ideal ingredient for a pickle:

To pickle Mushromes

Take them of one nights growth, and peel them inside and outside, boil them in Water and Salt one hour, then lay them out to cool, then make a pickle of White Wine and White Wine Vinegar, and boil in it whole Cloves, Nutmegs, Mace, and Ginger sliced, and some whole Pepper, when it is cold, put them into it, and keep them for Sauces of several Meats.[15]

This recipe offers a glimpse into an early English-style pickle. Most of the population—probably north of 80 percent—ate primarily vegetables on a regular basis. In the spring and summer months, vegetables were eaten fresh, while the rest of the year, they were often eaten pickled. During the height of summer, it was therefore not uncommon to find a harried housewife or her overworked servant in the kitchen, furiously pickling vegetables to last throughout the long British winter.

Prior to the invention of refrigeration, pickling was a common way to preserve food, and the basic technique goes back thousands of years. Pickling operates by way of anaerobic fermentation in salty water (brine) or, more typically in the British Isles, vinegar (acetic acid). Vinegar can be made from any number of ingredients (apples, beer, cane, etc.), but the most common method at the end of the seventeenth century used white wine.

The basic technique for pickling vegetables involved boiling them in hot water (which killed the bacteria), then once they had cooled, adding them to jars filled with vinegar and spices. Every kind of vegetable imaginable was subjected to this preserving process, with onions being a British favorite. Fish, walnuts, samphire, and even fruits were earmarked for pickling.

It was the British tradition of pickling that would pave the way for the acceptance of imported fish sauces (ketchup) that contained anchovies.*

Ketchup catches British attention

Little is known about the first fish sauces (ketchup) to arrive in Britain. Even their names and various spellings are a source of confusion. But what is clear is that as British traders explored East Asia in search of spices and porcelain in the seventeenth century, they encountered two unanticipated items: arrack (distilled alcohol) and fish sauce. Both must have been a godsend to the sea-weary sailors who manned the ships: one quenched their thirst, while the other brought a little flavor to their otherwise dreary and monotonous shipboard fare. As both alcohol and salt are preservatives, arrack and fish sauce held up well under the

---

* The world of ketchup, condiments, sauces, and gravies can be tricky water to navigate. The difference between a ketchup, condiment, and sauce frequently depends upon the historical context, and they were often used interchangeably. Ketchup is a kind of condiment, and when combined with other ingredients, can be used to quickly create a sauce. However, traditional French sauces are typically made from meat reductions and then seasoned in a saucepan. Gravies, unlike sauces, are made from the juices and bits that fall off meats when they are roasted, which are then combined with a thickener. All gravies are sauces, but not all sauces are gravies.

punishing heat and humidity on their long voyages in East Asia. Even better, both could be easily procured in the numerous ports that dotted coastal China, Vietnam, the Philippines, Indonesia, and Malaysia.

Ketchup—or *catchup*, *catsup*, *ka'chup*, and innumerable other variants of the word—has been traced by linguists to the early trading ports that Dutch and British traders visited on the islands of Java and Sumatra.* Small enclaves of coastal Fujianese merchants who had settled on these islands traded their home-made fish sauce—which they called *ke-tchup* in their native Hokkien language (from southern Fujian and Taiwan)—with the Dutch and British. The local Indonesians called this transplanted Fujianese fish sauce *kecap*. Back in Britain, fish sauces became all the rage, and they were most often spelled "catchup."

The first printed mention of the word ketchup in English comes from an unlikely source, *A New Dictionary of the Terms Ancient and Modern of the Canting Crew*. This compendium of slang terms used by thieves and ne'er-do-wells, published in 1698, has an entry for "Catchup—a high East-India sauce."[16] By 1711, when his book *An Account of the Trade in India* was published, Charles Lockyer wrote of the importation of this sauce: "I know not a more profitable commodity."[17] Lockyer's advice was simple enough: after purchasing ketchup in large tubs, one could transfer the contents to small bottles to be sold in England at a great profit. "Soy comes in Tubbs from Jappan," he writes, "and the best Ketchup from Tonquin [northern Vietnam]; yet good of both sorts are made and sold very cheap in China."[18]

How ketchup came to colonize Britain is nevertheless poorly understood. On the one hand, it may have been a top-down phenomenon: Lockyer's "profitable commodity" in little glass

---

* To avoid confusion, the spelling "ketchup" will be adopted in this text unless otherwise noted.

jars might have followed the traditional route of imported spices, textiles, and porcelains, from trading ships to the wharves of London and the aristocratic households that dotted the city and countryside. Ketchup, like imported spices, may have become yet another way to enhance the flavor of food while simultaneously underscoring the social differences between classes. As ketchup spread in elite circles, it may not have taken long for knowledge of it to trickle down to members of the aspirational class who clamored for the exotic new flavor enhancer.

On the other hand, the introduction of ketchup to Britain may have been more of a bottom-up affair, with returning sailors from East Asia yearning for the lively fish sauce that fit right in with the pickling traditions they had grown up with. While British elites enjoyed umami-rich French reduction sauces, for most of the British population—those subsisting on far more humble fare—food had changed very little since medieval times. Basic pottages, bread, and coarse hard cheese were typical, with a rare treat of sheep's head or pig's trotters. In this lackluster gastronomic landscape, imported ketchup would have introduced the protein-rich taste of umami into their daily fare, much as *garum* had done in Roman society.

However, the high price of imported ketchup would likely have kept it out of reach of all but the wealthy. So, utilizing their long tradition of pickling as a starting point, crafty cooks and clever housewives set about reverse-engineering it. Asian ketchup (fish sauce) acquires its umami-rich flavor from anchovies (and other small fish) that are aged in wood barrels or clay jars for up to a year or more. During this time, the dual processes of saline fermentation and enzymatic autolysis take place. In other words, the cellular breakdown of the anchovies (due to the release of their own gut enzymes) creates the sauce's distinctive taste. Enterprising Brits rejigged the process and compensated for the reduced ageing and fermentation by adding a host of spices traditionally used in their pickles (along with the all-essential anchovy). Even though the results did not really mimic imported ketchup, they did succeed in creating savory and spiced hybrids that were eminently suited to the British palate. Indeed, in just a few short years, domestically made ketchups—many flavored with anchovies—would become commonplace, found in both the humblest one-room cottages and the grandest castle kitchens.

The quick and eager acceptance of ketchups in Britain reflected social realities. If one came from the middling to lower classes, homemade ketchups, like homemade pickles, were reasonably economical and had a long shelf life. While French reduction sauces also satisfied the longing for umami, they cost a fortune to produce, requiring vast quantities of meat, considerable labor, and cold storage to preserve them. Further, ketchups did not interfere with the fundamentals of British culinary grammar. Indeed, rather than replace the British tradition of pickling, pickling was a useful complement to the creation of ketchups. And lastly, ketchup was an exotic novelty from Southeast Asia, which caught the public's imagination without any of the baggage associated with their long-time foes, the French.

The first printed recipe for ketchup in Britain is in Eliza Smith's *The Compleat Housewife* (1727). Not only was Smith the first to publish a recipe for a sort of reverse-engineered ketchup, but her fondness for cooking with anchovies in all kinds of dishes crowns her the original "Anchovy Queen." Forty of her recipes include anchovies. In fact, the very first recipe in her book, "To make a soop" (note how she avoids the French term "pottage"), contains anchovies. But it is her "English Katchup" recipe that merits a closer look:

To make English Katchup

Take a wide mouth'd bottle, put therein a Pint of the best White-wine Vinegar; then put in ten or twelve Cloves of Eschalot, peeled and just bruised; then take a quarter of a Pint of the best Langoon White-wine, boil it a little, and put to it twelve or fourteen Anchovies washed and shred, and dissolve them in the Wine, and when cold put them in the Bottle; then take a quarter of a Pint more of White-wine, and put in it Mace, Ginger sliced, a few Cloves, a Spoonful of whole Pepper just bruised, let them boil all a little; when near cold, slice in almost a whole Nutmeg, and some Lemon peel, and likewise put in two or three Spoonful's of Horse radish; then stop it close, and for a Week shake it once or twice a Day; then use it: 'tis good to put into Fish Sauce, or any Savoury Dish of Meat; you may add to it the clear Liquor that comes from Mushrooms.[19]

With the addition of all the anchovies, spices, shallots, vinegar, and wine, what we are looking at is more in the neighborhood of modern Worcestershire Sauce (with its abundant spices) than a traditional Asian fish sauce. The role of ketchup versus whole anchovies in recipes would undergo profound changes in the coming decades as the convenience of ketchup moved it center stage, with whole anchovies diminishing in importance. But all that is in the future.

In the meantime, ketchup was catching on with the public, and cookbook authors—and savvy publishers—were quick to take note. Mary Kettilby's *A Collection of Receipts* was first published in 1714 and went through four editions during her lifetime, but not one of them included a recipe for ketchup. Upon her death, her estate authorized a posthumous and expanded fifth edition (1734), and the publisher astutely included two ketchup recipes. One of the new ketchup recipes, "To make Catchup, that will keep good Twenty Years," forms the basis of most anchovy-based ketchup recipes in the future. And yet, this recipe is distinctly different from Eliza Smith's version. What is even more surprising is that its popularity had less to do with its inner beauty—ingredients, flavor, and character—than with its fancy dress, that is, its clever and colorful marketing. Thanks to its clever sales pitch, it would become the most enduring and commonly plagiarized anchovy-based ketchup recipe in English history. It is the ketchup recipe that would launch a thousand imitators.

For the new "Catchup" recipe in the fifth edition of Kettilby's cookery book, a base of strong and stale beer was proposed. This was a departure from Eliza Smith's more reassuring base of vinegar and white wine, which, in conjunction with the lemon peel, would have lent it more pleasing acidic and floral notes. Nonetheless, the substitution did not hamper the fame of her recipe.

Perhaps the most convincing explanation for the success of the beer-based anchovy ketchup relates more to the promise in its title than its flavor. For the frugal, overburdened housewife, knocking out a huge batch of sauce that was guaranteed not to go off was a godsend. Even if everyone suspected it was pure hype, and no one would actually want a sauce that was that old on their food, it was a marketing bullseye in the era before mechanical refrigeration. Pickled ketchup, like pickled vegetables generally, doesn't go bad after one season (it just deteriorates in quality). By implying that ketchup could go bad, the recipe title homed in on every housewife's fears. In case readers still had any doubts, they included in her book that oft repeated and plagiarized line: "[t]his is thought to exceed what is brought from India."[20] Not only would the ketchup keep for twenty years; it was also even better than the imported stuff.

One cookbook author who brilliantly claimed Kettilby's recipe as her own is the second of our two great Hannahs: Hannah Glasse, who was brilliant not because she made any contributions to the recipe—all she did was the old trick of mixing up the order of the ingredients—but for her clever editorial additions, which served to cement Kettilby's ketchup as the standard-bearer of eighteenth-century ketchup. Whereas Eliza Smith had titled her original ketchup recipe "To make English Katchup," and Mary Kettilby's version followed with the caption

"To make Catchup, that will keep good Twenty Years," Hannah Glasse took things one step further by positioning her ketchup recipe as the lead-off in a chapter titled: "For CAPTAINS of SHIPS." Right beneath, she added a slightly modified version of Kettilby's line: "To make Catchup to keep twenty Years." Everyone knew that sailors spent months, if not years, at sea. What better way for a captain to keep his unruly crew happy than with some long-lasting and flavorful ketchup? The implication was that this ketchup would last equally long in your kitchen cupboard at home. Glasse's only other real contribution to the recipe was the line "You may carry it to the Indies." Whereas Kettilby's ketchup was thought to exceed what came from India, Hannah's plagiarized version was now so good that you could export it back!

Glasse cemented the fate of beer-based anchovy ketchup, as her *The Art of Cookery Made Plain and Easy* (1747) became the bestselling cookery book of the eighteenth century. Almost every cookbook author after her followed the beer-based formula that she pilfered from Mary Kettilby, as opposed to Eliza Smith's more nuanced vinegar and white wine version. Not until commercially made ketchup came into production at the end of the century would this be rectified. Commercial producers were quick to recognize that a vinegar base provided a more reliable level of acidity and a more satisfying taste.

Glasse's *Art of Cookery* captures a pivotal moment in time for anchovies, with whole salted anchovies starting to be replaced by anchovy-based ketchup. Although this trend can be detected earlier, the runaway success of Glasse's cookery book resulted in a large-scale shift. For example, up to this point, almost every cookbook recipe for "Calf's head" calls for the addition of various amounts of whole, salted anchovies. But in Glasse's cookery book, neither "To hash a calf's head" nor "To hash a calf's head white" contain whole anchovies; both call for an anchovy-based ketchup. And who could resist the delightful-sounding recipe,

"To stew a turkey brown the nice way"? The secret ingredient? A spoonful of anchovy-based ketchup.

Central to the success of Glasse's cookery book was the recognition that most cooks and servants struggled to understand the technical terms and French-named ingredients used by male cookbook authors. "If I have not wrote in the high, polite stile," wrote Glasse, "I hope I shall be forgiven."[21] Her goal, as she makes clear, is to craft a cookbook that could actually be used by home cooks—almost exclusively women. In contrast to her male colleagues, who often called for lardons, Glasse simplified the language and called for good old-fashioned English bacon, so everyone was clear. "The great Cooks have such a high way of expressing themselves," she wrote, "that the poor girls are at a loss to know what they mean."[22]

Glasse's straight talk and spirited defence of England's home-grown cookery was highly appealing at a time when many felt intimidated about living in the shadows of aristocratic French cuisine. Glasse's hostility to the French mirrored the sentiments of her countrymen and women, culminating in a new, non-elite English sense of identity. Contributing to her personal animosity towards French-trained male cooks, as Gilly Lehmann points out in *The British Housewife* (2002), may have been the practice of paying them an average of £60 per year, while female cooks would have been lucky to make £10. Glasse frequently lashes out at the former in her book:

> I have heard of a cook that used six pounds of butter to fry twelve eggs, when every body knows, (that understands cooking), that half a pound is full enough, or more than need be used: but then it would not be French. So much is the blind folly of this age, that they would rather be imposed on by a French booby, than give encouragement to a good English cook.[23]

Despite all her antagonism towards the French, Glasse (like Eliza Smith before her) could not deny that they knew a thing or two about cooking. Consequently, she included more than a few French-inspired recipes, although she anglicized the titles. "Boeuf a la mode" in Pepys' day was now given the more accessible name, "Beef a la mode the French way," in Glasse's book. It was precisely this kind of practical approach that made her book such a success. In a section titled "Rules to be observed in Roasting," she states that a pig would be sufficiently roasted after an hour if just killed, or an hour and a quarter if killed the day before. "But the best way to judge," she writes, and not for the squeamish, "is when the eyes drop out."[24]

Hannah Glasse created a cookery book that was truly British, despite drawing heavily upon French-inspired recipes. No less than Clarissa Dickson Wright considered her "one of the greats of English food history."[25] Yet sadly Glasse's domestic affairs did not match the success of her book: she was declared bankrupt in 1754, served time in a debtors' prison, and was eventually forced to sell the copyright of her book. Upon release, she wrote two more cookbooks, but neither enjoyed the success of her first.

Anchovies reach their high point: cookery books in the eighteenth century

The great English essayist George Saintsbury (1845–1933) once wrote: "All sensible and well-informed people know that cookery books are delightful reading," and none more so than British cookery books written in the early eighteenth century.[26] During this period, the authorship and audience of cookery books took a gendered turn, as female writers sought to address young women's daunting prospects of getting married and running a household. Tips on household management and etiquette were in high demand, as they were considered crucial for aspirational families hoping to claw their way up the social ladder. Since these female-authored books met an immediate need for house-wives and their overworked housekeepers, many of them went on to be published in numerous editions. These far outsold those written by their authors' male counterparts, who directed their works towards a narrower market of male chefs and their aristo-cratic employers.

Regardless of their intended audience, every cookery book author at the end of the seventeenth and beginning of the eigh-teenth century owed a debt of gratitude to François Massialot, whose recipe collection firmly planted the flag of French cuisine in the kitchen of British elites. One of the first English chefs to adapt Massialot's approach in a wholesale manner was Patrick Lamb, author of *Royal Cookery; or, The Complete Court-Cook*, published posthumously in 1710. As befitting a master chef who cooked for English kings, queens, and nobility of the highest rank and worth, Lamb dispensed with the more mundane aspects of household management to focus all his attention on food and the art of fine dining. The protocol surrounding meals taken at court was serious business, and Lamb included thirty-three fold-out diagrams to illustrate exactly how dishes should be arranged on a dining-room table. Each dish was placed in a symmetrical relationship to those around it, in a choreography of exacting precision that resembled a complex topiary garden. The entire undertaking was meant to impose order on the food served at the table, in contrast to the unruly natural world that lay just beyond the dining-room windows. This was formal, elite dining *à la française*, and it spoke to the power and good breeding of those present (Fig. 3.2).

The first recipe in *Royal Cookery* is for a "Soupe-santé." We know that Lamb means business, as the first sentence of the recipe calls for 12 pounds of beef, to which 6 pounds of veal and a quarter pound of bacon are added. Even the simplest of Lamb's recipes requires immense quantities of meat. A basic "Pea soup"

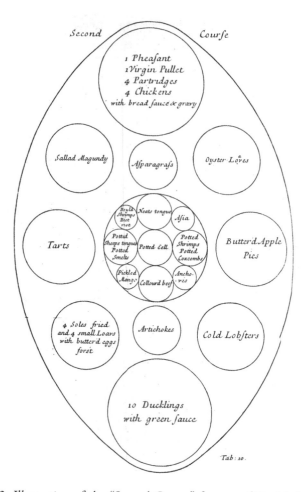

Fig. 3.2: Illustration of the "Second Course" for one of Patrick Lamb's elaborate place settings in *Royal Cookery*. Despite the formality of the arrangement and the presence of so many celebrated dishes, anchovies are right at home. In the outer ring in the 10 o'clock position is a "Sallad Magundy," an esteemed dish made with mounded cold cuts interspersed with anchovies and resting on a bed of lettuce. At the bottom of the illustration at 6 o'clock, the green sauce accompanying the ducklings also features anchovies. In the inner ring at 4 o'clock is a dish of plain anchovies, much as Samuel Pepys preferred to eat them. (*Library of Congress, Rare Book and Special Collections Division.*)

is a British classic going back at least to the medieval period, but his French-inspired version is an entirely different animal. To begin, Lamb's version calls for reducing tremendous amounts of veal, fowl, and beef down to their essence, a day-long undertaking. Meanwhile, the peas are cooked, mashed, and fried with a quarter pound of butter, an eighth of a pound of bacon, some onion, thyme, parsley, and pepper. Next, one adds the costly meat essence to the peas, skims off the fat, and strains it through a sieve. The dish is finally ready to serve, hours after it was begun first thing in the morning. This is precisely the kind of recipe that would have outraged many female British cookery book authors, as they would have seen it as an inexcusable waste of meat and time.

Lamb was quite judicious, however, in his use of anchovies. He even went so far as to point out that salt was unnecessary if one uses anchovies. For instance, his "Pigeon à la tartaré with cold sauce" calls for broiling the pigeons on a gridiron, while the sauce is made as follows:

> Mince a spoonful of parsley very fine, a shallot, or bit of onion, two spoonful's of pickles, one anchovy; separately mince all these very fine, then squeeze the juice of a lemon, half a spoonful of water, six spoonful's of oil, a little pepper, little or no salt, because of your anchovy: mix all these ingredients and just as you serve it, put to it a spoonful of mustard, and pour it cold on the bottom of your dish or plate, and put your broiled Pigeons on top of it. It is proper for a first course. So serve it.[27]

Breathing down the neck of Patrick Lamb was his court colleague Robert Smith, with his cookery book titled *Court Cookery* (1725). There appears to have been no love lost between these two, and Smith wasted no time in criticizing his former mentor. By the third sentence of Smith's introduction, he launches into his tirade:

I was near eight Years with Mr. *Lamb*, in His Majesty's (King *William*) Reign, and therefore knew most of His Receipts and Methods of Dressings; yet several of those Receipts, as they are now printed in his *Royal Cookery*, were never made or practis'd by him; and others are extreme defective and imperfect, and made up of Ingredients unknown to him; and several of them more calculated at the Purses, then the *Gôut* of the Guests, that it's impossible for a Cook to serve up a Dish, if they were only to follow the Receipts.[28]

And so on and so forth, with indignation and outrage at every step of the way. However, Smith was very much a man cut from the same cloth as Lamb: a French-trained English chef working at the highest rungs of court society, and whatever accusations he hurled at Lamb he was likely guilty of himself.

Anchovies became a key flavoring agent in the eighteenth century, as is evident in Smith's recipes. All three of his recipes for gravy contain anchovies, as do forty-four of his other recipes, making Smith a genuine anchovy aficionado:

To make good Gravy

Take a lean piece of beef, cut in thin slices ... and fry it brown with a lump of butter, till the goodness is out; then throw the meat away, and put into the gravy a quart of strong broth, and half a pint of Claret, four anchovies, a shallot, a little lemon peel, cloves, mace, pepper, and salt; let all boil well together; and when your gravy is ready, put it into a galley-pot, and set it by till called for.[29]

Like all of Smith's gravies, enormous amounts of meat went into them. Even though Smith does not spell out the quantity of beef, one can surmise that he was talking about at least several pounds, if not more. After cooking the beef in butter to extract its liquid essence, the meat itself is discarded—much to the horror of Hannah Glasse and anyone else on a budget—and a quart of some kind of unspecified broth, probably meat-based, is added. Red wine, anchovies, and seasonings deepen the flavor (with the cloves and mace a throwback to earlier times), while the prolonged boiling concentrates it and reduces the sauce to a rich, deep brown color. This is an all-purpose gravy of the kind the British excel at, one that can be added to hashes, stews, soups, and all kinds of meat and fowl, and even ladled onto a thick slice of bread.

Gravies and sauces also lay at the heart of Vincent La Chapelle's use of anchovies in *The Modern Cook* (1733). Anchovies had by now become a *de rigueur* flavoring agent in courtly circles. La Chapelle was considered the greatest French-born chef working in Britain at that time, and his cooking was the very pinnacle of sophistication. It was characterized by umami-rich sauces, fresh herbs, white wine (or champagne, which La Chapelle was wont to use), capers, and anchovies. Anchovies feature in 109 of his recipes, more than any other cookery book up to that time. La Chapelle consistently relied on anchovies to drive his sauces to their refined destination. For example, in his version of the classic French "Ravigotte sauce," he triples up on the umami by using gravy, cullis (or what the French would call a "*coulis*"), and anchovies in this creamy herb-intense sauce, which would have sent shivers down the spines of dinner guests.

It is difficult to appreciate how extraordinary each of these sauces was at that time. Nowadays, meat-flavored potato chips and cheap ramen noodle packs are engineered to deliver a wallop of umami and can be bought at any corner store. But in the early eighteenth century, umami-rich sauces were just coming into their own, and people were astonished at their incredible intensity of flavor. La Chapelle's recipe for sea bream captures the new infatuation with umami-rich sauces as it includes gravy (unspecified type), cullis (unspecified type), and the all-critical anchovy. This would have had an electrifying effect upon diners—an umami-rich current to which every synapse would have responded.

French-inspired cuisine hit its aristocratic peak in the first couple of decades of the eighteenth century. La Chapelle's recipes, especially his sauces, captured the rich and decadent flavors that became all the rage. But outside of courtly circles, few could afford to make these costly and time-consuming dishes. This created a fair amount of resentment, especially towards chefs like La Chapelle whose cookery book was filled with unattainable ingredients and recipes that were difficult to achieve in anything less than an aristocratic kitchen.

One cookery book author who took a more practical approach was William Verral, who published his *Complete System of Cookery* in 1759. While Verral was an Englishman, born and bred, his cookery cleverly combined elements of French cuisine with homegrown traditions. His father, Dick Verral, who owned the White Hart Inn in Lewes in East Sussex, had managed to secure a position for him in the kitchen of the Duke of Newcastle. Fortunately for young William, he was apprenticed to none other than the highly talented French-born chef Pierre de St. Clouet. The young lad spent years learning the tricks of the French culinary trade, and when his father died, Verral left the duke's service to take over the restaurant at the White Hart Inn. Armed with the latest French techniques, he judiciously applied them to his cookery, and the restaurant found its tables in high demand.

Adopting a sensible approach that resonated with the purses of his audience, he reassured his readers in the preface to his cookery book about what to expect: "I would venture myself to make a better soup with two pounds of meat, and such garden things as I liked, than is made of eight pounds for the tables of our gentry, and all for want of better knowing the uses of roots and vegetables."[30] For housewives working on a budget, this was music to their ears. There was also something immensely pleasing about his recipes, as he guided the reader forward with a gentle hand and prioritized common sense over exotic ingredients or fancy footwork. Despite his classical training in French cuisine, Verral did not throw the baby out with the bathwater, recognizing that some traditional English dishes were best: "I hope nothing is said disagreeable or in prejudice of our English and plain way of dressing a hare, for I think it best."[31] No doubt many of his readers would have agreed with him.

Anchovies assumed a very limited role in Verral's cookery. Only a handful of his recipes include them, and in others he substitutes them with English bacon. His "Ravigotte sauce," for instance, contains no anchovies, nor does his "Pea soup." In fact, in contrast to La Chapelle, Robert Smith, and Patrick Lamb, not one of Verral's sauces, gravies, or pies contains anchovies. Nor will one find any cooked with meat or fowl. Only when it comes to fish do we find a few anchovies sprinkled here and there. One could be forgiven for thinking that Verral had a problem with anchovies, but then, near the end of his cookery book, he includes this little gem:

Anchovies, with Parmesan cheese

Fry some bits of bread about the length of an anchovy in good oil or butter, lay the half of an anchovy with the bone upon each bit, and strew over them some Parmesan cheese grated fine, and colour them nicely in an oven, or with a salamander, squeeze the juice of an orange or lemon, and pile them in your dish and send them to the table.[32]

Verral summarized the success of this dinner savory when he wrote: "This seems to be but a trifling thing, but I never saw it come whole from the table."[33]

The ketchup and condiment craze hits England

If Eliza Smith was the Anchovy Queen, then Elizabeth Raffald was the patron saint of ketchup and condiments: she included one or the other in an astounding 144 recipes in her cookery book, *The Experienced English Housekeeper* (1769). Raffald was one of those indefatigable characters in history: she published a book on midwifery, was a long-time housekeeper, managed a number of inns, opened a confectionery store, ran a registry office and a cooking school, and compiled several directories for Manchester, the city where she lived for most of her life. Leonard N. Beck notes that her prodigious output also extended to biological reproduction: she produced sixteen daughters over the course of eighteen years.[34] While some question this number, her achievements were nonetheless exceptional. But it was her cookery book for which Raffald was best remembered, as it remained a bestseller for some fifty years and was plagiarized many times over. While La Chapelle's recipes lifted anchovies to their peak for the aristocratic crowd, Raffald's did the same for the aspirational middle and upper classes.

Raffald's generous use of condiments and ketchups illustrates how the convenience of pre-made flavoring agents was displacing traditional French sauces in English cookery. Elaborate French cullis was on the way out, and condiments and ketchup were marching in. "I have given no directions for cullis," she wrote, "as I have found by experience, that lemon pickle and browning answers both for beauty and taste (at a trifling expense) better than cullis, which is extravagant."[35] Claims of anti-extravagance went a long way with practical English women. Mrs. Raffald placed so much confidence in her lemon pickle and browning sauce that they are the first two recipes listed in her cookbook, an honorary position typically occupied by a French broth, stock, or soup.

We can get a taste of Raffald's enthusiasm for condiments and ketchup in the recipe "To make a Sauce for Salmon." It consists of both lemon pickle and browning (with its strong undercurrent of caramelized sugar), some walnut pickle (with anchovy), a little brown gravy, one anchovy, some water in which the fish was cooked, salt, flour to thicken it, and a healthy knob of butter. This kind of all-purpose sauce with vigorously contrasting flavors was about as far as one could get from the refined notes sought after by French-trained chefs.

Trying to make sense of all the dissimilar flavors, the esteemed scholar Stephen Mennell describes Raffald's browning as "a none too attractive sounding concoction."[36] Similarly, the culinary historian Kate Colquhoun notes that Raffald's ketchup marks "the beginning of a decline in culinary skills in Britain and the relinquishing of centuries of pride in the slow refinement of a sauce."[37] While some of the blame is rightly laid at Raffald's doorstep, her successors should not be exempt from criticism—especially those who ruthlessly plagiarized her recipes. Instead of creating a sauce from scratch, one now added a tablespoon or two of pre-made ketchup to a dollop of butter and sent the dish on its way.

To be fair, though, such criticism fails to consider Raffald's approach as a uniquely British development: her flavoring agents enlivened just about anything, in no time at all, and for next to nothing. Her recipes drew upon time-honored pickling traditions, imported fish sauces, and high-end French sauces to meet a particular British need, one that required flavor to be fast, cheap, and easy. People of modest means wanted to prepare meals in a practical and dignified way, within the limits of what they could afford. Raffald's work spoke to this portion of the population—which was a very large swath indeed.

Charlotte Mason, author of *The Lady's Assistant* (1777), was another notable advocate of ketchup, and her cookbook lists three different kinds. Anchovies were near and dear to Mason, and she wrote that "no other fish has the fine flavour of the anchovy."[38] Maria Eliza Rundell was also a fan of anchovies, and her cookery book, *A New System of Domestic Cookery* (1806), became one of the culinary blockbusters of the nineteenth century. Anchovies feature throughout her recipes and are particularly well represented in her sauces, gravies, and ketchup. Some recipes (such as carp sauce) use as little as half an anchovy, while others (such as "Fish sauce") pack a full-bodied anchovy punch, loaded with up to a dozen.

By the early decades of the nineteenth century, ketchups were a kitchen staple and every cookbook author offered up their own version (or one lifted from a colleague). One of the quirkier recipes from this period came via the eccentric Dr. William Kitchiner in his odd, though mesmerizing, cookbook, *Apicius Redivivus; or, The Cook's Oracle* (1817). Much like our man Pepys, Dr. Kitchiner was wildly curious about the world around him and was endlessly tinkering with it through writing ("The Pleasures of Making a Will," *inter alia*); optics (he developed a type of telescope); music (he composed and played a variety of instruments); and cooking (he invented the potato chip!). He was also prone to wild exaggeration, like his false claims that he attended Eton College and obtained a medical degree from Glasgow University. Be that as it may, Dr. Kitchiner's cookbook makes for fascinating reading due to its recipes and his frequent digressions into culinary lore.

Following in the footsteps of his culinary idol, the semi-mythical Apicius (the title of his book, *Apicius Redivivus*, roughly translates as "Apicius Recycled"), Dr. Kitchiner urged his readers to taste-taste-taste their cooking. "The most experienced artists," he wrote, "cannot be certain of their work, without tasting; they must be incessantly tasting. The spoon of a good cook is continually passing from the stewpan to his tongue."[39] All this tasting no doubt made his "Wow wow sauce" and the equally grand "Sauce superlative" even better. His recipe for essence of anchovy one-upped those of his colleagues with its title, "Quint-essence of anchovy," which contains a typical Dr. Kitchiner-esque footnote: "Epicure QUIN used to say, 'Of all the Banns [proclamations] of

Marriage I ever heard, none gave me half such pleasure as the union of delicate ANN-CHOVY with good JOHN-DORY."[40]

Dr. Kitchiner was exceedingly fond of condiments and ketchup, and he did not hold back on either anchovies or spices in his recipe for "Tomata Catsup":

Dr. Kitchiner's Tomata Catsup

Gather a gallon of fine, red, and full ripe Tomatas; mash them with one pound of salt; let them rest for three days, press off the juice, and to each quart add a quarter of a pound of anchovies, two ounces of shallots, and an ounce of ground black pepper; boil up together for half an hour, strain through a sieve, and put to it the following spices; a quarter of an ounce of mace, the same of allspice, ginger, and nutmeg, a drachm of coriander seed, and half a drachm of cochineal; pound all together; let them simmer gently for twenty minutes, and strain through a bag: when cold, bottle it, adding to each bottle a wineglass of brandy. It will keep for seven years.[41]

With its quarter pound of anchovies and a shelfful of spices, the origins of this ketchup can be traced all the way back to Hannah Woolley's "Pickled mushroom" recipe of 1672. While the pickle varied (white wine vinegar, white wine, beer, brandy), as the base (mushrooms, walnuts, anchovies, tomatoes), the fundamental seasoning of ketchup remained fairly consistent: black pepper, mace, ginger, cloves, and nutmeg. Some ketchups were also flavored by ingredients such as allspice, coriander seed, lemon peel, and horseradish, but this was far less common. Without the early pickling tradition in England, the development of ketchups may not have taken off, and the trajectory of Britain's beloved condiments would have been very different.

The second-to-last recipe in Dr. Kitchiner's cookery book is for "Anchovy toast," a savory snack that had been eagerly embraced since the late 1600s, particularly by the landed gentry. In Dr. Kitchiner's version, anchovies and butter are pounded, sieved, and spread on hot toast. Savories like this signaled the end of supper and the beginning of the after-dinner festivities. For those adventurous souls seeking a more piquant note, Dr. Kitchiner suggested that "[y]ou may add, while pounding the anchovies, a little made mustard and curry powder, or a few grains of cayenne, or a little mace or other spice. It may be made still more savoury, by frying the toast in clarified butter."[42]

And his final recipe? "Devilled biscuit." Curiously, the recipe merely replicates the preceding recipe for anchovy toast, with the caveat that upon eating the anchovy toast, the conviviality should commence in earnest. Specifically, "when the votaries of Bacchus are determined to vie with each other in sacrificing to the Jolly God" [i.e. when everyone is sufficiently drunk], let the singing begin![43] In order to facilitate the festivities, Dr. Kitchiner helpfully provided the sheet music to "The Anacreontic Song," a musical number associated with a gentlemen's drinking club in London known as the Anacreontic Society, of which he was an esteemed member. Anacreon was a Greek poet who was well known for his drinking songs. Taking their cues from him, the club members would meet once a month to indulge in food, music, and copious amounts of alcohol. And the significance of the song? Well, Francis Scott Key would add new lyrics to the melody—known as a contrafactum—and retitle it "The Star-Spangled Banner," and *voilà*: in 1931 it became the national anthem of the United States of America.

The Industrial Revolution and an expanding market for anchovy products

The year 1760 marked the beginning of the Industrial Revolution, a period of rapid technological innovation and social change in Britain that would also have major implications for anchovies. Up to this point, more than three quarters of the population still lived in the countryside. The promise of work in the cities soon resulted in an influx of the rural poor. Crowding into squalid tenements with poor lighting and ventilation and limited bathing facilities, the new arrivals sought work in mills and factories. Twelve-hour shifts were the norm, and children as young as six or seven toiled alongside their parents in dimly lit, smoke-filled sweatshops.

While life in the countryside did not always provide enough to eat, at least food was somewhat nutritious. People had access to grains and ale, vegetables from scattered plots, and foraged foods, with an occasional piece of meat (often poached from a nearby estate) rounding out their diet. But as the poor migrated into the cities, their diets—at least initially—suffered tremendously. Mostly, they subsisted on adulterated bread,* tea, sugar, hard cheese, and perhaps some watery soup. Many tenements had only communal cooking facilities, where food would stealthily disappear into the hungry mouths of one's neighbors. Cookbooks of this era cannot be relied upon as a reference for the eating habits of this large segment of society. Most food consumed by the poor was under-seasoned and insufficient in calories. Further, few had the time or money required for cooking, as coal cost a small fortune. When they did manage to cook, the food was prepared and eaten quickly; hard-boiled eggs were a staple at all hours of the day.

Britain's small but growing middle class fared much better, particularly those with an education. An entrepreneurial frenzy

---

* Much like cocaine and heroin in our own era, almost all bread was adulterated with impurities of varying degrees of toxicity in the eighteenth and nineteenth centuries. In one *Lancet* study published in 1855, all forty-nine samples of bread tested were found to be adulterated. The same study also noted that anchovies were often contaminated with "Venetian red," a colorant containing iron and lead that was used to turn their flesh a deep red.

set in across the land as ambitious men, often aided behind the scenes by their wives, scrambled to form partnerships and open new businesses that catered to the emerging middle class. New shops sprang up overnight offering a slew of different goods and services, during the so-called "consumer revolution" of the later eighteenth century. Bolstered by expanded trade across the British Empire, vast amounts of imported foods began to arrive at the wharves of London. As volumes increased and prices came down, many items such as Italian dried pasta and Indian pickles were for the first time within reach of the middling sort. Anchovies also found their way into more modest cupboards, as did Parmesan cheese, olives, tea, coffee, sugar, figs, pistachio nuts, and various spices such as cinnamon, ginger, and mace.

While London's markets provisioned the rapidly expanding city with meat, fowl, fish, and vegetables, a number of small business owners also imported luxury fabrics and food from abroad. They were called "warehousemen" as their industry first arose on the wharves of London. Over time, they migrated to more fashionable parts of the city, where their customers lived and worked. In addition to targeting London's rising middle class and the gentry, these warehousemen also sold wholesale to inn-keepers and the burgeoning restaurant scene. Like an upscale modern boutique with a high-end delicatessen at the back, these warehouses play an important role in our story, as do the shop-keepers to whom they sold their goods.

Elaborate advertisements were placed on calling cards and in newspapers enticing customers into their shops. In the finely etched illustration of Mrs. Holt's Italian Warehouse (circa 1740), the entire narrative aims at tempting the customer to consume Italy's bounty. To the right of the Roman God Mercury, who is associated with commerce, a ship is being loaded with treasures bound for Britain; a dockworker carries a box on his shoulder (silks? damasks?) up the gangway, while another positions a barrel (wine? olive oil? anchovies?) to be stowed on board. In the four corners are depictions of Italy's four great ports: Naples, Venice, Genoa, and Leghorn (Livorno) (Fig. 3.3). In cursive script below the illustration (not pictured in the image below), the text proclaims that a wide variety of Italian products can be found at Mrs. Holt's, including "Italian Wines, Florence Cordials, Oil, Olives, Anchovies, Capers, Vermicelli, Bologna Sausages, and Parmesan Cheese."[44]

Such warehouses soon progressed from selling imported anchovies to creating the first commercially made condiments, ketchups, and sauces. John Burgess is often credited as the first warehouseman to commercially manufacture and market his own sauce to the public. His father was a successful grocer in

Fig. 3.3: A detail of the shop card of Mrs. Holt's Italian Warehouse (circa 1740). And the artist who etched the illustration? None other than the acclaimed English artist and social critic, William Hogarth. (*Penta Springs Limited/Alamy Stock Photo.*)

Hampshire, and he sent his son to London to learn the trade. After completing his apprenticeship in the city, Burgess started his own warehouse business and began tinkering with recipes. The details are not clear, but it appears that by 1760 he was manufacturing and selling what he called a "Devonshire sauce." Although this early concoction failed to take hold in the marketplace, in 1775 he released the condiment that would take Britain by storm: the Original and Superior Essence of Anchovy. It was the first commercially made condiment that achieved national recognition in Britain (Fig. 3.4).

Creating an anchovy essence was a shrewd move, as Burgess was already importing salted anchovies from Gorgona in Italy, and he had a warehouse full of all the necessary spices. Although the exact ingredients of his original recipe are unknown, it is thought that it was made by gently heating a giant vat of water and salted anchovies, letting it simmer for a while, and then adding an unknown number of spices. It may also have been aged. At some point, the brew was strained, bottled, and sold to the public. It was an instant success. Within a decade, Burgess's anchovy essence was the most popular product in his crowded product line. In 1800, Burgess and his son released another hugely popular product: Burgess's Genuine Anchovy Paste (Fig. 3.5). "Over the years the Burgess products have been taken far and wide," writes patents scholar David Newton, "and it was reported that Admiral Lord Nelson took some to the battle of the Nile in 1798 and that in 1910 Captain Scott took some on his ill-fated Antarctic expedition."[45]

In the late 1790s, another commercially manufactured condiment appeared: Harvey's Sauce. This filled a pressing need in the marketplace as it required no refrigeration, had a long shelf life, and, most importantly, complemented a wide variety of foods. The ingredients remained a closely guarded secret for decades, but from later sources we learn that it was basically a traditionally made ketchup with a vinegar base:

Fig. 3.4: *The Sauce Shop* (detail) by Thomas Rowlandson (1776). Sauces of all sorts were carefully considered before customers handed over their hard-earned coin. The seated man on the far right appears to have his favorite, which the poodle eagerly investigates. (©*The Trustees of the British Museum. All rights reserved.*)

Harvey's Sauce
6 anchovies
1 pint vinegar
3 tablespoons soy sauce
3 tablespoons mushroom catchup
2 cloves garlic
1¼ ounce cayenne pepper
cochineal powder (for color)

Countless shopkeepers soon stepped up to try their hand at making a successful condiment. One such early manufacturer was

Fig. 3.5: Featured prominently on the ceramic lid of every Burgess's Genuine Anchovy Paste was the Royal Coat of Arms. Modern antique collectors covet these ceramic lids with their links to the foodways of Britain's past. (*Some Wonderful Old Things/Alamy Stock Photo.*)

James Cock, who worked as a fishmonger in the town of Reading, 56 kilometers west of London. In 1802, James Cock and his wife developed and sold a fish sauce at their market stall. Several years later, they also developed an anchovy essence, a lemon pickle, and mushroom and walnut ketchups.* Not much

---

* Many wives had their own "secret" recipe for mushroom or walnut ketchup. Mushroom ketchup was made by layering chopped mushrooms and salt in a pot which was then left to ferment for several days or weeks. The resulting liquid was strained, simmered, and a host of seasonings were added: spices, herbs, and vinegar or beer. Similarly, walnut ketchup was made using young and immature walnuts, known as green walnuts. Both ketchups—along with anchovy ketchup—were widely used to add a punch of flavor during cooking or at the table.

is known about these early condiments, but a few years later, they hit the jackpot with their Reading Sauce.

Based on a family recipe, the original Reading Sauce was said to be composed of 110 gallons of walnut ketchup (probably containing anchovies, as most walnut ketchups did), 25 gallons of mushroom ketchup (which usually did not contain anchovies), 12 gallons of soy sauce, 2½ gallons of chilies, 1 gallon of salt, 1 gallon of garlic, various spices, including ginger and cloves, and a barrel of salted anchovies. The mixture was simmered, then aged in barrels for twelve months. "They seem to have combined several well-known ketchups," writes British historian T. A. B. Corley, "probably from household recipes, and added soy sauce from China, anchovies from the Black Sea and spices from the West Indies or the east."[46]

Two decades into the nineteenth century, most shopkeepers across the country stocked industrial condiments in one form or another. Although many of the poor still could not afford them, the convenience of these condiments ensured that every housewife with the means had a bottle or two on hand. After-dinner savories also enjoyed an increase in popularity among the elite, and anchovies on toast remained a favorite. Capitalizing on the trend, John Osborn unleashed his Patum Peperium in 1828—The Gentleman's Relish. Osborn was an expatriate Englishman working as a warehouseman in Paris when he devised his recipe, a sort of potted anchovy mixture. Said to contain anchovies, butter, herbs, and spices, the exact recipe remains a secret to this day. In contemporary writing, it has been called the "quintessential English delicacy," most likely as much for its unique flavor as for the fictional England that it conjures up. "It recaptures imaginary memories of high tea in front of an open fire," writes journalist Adam Edwards, "as joyous to the dark December days of winter as the cucumber sandwich is to the picnics of high summer" (Fig. 3.6).[47]

Fig. 3.6: The name "Patum Peperium" is an odd etymological amalgamation of Greek and Latin meaning roughly "paste of peppers." While peppers may be present, it is the composition of 60 percent anchovies that gives Gentleman's Relish its kick.

While the success of a commercially made condiment depends primarily on taste, a host of other factors also come into play. A good founding myth, for example, works wonders. This is what launched Worcestershire Sauce* to worldwide fame.

Early company literature for Lea & Perrins Worcestershire Sauce recounts the chance meeting of "Lord Sandys," a certain "nobleman of the country," with two chemists, John Wheeley Lea and William Henry Perrins, to discuss the replication of a sauce that Lord Sandys had discovered in India when he was a Governor of Bengal.[48] Working from his secret recipe, the two aspiring food

---

* The brand name Worcestershire Sauce has caused no end of debate regarding its proper pronunciation. Locals from the town of Worcester drop the "shire"—the British equivalent of "county"—as well as the first "r," with the resulting pronunciation "Wooster sauce." But countless other variations exist, as many fiercely argue.

purveyors dutifully tried to recreate the sauce in their shop in Worcester. Alas, the end result was a disaster: a ghastly, overpowering concoction that rendered the entire undertaking a complete failure. The disheartened chemists consigned the remaining sauce to their cellar, where it was quickly forgotten.

Three years later, during a spring clean, Messieurs Lea and Perrins happened upon the sauce. Upon opening a bottle, they discovered that the sauce had miraculously mellowed and finally lived up to its promise. Equally as important, the "secret" recipe came from a great and illustrious man. No other sauce could boast such a pedigree. Similar to ketchup, but in a league of its own, the sauce brought a tantalizing spark to even the most insipid foods. In 1837, Lea and Perrins started selling small bottles of Worcestershire Sauce. It flew off the shelves.

Worcestershire Sauce made Lea and Perrins fabulously wealthy, despite its founding story turning out to be pure fiction. In his book *The Secret Sauce* (1997), Brian Keogh—a former accountant for Lea & Perrins—notes that "no Lord Sandys ... was ever a Governor of Bengal or, as available records show, ever in India."[49] Nonetheless, the story of Lord Sandys is still repeated over and over in countless books and articles, imbuing Worcestershire Sauce with the mystical aura of a great man's secret recipe. At least one aspect of the story is true: Lea & Perrins Worcestershire Sauce is still aged for three years prior to bottling. Although the recipe had been a closely guarded secret for over 150 years, Mr. Keogh discovered the original recipe in a dumpster outside the offices of Lea & Perrins in 2009.

Worcestershire Sauce's ingredients place it firmly in the line of anchovy-based ketchup. But it also contains molasses, sugar, and tamarind extract, perhaps in a nod to the fruit-based chutneys of India that were all the rage in Britain. Onions, peppers, and garlic, along with "natural seasonings," some soy sauce, lemon, and pickles, round out the recipe along with the all-critical anchovy. The sauce's sweet notes harmonize with its ultra-savory anchovy and vinegar bite to create a condiment that pairs exceptionally well with meat, fowl, and fish. It also adds a piquant note to salad dressings, eggs, and that world-famous hangover drink, the Bloody Mary (Fig. 3.7).

Worcestershire Sauce helped to democratize the taste of umami in British cuisine, both near and far. On the home front, a dash or two of Worcestershire Sauce saved housewives countless hours in the kitchen creating complicated, time-consuming reduction sauces or cullis. Further afield, it served as a signifier of all things British and the country's rational approach to

Fig. 3.7: Condiment labels were important not just for marketing purposes, but also to distinguish products from imitations, as copyright infringement was rife. For this reason, many condiment bottles like those of Lea & Perrins were originally signed by hand. (*Urbanbuzz/Alamy Stock Photo.*)

seasoning. Unlike French *haute cuisine*, with its fussy sauces requiring trained chefs, an array of pots and pans, and hours upon hours of simmering to reduce stocks down to their umami essence, a simple bottle of Worcestershire Sauce sufficed for the Englishman abroad. There is something eminently practical, and as such, quintessentially English about all this. One can easily imagine an Englishman setting off on a steamer with bottles of Worcestershire Sauce tucked away in his luggage. As the nineteenth century gained momentum, and British colonization was in full swing, Worcestershire Sauce was transported to the far-flung corners of the Empire, where it brought a little taste of home to Brits abroad.

The Mrs Beeton beating: anchovies fall out of favor in England

As condiments rose in popularity, many argue that the quality of British cuisine declined. The British also lost interest in eating whole salted anchovies on their own. Clarissa Dickson Wright laid much of the blame for the downturn of British cooking in this period at the feet of Isabella Mary Beeton and *Mrs. Beeton's Book of Household Management*, first published in 1861. Not only did her cookery book cast a shadow over British cuisine for the rest of the nineteenth century, but it also signaled the end of anchovies' glorious run in British cuisine. Not even ketchups or condiments got a fair shake in Beeton's book.

It is difficult to overstate the impact that this cookery book had on British culture at the end of the nineteenth and in the first half of the twentieth century. It was an instant success, selling over 60,000 copies in its first year of publication. By 1868, over 2 million copies were in print. It is still being printed to this day. It did not merely outsell its competitors; it crushed them, and it came to define cuisine, household management, and etiquette in the Victorian era. If there was one book every house-wife had to have other than the Holy Bible—which some argue was the only book in England that outsold hers at that time—it was *Mrs. Beeton's*.

Beeton was known for the phrase "everything in its place." When applied to her cookbook's format and layout, this was nothing short of revolutionary. Thanks to its excellent table of contents and functional index with cross-referencing, finding a recipe had never been so easy. She also presented a concise list of ingredients at the head of each recipe, followed by straightfor-ward directions, a format we still follow to this day. She even told her readers how much a recipe cost, as well as the number of servings each recipe made. Prior to *Mrs. Beeton's*, ingredient lists were vague, cooking times practically non-existent, and all of it was jumbled together in a chaotic mess, resulting in recipes that required a fair amount of interpretation. Beeton's rational and structured approach is perhaps her book's greatest asset, for its culinary shortcomings, sadly, are legion.

So how did one of Britain's most famous cookery books come about? In 1856, twenty-year-old Isabella Mary Mayson married Samuel Orchart Beeton. Shortly after their marriage, Isabella started to assist her husband as a columnist for the "Pickles, Pies, and Preserves" section of his thriving publication, *The English-woman's Domestic Magazine*. Even though she lacked any mean-ingful experience in cookery, Isabella jumped enthusiastically into her new role. During the eight short years of their marriage (she died at the age of twenty-eight), they published a flurry of books and magazines culminating in their most successful undertaking, *Mrs. Beeton's Book of Household Management* (Fig. 3.8).

At the beginning of the Victorian era, Britons were yearning for knowledge of the world around them, and Sam shrewdly planned a series of books to feed their appetites and cash in on the phenomenon. He had already started work on one book,

Fig. 3.8: The title, *Beeton's Book of Household Management*, was a nod to a series of books that Sam Beeton had planned to publish in the coming years. Rather tellingly, Isabella was not listed as the author but given an "Edited by" credit in the first edition. However, given the immediate success of the book and in order to further capitalize upon her persona, the title on all subsequent editions was changed to *Mrs. Beeton's Book of Household Management*.

Beeton's Dictionary of Universal Information, when he and Isabella hit on the idea of publishing a cookery book in the same vein. "In time," writes Professor Kathryn Hughes, "there would be *Beeton's Book of Birds, Beeton's Historian, Beeton's Book of Songs*— titles that would typify the totalizing categorizing culture that drove the early Victorians and which Sam Beeton would come to exploit so successfully."[50]

Isabella and Sam conceptualized *Beeton's Book of Household Management* precisely in this "totalizing" fashion, that is, as a book designed to include not just recipes and guidance on household management, but also deep dives into arcane knowledge.

Hardly a page goes by without something catching your eye, but unfortunately, many of the recipes are disappointing. The book presents a curious hodgepodge of recipes that range from bare-bones dishes to elaborate three-course dinners (with multiple entrées) for eighteen people. The enormous range of recipes makes little sense, until one learns that Isabella lifted at least a third of them from earlier cookbooks. She also filled out her book with recipes drawn from submissions to *The Englishwoman's Domestic Magazine*. At least she had enough common sense to mix up the order of ingredients and make a substitution or two, so that she could call these recipes her own.

Tracing Beeton's recipes back to their rightful authors has turned into a bit of a cottage industry in Britain. Kathryn Hughes traces some of the more elaborate recipes to chefs such as Carême, Louis Eustache Ude, Charles Elmé Francatelli, and Alexis Benoît Soyer. Even the eccentric Dr. Kitchiner's cookbook was strip-mined for recipes. Beeton also ransacked the recipes of the greatest female cookery book authors of the era, including Hannah Glasse, Elizabeth Raffald, Maria Eliza Rundell, and, most significantly, Eliza Acton. Acton's cookery book, *Modern Recipes for Private Families* (1845), was a goldmine of simple, tasty, and cost-effective recipes to which Beeton helped herself.

Looking back at the recipes in *Mrs. Beeton's* from the gastronomic perch of the twenty-first century, it is hard to account for its success. Attempting to simplify cooking for the masses, many of her recipes dumbed down what had previously been a vibrant and distinctive national cuisine. Tasteless, bland, and insipid are a few of the adjectives that critics have used to describe her work. She often economized by reducing or even eliminating seasonings, as is the case with her "Onion soup," which does not contain a single herb or spice. And you know you are in trouble when the first ingredient of her fish stock recipe calls for 2 pounds of beef or veal. Massialot is surely rolling over in his grave. Vegetables, needless to say, are invariably overboiled, and sugar has a way of creeping in far too often. In fact, sugar seemed to be Beeton's secret weapon, and she never missed an opportunity to insert a "teaspoon or two" into her recipes. Of her soup recipes, 17 percent include sugar, unlike those of the sure-footed Eliza Acton, who included sugar in only one ("Sago soup").

Mrs. Beeton's also had serious consequences for anchovies and anchovy-based condiments. For example, while Beeton copied roughly one third of Acton's fish recipes (and 25 percent of Acton's soups), she excluded almost every fish recipe that contained an anchovy-based condiment. Why would Beeton do this? The most likely explanation is that she wanted to economize her recipes. But two problems arise with this. First, if someone could afford to purchase her cookery book, complete with color plates (the first cookery book to ever include them), then they could certainly afford a bottle of Harvey's Sauce or Essence of Anchovy. Second, Beeton included other recipes that call for extremely expensive cuts, such as veal, venison, and sturgeon. Might Beeton's choices have reflected the way in which condiments were by then often utilized at the dining-room table, rather than during the cooking process itself? Perhaps. Or perhaps the simplest explanation may be that she herself did not like anchovies.

A sweeter sauce: bold, brown, and devoid of anchovies

Despite Mrs. Beeton's lack of interest in including condiments in her book, Britons were still consuming them, and sales steadily increased throughout the nineteenth century. Commercially made condiments evolved along two distinct lines: traditional condiments such as Worcestershire Sauce, Harvey's Sauce, and Reading Sauce, all of which were made with anchovies and remained bestsellers; and a new kind of condiment, known as "brown sauces." Brown sauces occasionally contained anchovies in the early days, but by the 1850s they had become sweeter and tangier. Brown sauces derived their distinctive flavors from dried fruits (raisins, dates, mangoes, or oranges), sweeteners like molasses, and imported spices.

The most popular brown sauce in the Victorian era (according to sales) was Yorkshire Relish. Developed by a chemist in northern England and launched in 1865, Yorkshire Relish was a thin sauce with loads of spices, similar to Worcestershire Sauce, but it was fruitier and lacked anchovies (Fig. 3.9). Conjuring up the glories of Empire and the exoticism of the East, George Batty's Nabob Sauce and Joshua Fletcher's Tiger Sauce were two more brown sauces whose flavor profiles also exhibited more fruit and spice notes. Tamarind and star anise were just two of the alien, yet alluring, imports that found their way into this new class of condiments. The public clamored for these flavorful brown sauces, and as their sales rose, their prices came down. When the earning power of the poor increased at the end of the nineteenth century and the beginning of the twentieth, brown sauces found their way into more households. By the 1950s, almost every abode in Britain was equipped with at least one or two of these treasured condiments.

Britain's most successful brown sauce of all time was HP Sauce, and its earliest version dated to 1884. It was invented by a grocer in Nottingham, Frederick Gibson Garton, and was initially called "The Banquet Sauce." A few years after beginning production, Garton got wind that his sauce was being served in the Houses of Parliament, and he promptly renamed it "Garton's

Fig. 3.9: Said to be flavored with twenty-seven "eastern spices," a bottle of Yorkshire Relish was what everyone wanted to perk up their food, whether it was for breakfast, lunch, or dinner. (*Lordprice Collection/Alamy Stock Photo.*)

HP Sauce." At this point, Garton stepped out of the story. "He was deep in debt to a vinegar malting factory," writes Ameer Kotecha, "and despite his repeated attempts to brown-nose the debt collector to keep the bailiffs at bay, he was forced to sell his trademarks and recipes."[51] The new owners dropped "Garton's" from the title, added a picture of the Houses of Parliament to the label, and the rest is history.

While HP Sauce conquered Britain, it was another brown sauce that went on to conquer the world. The story begins with a twelve-year-old lad, working as an apprentice in the kitchens of the Prince Regent, soon to be King George IV. His name was

Henderson William Brand, and over the years, he worked his way up the kitchen hierarchy. Having eventually attained the title of cook, one story has him serving his version of a brown sauce to the future King of England who promptly replied that it was "A1." Another version has the sauce acquiring its iconic name at the 1862 International Exhibition in London where it was judged "A1." Perhaps the most likely version of the story has the name evolving out of a patent dispute between Brand and one of his former partners, with Brand adding "A1" to distinguish his product. Brown sauces like A1 and HP soon became household favorites, with a corresponding decline in anchovy-based sauces.

"A is for Anchovy": Modern British cooking

The twentieth century saw a big shift in the way condiments were used. They were less frequently added to a dish in the kitchen, and more commonly found on the dining-room table for people to help themselves. In the post-World War years, condiments came to occupy a cherished role in every British household, with fierce debates erupting over the merits of brown sauce versus red sauce (American-style tomato ketchup) and Worcestershire Sauce versus malt vinegar.

However, whole anchovy fillets only found their way back into British cuisine in the form of appetizers served by upscale restaurants several decades later. Since then, two popular menu items that never went out of fashion were anchovy-stuffed olives and anchovy canapes, featuring hard-boiled eggs on a slice of toast with an anchovy fillet draped on top. Accompanied by a glass of champagne or a Martini, it was how the smart set began an evening of fine dining.

Anchovies also underwent a revival with the publication of Elizabeth David's *French Provincial Cooking* (1960). As Colquhoun notes, David's book "evoked the vibrant colours, touch and smell of the French market, the piquant, earthy and aromatic flavors of garlic, anchovies, olives, marjoram, saffron and thyme, lemons, apricots and figs; and a spirit of cooking that was more about adventure, devotion and satisfaction than martyrdom and boast."[52] Postwar housewives did not need to be told twice. They embraced David's vision of food that did not just nourish ("rustic" cuisine) and was not pretentiously northern French (highbrow cuisine), but rather celebrated new gastronomic possibilities. Sometimes this involved whole anchovies and not just those in a condiment bottle.

Another big boost for anchovies in Britain came about with the appropriation of French *la nouvelle cuisine* in the 1960s and 1970s. British chefs such as Marco Pierre White and his one-time protégé Gordon Ramsay gave new life to anchovies in the 1980s and 1990s. Marco Pierre White's "Grilled Angus strip loin and Café de Paris butter" elevates a simple steak to a new realm of flavor with his enhanced butter. To make his butter, he combines anchovies, Worcestershire Sauce (more anchovies), ketchup, mustard, shallots, garlic, and lemon juice and zest, along with a slew of fresh herbs and spices. After marinating overnight, the ingredients are combined with the butter, and a dollop is placed upon the seared steaks. Heaven. Another big boost to anchovy consumption came from the enormously successful cookbooks of Jamie Oliver, whose impact upon British cooking is still not fully appreciated to this day. In *Jamie's Italy* (2005), a basic recipe like "Anchovies in tomato sauce with pasta" introduced a new generation to the joys of cooking with anchovies.

In keeping with the tastes of this generation, in Nigella Lawson's cookbook, *Cook, Eat, Repeat* (2020), anchovies assume pride of place. Lawson's recipes appeal to our contemporary sensibilities, which seek to celebrate a few key flavors when putting together a dish, in contrast to earlier periods which often luxuriated in a host of spices and seasonings. Nonetheless, a line can be drawn from many older recipes straight through to Lawson's anchovy-infused creations, linking the past with the present in a culinary continuum.

"For cooks, and certainly—if not emphatically—for this cook," writes Lawson, "anchovies are of the essence. Few other ingredients arrive in the kitchen with such confrontational pungency, and yet manage to imbue so many dishes with transformational subtlety."[53] Such is her enthusiasm for anchovies that she refers to them as the "bacon of the sea"—an expression that captures all their flavor-enhancing possibilities. One of Lawson's recipes that benefits from anchovies is her beef stew, a dish that she has made for over twenty years without dissent (other than from her children). Eliza Acton would no doubt agree, as in *Modern Cookery* (1845), she included a recipe for "A good English stew" enhanced with anchovies. Maria Eliza Rundell's 1810 recipe for "Stewed rump of beef" took things one step further with the addition of both an anchovy-infused ketchup and salted anchovies. All three recipes capitalize on anchovies to nudge them along in their quest for flavor.

"Eggs and anchovies are the perfect union," enthuses Lawson in her chapter, "A is for Anchovy."[54] She likes nothing more than a poached egg with anchovies on top, much like Charlotte Mason (1777) who added anchovy-based ketchup to her eggs. Eliza Smith (1727) created a slightly more involved recipe for hard-boiled eggs, topping them with a sauce of anchovies, morels, white wine, shallots, thyme, oysters, and butter. Even the great French chef Escoffier (1903) could not resist combining anchovies and eggs. As befitting the fancy venues in which his dishes were served, Escoffier upscaled them with a decorative flourish. Hard-boiled eggs were peeled and their bottoms trimmed flat, and then they were arranged upright on a dish, with anchovies wrapped around them horizontally like the rings of a barrel.

Lawson is a little more informal with her anchovies and eggs, simply calling for them to be "striated" on top of the eggs. Either way—or in whatever arrangement—anchovies and eggs have long proven to be natural bedfellows: a perfect way to begin the day.

Lawson singles out anchovy toast as a particularly delightful way to celebrate anchovies, but saves her greatest praise for what she calls her "Anchovy elixir." Blending anchovies, garlic, lemon juice, and olive oil, Lawson describes her umami-rich sauce as "the very apogee of anchovydom ... For the anchovy lover, there can be no purer celebration of its qualities."[55]

Anchovy sauces have been improving British cookery for hundreds of years, with their various forms reflecting the prevailing tastes of their time. Aside from the addition of garlic, Lawson's "Anchovy elixir" is a kissing cousin to all the anchovy sauces that came before her, including those created by Hannah Glasse (1747), Maria Eliza Rundell (1806), Dr. Kitchiner (1817), and Eliza Acton (1845), to name a few. Each version reflected the tastes of the day. An anchovy combined with "[p]lain butter melted thick," wrote Glasse, "is a good sauce: In short, you may put as many things as you fancy into the sauce."[56] Lawson would undoubtedly agree. While her taste buds lead her to olive oil instead of butter, the humble anchovy is the engine that powers both sauces.

While chefs like Lawson fully embrace anchovy fillets—whether draped on top of a dish or tucked away in a sauce—anchovy-based ketchup and condiments have never gone out of style in Britain. If you look closely at the supermarket shelves, you can still find a quintessentially British condiment that harks back to the past: Geo Watkins Anchovy Sauce (Fig. 3.10). First produced in the mid-nineteenth century, its high anchovy content (34 percent) leaves no doubt that it is the real deal, a genuine Victorian-period flavor enhancer. As one of its contemporary advertisements proclaims, "This is instant anchovy in a bottle," and there is nothing more British than that.[57]

Fig. 3.10: Anchored in tradition and aged to perfection: Geo Watkins Anchovy Sauce. (*Martin Lee/Alamy Stock Photo.*)

Atlantic Ocean

Bay of
Biscay

Santoña   Castro Urdiales
Santander   Lekeitio
Laredo
Guernica   San Sebastián

L'Escala

Douro River   Duero River   Ebro River

Barcelona

Madrid

Yuste

SPAIN   Valencia

Mallorca

Lisbon   Ibiza
Tróia

Guadalquivir River

Seville   Granada

Málaga   Mediterranean Sea

Atlantic
Ocean

N

0   50   100 miles
0   50   100 km

4

THE SPANISH ANCHOVY

FROM NOSES UP TO FORKS DOWN

Modern Spaniards are the top consumers of anchovies in the world. In the south, they have always eaten them, albeit in a uniquely Andalusian way: fresh, floured, and deep-fried. But in the north, people barely considered them, even though anchovies flourished in the waters surrounding their lands. Why the north was so late to the anchovy game is a story of how status can dictate taste. Not until the cataclysmic events of the twentieth century were anchovies embraced across all of Spain. Perversely, the Spanish Civil War opened the door for anchovies to enter the world of mainstream Spanish cuisine. Soon many, but not all, Spaniards embraced anchovies, and those that did never looked back.

Religion, hierarchy and the missing fish: Spain's early disdain for anchovies

Locating anchovies in the gastronomic traditions of Catholic Spain (in the north of the country) is a challenging task. Delving into documentary sources, the first thing that one is confronted with is negative evidence: anchovies are missing in action. Early Spanish cookbooks, official documents, correspondence, and literature shed very little light on the consumption of anchovies. In fact, few sources mention them until the late eighteenth and nineteenth centuries. We know that anchovies were being consumed in earlier periods, but how widely, by whom, and how they were being prepared is largely speculation. This can be explained, in part, by the unique relationship between anchovies and national identity, as well as the emergence of Catholic food hierarchies in the early modern period.

The roots of Catholic Spain's peculiar relationship with anchovies begin in the late Middle Ages. The *Reconquista* period, which some historians date back to around the eighth century CE, is typically understood as the triumph of Christian forces in the north against their southern Muslim neighbors over a period of some 700 years. More recent scholarship challenges this characterization as little more than late nineteenth and early twentieth-century revisionist propaganda, as the battle lines were never clear-cut. Some Christian forces allied with their Muslim neighbors, and there were significant stretches of peaceful coexistence. This period was characterized as much by shifting political alliances as religious affiliations. Caught in the middle, as usual, were the Jews, who occasionally found refuge under some of the more benevolent and enlightened Christian and Muslim rulers who still held sway over their territories.

Towards the end of the *Reconquista* period, in 1478, Ferdinand II of Aragon and Isabella I of Castile inaugurated a new Catholic Inquisition (there had been several preceding this) to assume control over the entire Iberian Peninsula and create a common Catholic identity. As the Catholic Crown consolidated power, and the Spanish Inquisition intensified, proclamations required all Jews and Muslims to convert to Christianity. Central to the entire undertaking was the surveillance of society to ensure that everyone was acting in line with Catholic orthodoxy and not secretly practicing the heretical religions of Islam or Judaism behind closed doors.

Food has always operated as a signifier of religious identity, and in early modern Spain it became a key litmus test by which religious beliefs were ascertained. Perhaps nothing symbolized religious identity more than pork, which Muslims and Jews do not eat. In the hysteria of the Inquisition, avoiding pork or not working on the Sabbath could be potentially life-threatening. One was not even safe behind closed doors, as observing the Sabbath could be detected by the lack of chimney smoke (lighting a fire was prohibited on the Sabbath), and Christian neighbors were recruited to keep an eye on those who refrained from work. Another tell-tale marker of Judaism was purchasing large amounts of vegetables before the Sabbath (thereby avoiding work on the day of rest). Butchers were closely watched to verify which families avoided pork, and fishmongers kept track of those who abstained from shellfish. Islam had fewer food restrictions than Judaism, but with alcohol prohibited and animal butchering following closely prescribed rules, church officials were ever vigilant in their search for signs of "Muslim" transgressions.

Christians had their own dietary restrictions, and foremost among these was the practice of fasting. The Christian tradition of fasting did not really commence in earnest until the fourth and fifth centuries CE, and its primary purpose was to perform religious penance modeled on Christ's forty days in the desert, when he withstood the temptations of sin by foregoing food. While meat was widely held to be the most beneficial food for good health in medieval Spain and the rest of Europe, it was also thought to symbolize and trigger the more "base" aspects of humanity, such as sexuality and hunger, over spiritual purity and enlightenment. Fasting days grew in number throughout the

Middle Ages until they came to occupy close to half the calendar year. Chief among the prohibited items on fasting days was meat. Fish became the go-to substitute for animal flesh for those who could afford it, and a thriving trade in seafood evolved around fasting days and the forty-day period of Lent. Fasting became a key way in which Christians could differentiate themselves from their Muslim and Jewish neighbors.

Food not only signified religious identity in early modern Spain, but it also revealed one's place in the social hierarchy. In her book *Food Matters: Alonso Quijano's Diet and the Discourse of Food in Early Modern Spain*, Hispanic studies professor Carolyn Nadeau details how the consumption of food became a performance in which hierarchy and status were enacted, from seating arrangements to serving sizes, the types of courses received, and the order in which you were served. The categorization of food had little to do with taste or nutritional value; rarity and exclusivity were key. In this context, the expression "you are what you eat" rang true, with the food you ate defining your hierarchical rank in society.

At the top of the food hierarchy in Spain during this period was meat. As Nadeau notes, "[A]ll meats were not created equal," and this extended to the entire food chain, including seafood, grains, vegetables, and pulses.[1] At the top of the meat hierarchy was *carnero* (mutton), but *carnero* did not refer to any mutton, but lamb less than one year old. Close behind was baby goat (kid) and baby cow (veal). Wild game was also highly ranked, as much for its taste as for its exclusivity, as it was only hunted on the very largest of estates. Fowl, especially the rarer game birds, were highly esteemed.

The type of bread you ate also spoke to your position in society. At the top of the bread hierarchy were those loaves made with wheat and extensively bolted to yield the purest white bread. Lower down the hierarchy were wholegrain wheat breads, which were coarser and less refined. By far the most common breads for the majority of society were black breads or those made from rye. Rye was a staple used in many forms; in the cities, the poor often subsisted on a gruel of rye, onions, and a scrap or two of animal fat, along with anything else they could scrounge.

Vegetables, and lentils in particular, were a paradox, as Nadeau notes. On the one hand, they were recognized as an ideal fasting-day food, and, as such, were associated with religious abstinence and spiritual purity. By foregoing meat and eating vegetables instead, one was tempering one's "base" instincts and moving closer to God. On the other hand, vegetables and pulses were ranked at the bottom of the food hierarchy, deemed as little better than animal fodder. While lentils were viewed somewhat dubiously across Europe, nowhere was this more pronounced than in Spain. Nadeau notes that early Spanish cookbook authors often included chapters or sections with recipes for abstinence days, but rarely mentioned lentils. Thus, social stigma outweighed the moral imperatives of religious abstinence.

Above all, in elite households, religious abstinence meant one thing: fish days. But fish days, according to records, did not appear to include anchovies. Given the high number of fasting days—the weekly calendar was often understood in terms of meat days and fish days—and the abundance of fish recipes in cookery books, the lack of anchovies bespeaks their extremely low hierarchical rank. In an era obsessed with status, our tiny, bony, inconsequential anchovies fared terribly.

Early cookbooks and the elusive anchovy

Cookbooks in the "Golden Age" of Spain—*El Siglo de Oro* (circa 1492–1659)—reinforced a hierarchical understanding of fish, with dire consequences for anchovies. Just as the earliest English, French, and Italian cookbooks originated in courtly kitchens and operated socially as statements of power, so too did their Spanish counterparts. The authors of these manuscripts worked for royalty and aristocrats, and their well-stocked larders full of exotic ingredients bore little resemblance to what was found in the cupboards of humbler households.

One of the first Catholic cookbooks published in Iberia was the *Lybre de doctrina pera ben servir: de tallar y del art de coch*, "The Doctrine of Serving and Carving Well and the Art of Cooking" or, as it is more commonly known today, "Book of Cookery." The first edition was written by Maestre Robert in Catalan in 1520. Five years later, it was published in Spanish under the title *Libre del coch* with the author listed as Ruperto de Nola, the name by which he is known to this day. While most accept that he was a Catalan, he may have been Italian (and possibly even served at the pleasure of King Ferdinand I of Naples), as his recipes show some Italian influences. Whoever he was and wherever he was born, de Nola's cookbook served as a foundation for the emerging culinary traditions of Spain, having one foot planted in the medieval past, with some recipes drawn from the earlier fourteenth-century *Libre de Sent Soví*, and the other foot stepping forward into the Renaissance, influenced by more contemporary Catalan and Italian practices (Fig. 4.1).

There is much to admire about de Nola's cookbook. Somewhat surprisingly, vegetables are treated with a modicum of respect. Drawing upon Arab traditions, nuts such as almonds and pine nuts are often ground in a mortar along with crustless bread to act as a thickener and texture enhancer for soups and sauces. Ginger, cinnamon, saffron, nutmeg, mace, and grains of paradise, as well as generous quantities of sugar, are common throughout his recipes. Such ingredients are often combined with verjuice or orange juice to strike the sweet-sour-spice balance to which

Fig. 4.1: The "Golden Age of Spain" could just as easily have been called the "Golden Age of Hierarchy," as the cover illustration of Ruperto de Nola's *Libre del coch* illustrates visually through the respective heights of the king, cook, and server.

medieval cooking aspired. His "Pottage called peach dish" (*Potaje llamado persicate*) captures these notes perfectly, with the peach soup cooked in a savory meat broth with blanched and ground almonds that no doubt hit all the right notes for a satisfying sixteenth-century soup.

Of all the cookbooks published in this period—and for the next 225 years—de Nola's is the only one to contain an anchovy recipe. Significantly, the recipe calls for fresh anchovies, which were widely available along the Catalan coastline:

Anchovy casserole (*Saiton en cazuela*)

The anchovy is commonly bitter, and because of this you must remove the head together with the intestines and wash it, and clean it well, and then take all common spices, and also put in raisins, and almonds, and pine nuts; and the almonds must be scalded and blanched; and then mix them with the raisins, and almonds, and pine nuts, and with all the good herbs, and with the fish. And let everything be mixed in the casserole with a little oil. These casseroles are better to cook in the house than in the oven; and for the most part, they should be eaten in the month of April.[2]

The notion that fresh anchovies are "commonly bitter" is perplexing. This is a characterization that de Nola made about no other fish in his cookbook. All fish intestines can be bitter, but de Nola specifically called for removing them along with the head, so we must assume he was talking about the flesh itself. Although this was not presented as a value judgment but more as a simple statement of fact, it does not seem to have been based on any objective analysis of how fresh anchovies actually taste. One cannot help but wonder how much of de Nola's description was rooted in the bias against anchovies that was common at the time: too small, too bony, too low-ranked. Given the prominence of de Nola's cookbook and its huge impact on royal Spanish cuisine over the next 200 years, might his characterization have acted as a nail in the anchovy coffin?

Anchovies are absent from Diego Granado's *Libro del arte de cozina* (1599), although it is filled with several promising recipes, many with a new culinary sensibility. It is too bad that they are almost entirely poached from Bartolomeo Scappi's Italian cookbook, *Opera*, and, to a lesser extent, de Nola's Catalan cookbook. Anchovies are also absent in Domingo Hernández de Maceras' (1607) cookbook of the same name, *Libro del arte de cozina*. De Maceras was the head cook at the College of Oviedo in Salamanca, where lesser nobility sent their children to become functionaries in the burgeoning Spanish bureaucracy. In the hunt for an anchovy recipe in early seventeenth-century Spain, this seems like a good candidate, as it addresses a stratum of society a notch or two below courtly cuisine. But alas, despite the book's inclusion of over thirty-seven recipes with fish, not one of them contains anchovies.

Anchovies are even absent from royal chef Francisco Martínez Montiño's *Arte de cocina* (1611), the greatest cookbook of the Golden Age of Spain and the most published Spanish cookbook up until the twentieth century. While anchovies could complement many of his recipes (as they did in recipes from this period in Italy), they are, rather tellingly, nowhere to be found. Thus far, anchovies make a grand total of one appearance in all the Spanish cookbooks published up to this time. And with no new Spanish cookbooks published between 1611 and 1745, it would be a long while before we would see them in a recipe again.

A man who liked his fish: Holy Roman Emperor Charles V

While highbrow Iberian cookery books effectively barred anchovies from the upper-class table, they found an unlikely patron in none other than the Holy Roman Emperor, Charles V. How exactly did our little fish make it all the way to His Grace?

Charles V, born in the Flemish city of Ghent in 1500, became king of nearly one third of Europe through that most time-tested of methods: inheritance and marriage. Through one branch of his family, Charles inherited the Netherlands; another branch brought him the Hapsburg holdings, including Austria and a large swath of central Europe; and a third branch brought him his Mediterranean empire, including parts of Spain and the kingdoms of Naples, Sardinia, and Sicily. He also ruled over a huge chunk of the New World, which led to his vast holdings being called "the empire on which the sun never sets." With such extensive territories, and the gold and silver of the New World financing his Catholic agenda, he had many reformation-minded enemies testing his borders. Holding together his vast empire required constant military campaigns, and over the years, this took a severe toll on his health, contributing to his decision in 1556 to abdicate the throne in Brussels.

Seeking a milder climate to cope with his ailments—gout in particular—Charles decided to retire to the Monastery of Yuste in 1557 in the western region of Extremadura in Spain. A fleet of sailboats carried Charles and his entourage of family and court sycophants from the Dutch province of Zeeland to Laredo on the north coast of Spain. From here they set out on their overland journey, with Charles's poor health often requiring him to be carried in a litter. Lousy weather, bad supply lines, and pretentious rural incompetents added to the difficulties of the journey. But it is on this journey that we see the first references to anchovies, as William Stirling's *The Cloister Life of the Emperor Charles V* of 1853 noted:

> The fourth day was marked by an improvement in the weather, which had hitherto been rainy, and by the arrival of a courier from court with a supply of potted anchovies and other favorite fish for the emperor.[3]

While Charles awaited final renovations to his lodgings in Yuste, we catch another glimpse of anchovies in Spain:

> The weekly courier from Valladolid to Lisbon was ordered to change his route that he might bring, every Thursday a provision of eels and other rich fish (pescado grueso) for Friday's fast. There was a constant demand for anchovies, tunny, and other potted fish, and sometimes a complaint that the trouts of the country were too small ...[4]

Eventually, with Charles having dismissed almost the entirety of his staff and servants, the residence at the monastery in Yuste was ready for occupation (Fig. 4.2). By now, the enfeebled former ruler had become somewhat of a glutton, reputedly so obese that he could not even walk between the tables in the refectory. Robert Goodwin notes our next reference to anchovies in the life of Charles V:

> He indulged his great love of fish and was sent plaice and lamprey from Lisbon, sole and oysters in *escabèche*, smoked herring and salmon, and on one occasion his physician, Dr. Quijada, had to dissuade him from eating a barrel of anchovies that had putrefied in the transit.[5]

So why were Charles V and his entourage eating anchovies in Spain when Spaniards themselves seemed to disdain them so? The former king was born and bred in the northern European

Fig. 4.2: After nearly four decades leading military campaigns across Europe, Charles V desired little more than to retire to the monastery in Yuste, Spain, where he could contemplate life and enjoy the occasional anchovy. This painting by Titian (1548) commemorated the emperor's victory over the Protestant armies at the Battle of Mühlberg in 1547. (© *Photographic Archive Museo Nacional del Prado.*)

city of Ghent, with access to an abundant supply of salted and potted fish. Might he have acquired a taste for anchovies early in life? Or might he have discovered anchovies later in life, perhaps while on one of his numerous campaigns to his Mediterranean kingdoms of Naples, Sardinia, or Sicily, all of which were major anchovy-consuming regions?

Whatever the case, the only other consistent reference to anchovies in this period is found at the other end of the social spectrum: among poor coastal fishermen.

French fishermen refine the Spanish fishery

Around the time that Charles V was retiring to his monastic retreat at Yuste in the mid-sixteenth century, a revolutionary change in fishing technology occurred along the Catalan coastline in northeastern Spain. This marks a turning point in our story, as it is the start of one of the great anchovy production booms in Spain. And the impetus for this historic anchovy event? Rather tellingly, it was not local consumption that drove these changes, but the French. More specifically, French fishermen. Departing from their ancestral fishing grounds in the south of France, a small fleet of no more than five or ten boats, carrying four or five men per vessel, sailed into the waters of Catalonia and changed fishing practices forever. They introduced new boats, nets, and fishing techniques to an industry that had changed remarkably little since the Roman era. On an uninhabited rocky peninsula jutting into the sea would arise the most famous anchovy town along the Catalonian coastline: L'Escala.

This curious chapter in Spain's anchovy story began not in the town of L'Escala itself, but in the neighboring settlement of Empúries nearly 2,000 years earlier. Located just 1 kilometer northeast of L'Escala on a wide sandy beach, Empúries was founded as a colony in 575 BCE by Ionian Greeks from the west coast of modern-day Turkey. After several centuries, the Romans arrived (as they always seemed to do), and things took an inevitable Roman turn, including the emergence of *garum*. The waters off Empúries teemed with sardines, mackerel, and anchovies, collectively known as "bluefish," and Empúries was ideally situated for *garum* production: year-round running water, front-door access to the sea, and a nearby lagoon that was engineered to create salt pans. Empúries thrived for centuries as a trading town (its original name, *Emporion*, means "trading place" in ancient Greek), but its exposed location on the beach with no natural defences left it vulnerable to invasion, and the Vikings promptly plundered it in the mid-ninth century. Empúries was soon abandoned, with sand, dune grass, and scrub brush reclaiming the landscape.

With the passage of time, several local families moved into the derelict site. By the late eleventh century, it was under the control of the Count of Empúries, Hugh II. At that time, fishing techniques were still rudimentary, handed down from father to son stretching back generations. No one was getting rich from fishing, but when coupled with a small plot of land on which to grow vegetables, one could precariously raise a family.

Why the first French fishermen set sail for Empúries in Spain is not fully understood. Lurdes Boix, Director of L'Escala's Anchovy and Salt Museum (MASLE), posits that a combination of factors may have played a role, such as high taxation in France and the pristine state of the fishing grounds off Empúries. Further research is ongoing. What we know for sure is that the arrival of the French in Catalonia around 1575 was a game-changer. Bigger boats, better nets, and, most importantly, a paradigm-changing understanding of how bluefish respond to celestial phenomena, had profound implications for the fishing industry.

The key to the whole shift was an astute observation: precisely twice a day, bluefish school together and swim towards the rising or setting sun. As soon as the first rays of sunlight break the plane of the horizon each morning, bluefish are drawn towards the surface which is associated with feeding habits and predator avoidance strategies. It is at this moment that a net laid in their path will intercept them, resulting in a colossal catch. Once the sun has risen and its light diffused across the entire sky, the fish calm down and resume more informal feeding patterns. Contemporary anchovy fishing around the world exploits this same phenomenon, with powerful arc lights shone into the sea at night, attracting great schools of anchovies to the surface.

French fishermen also brought with them a new technology: gillnets. Traditional nets trapped fish in an enclosed area, as their mesh was too fine for the fish to escape. With gillnets, however, the mesh was just large enough for a fish's head to get through but too small for the entire body, thereby trapping the fish at their gills, hence the name "gillnet." If the fish tried to back out, their gills would become further entangled in the mesh. Interestingly, the nets were not made of cotton, but of cannabis hemp. To preserve the nets against the deleterious effects of UV rays and salt water, fishermen would boil the natural hemp with pine bark, which contains resinous oils that saturate the hemp fibres and served as a protective coating.

The other major change brought by the French was the introduction of bigger and better boats, called *llagut* in Catalan, *sardinals* in Spanish, or sardine boats in English. The traditional fishing boats were little more than small rowboats, that usually lacked a sail and could comfortably hold only two or three men at most. The new French-style sardine boats boasted a Latin sail, could accommodate up to five men, and had enough room to process and salt fish right in the boat. Depending upon where the fish were running, the boats were still small enough to be effectively rowed close to shore or near rocks, but if conditions dictated, the fishermen could hoist the sail and pursue the fish further out at sea. The result was a huge increase in sardine, mackerel, and anchovy catches. The combination of larger boats, better nets, and a new understanding of bluefish behavior transformed the small rudimentary fishery industry, leading to the first commercial exploitation of bluefish in Spain (Fig. 4.3).

A fishing frenzy: L'Escala scales up

Everyone got in on the bluefish boom. So many fish could be caught with the new boats and technology that long-time local farmers such as Cincluas and Cortes dropped their hoes, sold their land, and bought boats. Documents indicate that even the local priest, Father Bessedes of Empúries, sold his land to get in

Fig. 4.3: An engraving of a French-style sardine boat with a Latin sail and rigging. These highly maneuverable boats allowed fishermen to quickly locate and target the fast-moving schools of bluefish from the shoreline to further out at sea.

on the new gold rush. For the first time, there was real money to be made from the sea, and the numerous fasting days and religious holidays provided a constant market for reasonably priced bluefish, at least in comparison with the larger and more desired salmon, swordfish, and trout. The faster you could get a boat into the sea, the sooner you could start making money.

One impediment was the distance from Empúries to the uninhabited rocky point with the best fishing grounds a kilometer south of town. If the boats and all their gear could be stowed nearby, an hour or two of travel could be saved each day. A request was made to the Count of Empúries to allow for a few simple fishing huts to be constructed on the barren peninsula, forming the foundation of the future town of L'Escala. In 1591, an inhabitant of Empúries called Joan Andreu took things one step further and approached the count requesting permission to build a small, two-story house/workshop at the point, measuring 14 meters by 8 meters. The bottom floor was his workshop, devoted to his fishing gear, supplies, and a small salting operation. His family lived upstairs. Soon, others followed, and the catches increased.

L'Escala grew quickly in size and importance, and by the beginning of the eighteenth century almost 1,400 inhabitants, 90 percent of whom were involved in fishing, called it home. Men worked the boats, women processed the fish onshore, and the kids did a little of everything. Fresh fish was sold to wholesalers, who transported it on ice to nearby towns and villages, with Barcelona being a key market. But the bulk of the fish was salted, with much smaller amounts being smoked or sun-dried. The fish destined for salting was gutted and packed in barrels with alternating layers of fish and salt.

An ample supply of salt was essential to the entire undertaking. One key source of salt was the island of Ibiza, known at that time as the "saltshaker of the Mediterranean."[6] Salt was also imported from the salt pits of Torrevieja and Tortosa, on Spain's east coast on the Mediterranean Sea. Further afield, it was imported from Trapani, Sicily, a town that would loom large in Spain's second great anchovy production boom. Salt was such a key commodity that King Philip II—Charles V's son—passed a proclamation in 1586 that effectively created a state monopoly on its sale. With salt taxes bringing so much into the state's coffers, sales were closely regulated, and meticulous records were kept. These records provide a key documentary source for L'Escala, as they reveal not just the quantities of salt that were purchased by fishermen, but also which kinds of fish it was used for and how much was left over. From these records, we learn that between March 10 and June 3, 1726, Francesc Molinas produced 142 barrels of salted anchovies, Bernat Poch produced 103, and Rafel Maranges managed—for whatever unfortunate reason—a paltry 2 barrels.

Sardines were the predominant catch and moneymaker in L'Escala, with anchovy production a distant second, at roughly 10 percent of the total catch. Clearly, L'Escala was producing salted anchovies, but who was consuming them? One hint is provided in a diary of Francisco de Zamora, a highly regarded royal bureaucrat in the Catalan court who detailed his observations of Catalonia in 1789. Writing about L'Escala, Zamora wrote:

> The women take care of the anchovy. There is salt from the Neapolitans of Tortosa ... There are 18 boats and 60 laúdes [sardine boats], they fish a lot of anchovies and a little coral; their neighbors work in all branches [of the fishery], earn good wages and there are no poor people.[7]

Aside from the encouraging observation that there are no poor people, Zamora's comment that there are eighteen larger vessels engaged with the fishery is revealing. Lurdes Boix suggests in her article, "La saló de peix a l'antic port de l'Escala, segles XVI al XIX," that these vessels were engaged in "Cabotage," transporting goods and people to various ports, often for foreign operators. This drives the conversation towards the export of L'Escala's salted anchovies, perhaps to more lucrative foreign markets in France and Italy where demand may have been greater, leading to overall higher profits.

Further support for this "foreign market" theory for Spanish anchovies, albeit indirectly through sardines, comes from a L'Escala native, Ramon Balaguer, who was involved in long-distance trade. In 1802, his vessel, the *San Antonio*, exported salted sardines and oil to Livorno, Italy, and imported Alexandrian (Egyptian) wheat, hemp from Bologna, and dried *bacalao* (which originated off Newfoundland) back to L'Escala. Spanish records for salted sardines were few, though religious and state documents indicate that they were shipped to markets across the country, for consumption on Spanish fasting days and religious holidays.

Despite the value of anchovies as an export commodity, local fishermen and their immediate and extended families likely consumed far more of them than they could stomach. Such is the universal fate of fishing families around the world. A similar scenario would have played out in the nearby coastal communities that formed natural trading partners with L'Escala, although it was probably only those at the lowest rungs of society who were consuming anchovies. In the Muslim south, to the contrary, anchovies had been celebrated for centuries.

Turning south: Málaga boasts bountiful boquerónes

While the rest of Catholic Spain was sorting out its complicated relationship with anchovies, the inhabitants of one city in the southeast of the country, Málaga, were eating them with enthusiasm. Not only have the Malagueños—as the locals are called—

always eaten anchovies, but they have been eating them in a uniquely Malagueño way: fresh, lightly floured, and deep-fried. The Malagueños' love of deep-fried anchovies, which they call *boquerónes*, is so great that they are affectionately known to this day as *boquerónes* themselves. Even more curiously, they also call deep-fried anchovies *victorianos*, a name linked to an obscure Catholic order of friars that played an outsized role in popularizing them. Irrespective of their name, Malagueños (and Andalusians more generally) were the only ones consistently eating anchovies this way until the twentieth century. This is nothing short of remarkable, given that deep-fried anchovies are now ubiquitous in modern Spain, served everywhere from the humblest cafés to the fanciest restaurants.

To understand Málaga's unique appreciation for anchovies, we begin with the founding of the city. Málaga is located on the southeast coast of Spain on the Costa del Sol (coast of the sun) about 100 kilometers east of the Strait of Gibraltar. Its natural port no doubt appealed to the Phoenicians, who founded the city around 770 BCE. It quickly became an important trading city with links to the wider Mediterranean world. Blessed with a generous 300 days of sunshine a year—ideal for its famed oranges, lemons, and pomegranates—water, and ample fishing grounds just offshore, it quickly attracted the attention of foreign powers. Ancient Carthage, then the Romans, the Visigoths, and a succession of Muslim rulers held sway over the city and left their mark.

The Muslim conquest of Iberia is traditionally dated to 711 CE, the year when the Arab forces of the Umayyad Caliphate of Mecca defeated the Visigoth Kingdom of Hispania. Sweeping across the Strait of Gibraltar on ships from North Africa, the Arab forces scored a decisive victory at the battle of Guadalete, where the Visigoth king, Roderic, was killed. After consolidating the lands in the southern part of the country, which they called

Al-Andalus (from which the modern name Andalusia derives), they advanced northward, eventually crossing into France, where they met stiff resistance. After a fateful defeat at the city of Toulouse, they retreated over the Pyrenees back to the Iberian Peninsula, where they would remain for the next 800 years. Their forces included a large contingent of Moors (from the Latin "mauri," meaning people from ancient Mauretania, namely the modern states of Morocco and Algeria). Collectively, these different Muslim groups intermarried and laid their imprint upon the land, merging their Arab and North African culinary traditions with local Christian and Jewish practices.

The Moorish golden age in Spain brought huge advances in science, engineering, medicine, and the culinary arts. During the tenth century CE, Córdoba was the most advanced city in Europe, a relatively tolerant society with a mixed population of half a million Muslims, Christians, and Jews. At a time when many parts of Europe were struggling economically, Moorish cities were flourishing, with fresh water, irrigated agriculture, and vibrant centers of learning that attracted scholars from around the Mediterranean world. Christians and Jews were forced to pay a special yearly tax to the Muslim state, but this afforded them more rights than minorities in any other country in Europe. Such legal protections would become a distant memory under the Catholic Crown, which stripped Muslims and Jews of all rights, confiscated their property, and forced them into exile with only what they could carry on their backs. But such dark days lay in the future. During the Moorish golden age, society and the arts flourished, with elites commissioning hand-crafted cookbooks to showcase their culinary sophistication and good taste.

The origins of floured fried fish

The most famous Moorish cookbook known to modern readers is the *Manuscrito anónimo*, known in English as "The Anonymous Andalusian Cookbook," and dated to the thirteenth century. The cookbook covers a tremendous amount of culinary terrain, drawing upon Moorish, Arab, Jewish, Christian, Sicilian, Middle Eastern, and Persian influences in its more than 500 recipes. Just as the Roman cookbook *Apicius* is a collection of earlier recipes compiled by different scribes over time, so too is the *Manuscrito anónimo*. The recipes it contains are like DNA snippets that carry gastronomic traces of past cultures. Some of its recipes can be found in an earlier cookbook of 1226 called *Kitāb al-Tabīkh*, "The Book of Dishes," by Muhammad al-Khatib al-Baghdadi. Al-Baghdadi's recipes, in turn, draw upon various Persian dishes. Some of the *Manuscrito anónimo* recipes can be traced back even further to the ninth century and the half-brother of the reigning Caliph—a prince, poet, gastronome, and man about town named Ibrahim ibn al-Mahdi. This all helps to explain how Middle Eastern and Persian food made its way to the Iberian Peninsula and onwards to influence European cooking.

But for all its connections to the Muslim east, the *Manuscrito anónimo* also highlights the changes that cuisine can undergo when afforded new ingredients in new lands far from their place of origin. Olive oil is a case in point. In tenth-century Iraq, olive oil was exceedingly costly, and was reserved for the most exceptional of courtly celebrations. This is evident in al-Baghdadi's cookbook, which makes far more use of *alya*, a cooking fat derived from the tails of sheep. "Many, if not most of the recipes in al-Baghdadi's *Kitāb al-Tabīkh* begin with instructions to render out tail fat in a hot pan," writes American historian H. D. Miller, "fat which is then used to brown meat for stewing, or as the medium for frying *kubabs*."[8] But in

Andalusia, olive oil was plentiful and was incorporated into all types of dishes, lending a distinctive taste that came to redefine Moorish cooking.

Seafood also sets Moorish cooking apart from its Middle Eastern and Persian counterparts. Al-Baghdadi's cookbook only lists twelve recipes for fish—not surprising given that Baghdad is located far from the Persian Gulf and is limited mostly to freshwater fish. While fish were appreciated and even praised in Baghdad, above all it was meat that held pride of place. But Andalusia's coastline includes the Strait of Gibraltar, one of the richest fisheries in the entire Mediterranean Sea. Its abundant seafood became a defining and celebrated characteristic of Moorish cuisine. Miller elaborates: "The true fish lovers of the medieval Muslim world, however, could be found in Iberia and the Maghreb, and in the Nile River valley."[9] The *Manuscrito anónimo* contains dozens of recipes for fish, with at least seventeen individual species (mostly saltwater varieties) mentioned by name. In that book, fish is prepared in every way imaginable, from roasting to frying, to stewing with yoghurt.

While floured fried fish is a common indulgence in today's world, its inclusion in the *Manuscrito anónimo* was a world first. According to the book's translator, food historian Charles Perry, the recipe *hut mu'affar*, "dusted fish," was invented on the Iberian Peninsula "sometime in or before the 1200s."[10] Because the recipe calls for a larger fish, the initial direction is to poach the fish in boiling water to firm up its flesh prior to deboning and separating out the fillets:

hut mu'affar (dusted fish)

Take what fish you have which are good and esteemed, scale and boil with water and salt. Then take them out, wash and open the pieces as slabs [fillets] and remove from them whatever is there in the way of bones and spines.

Then take ground breadcrumbs or wheat flour and add some egg, pepper, coriander, cinnamon and spikenard. Beat it all together and roll the pieces of fish in it one after the other. Then fry with fresh oil until browned and repeat several times until browned and done [until all the fish is cooked].

Then make a sauce of oil, vinegar, a little *murri* [a fermented sauce made from barley or fish] … and cumin. Boil [it together] and throw it over [the fish].[11]

Like all the recipes in the *Manuscrito anónimo*, this is clearly a dish for elites, as the eggs, spices, and aromatic essence spikenard (to say nothing of the "esteemed" fish) would have been out of reach for all but the wealthy. The structural foundation of the dish lies in coating the fish with breadcrumbs and/or flour prior to cooking. Each addition to this foundation reflected the creativity of the cook, as always, in accordance with his or her means. This flexibility allowed for a wide range of variables, making it a popular dish across the socioeconomic board. Even with no further embellishments, save a bit of salt, crispy fried fish was (and is) an irresistible treat. Stripped down to its bare bones, the recipe for *hut mu'affar* is the culinary touchstone that many centuries later would give rise to Catholic Spain's love of deep-fried anchovies.

The Portuguese adopted the practice as part of their Lent festivities, one of the *quattuor tempura*, celebrated four times a year. Portuguese merchants took the recipe to East Asia, where the Japanese adopted it, with "tempura" becoming a staple part of their culinary repertoire. Sephardic Jews forced into exile from Spain brought the recipe to England, from which fish and chips became a national obsession. Even the original *hut mu'affar* sauce made the voyage overseas, with the English simplifying it to oil and vinegar before eventually dropping the oil entirely and settling on their own special malted vinegar. Mexican deep-fried fish tacos owe their origins to Japanese fishermen who were brought to the town of Ensenada in 1920, where they introduced their favorite way to deep-fry fish.

The Miracle of Málaga: north and south at war

Jumping forward several hundred years to the late fifteenth century, the long drawn-out war between the Catholic north and the Muslim south was lurching towards its conclusion in favor of the Catholic monarchs, King Ferdinand II of Aragon, aka "Ferdinand the Catholic," and Queen Isabella of Castile. But in the year 1487, Málaga was still under the control of the Lord of Granada, Muhammad XIII, known to the Catholics as El-Zagal. The centuries-long *Reconquista* had brought Christian forces to the very doorstep of Muhammad XIII's territory. It was crucial for him to retain Málaga, as the city was the key conduit to the Mediterranean world of lucrative trade and support networks. To lose the vital port city would mean that Muhammad XIII's territory would be cut off and landlocked. For these same strategic reasons, the conquest of Málaga was critical for King Ferdinand II, as once the city fell, the noose would tighten on Granada. If the Nasrid Kingdom of Granada fell as well, then the entire Iberian Peninsula would be under the Catholic flags of Ferdinand and Isabella.

Ferdinand assembled a massive army for the assault on Málaga. Some estimates peg the force at 80,000 strong, with up to 20,000 horsemen, 8,000 regular troops, and at least 50,000 support personnel, including traders, engineers, blacksmiths, leatherworkers, carpenters, cooks, and the usual motley crew of prostitutes and ne'er-do-wells.

Ferdinand intended to negotiate a quick surrender of Málaga to spare his forces a long, drawn-out siege, knowing that it would exact a terrible toll. But Muhammad XIII had placed the defence of Málaga in the hands of his most competent and trusted general, El-Zegrí, who had been instructed to hold Málaga at all costs. Well stocked with artillery, ammunition, and a contingent of fierce North African mercenaries known as *Gomeres*, El-Zegrí rebuffed Ferdinand's terms of surrender, and a long, brutal, four-month siege of the heavily fortified city ensued.

Ferdinand's forces pounded the city walls with a new type of cannon, more powerful than the world had ever seen. With repeated volleys of coordinated cannon fire—some cannonballs weighed up to 50 kilograms—sections of the wall started to collapse. But El-Zegrí's defenders were well prepared. Waves of arrows, darts, and rocks rained down upon the Catholics. Those who made it past the flurry of lethal projectiles to the base of the wall were met with boiling pitch and resin poured down from above. Surprise nocturnal raids became a common tactic on both sides, depriving everyone of much-needed sleep and fraying the nerves of all involved.

In the midst of a steely stalemate, the "miracle" of Málaga occurred. According to tradition, three friars from the Catholic Order of Minims were visiting the encampment, and Ferdinand invited them to make a prayer to the Virgin Mary requesting her assistance. They gathered in front of a small sculpture of the Virgin Mary that had been sent to Ferdinand by Hapsburg Emperor Maximilian of Austria. Through his heartfelt prayers to the Virgin Mary, and with the Minims at his side, Ferdinand learned that he would win the war in three days' time.

Sure enough, three days later, the city walls of Málaga were breached. After nearly 800 years of Muslim rule, the Catholic flags of Ferdinand and Isabella were raised over the city, and the following day the couple made their triumphant entrance. El-Zegrí held out for another week before surrendering the citadel. Ferdinand wasted no time in exacting his revenge upon the city. Except for the twenty-five leading Muslim families that were spared his wrath, the city's population was sold into slavery. Some were traded to North African kingdoms that held Christian captives, others were sold to help rebuild state coffers, and some were simply given away as presents, with Queen Isabella gifting fifty of "the most beautiful Moorish girls" to the Queen of Naples and thirty to the Queen of Portugal.[12]

In recognition of her miraculous intervention on behalf of the Catholics, a small chapel was constructed to house the sculpture of the Virgin Mary, right where the original prayer had been made. Over time, a *convento* was constructed and the small chapel was enlarged into a rudimentary church, so that pilgrims could pay their respects and conduct prayers. Ferdinand bequeathed the sculpture of the Virgin to the order, dubbing it *Santa Maria de la Victoria*, the new patron saint of Málaga. It was displayed prominently in the church where it rests to this day.

The Minims, or "Minimos" as they were known in Spain, were a humble order, but their name proved problematic to Ferdinand. The order was founded by Saint Francis of Paola in the early part of the fifteenth century in Italy. A central tenet of the order was a vow of poverty and austerity, which entailed wearing a habit of roughly woven black wool and following a diet based on the "Lenten way of Life," forsaking all meat and dairy.[13] Within the Catholic hierarchy, members of the order considered themselves minor friars—the least of the least—and this was reflected in their choice of the name "Minims," which derives from the Italian word *minimo*, meaning minimum, smallest, or least. But Ferdinand viewed such a humble and small name as entirely inappropriate for the outsized role that the "Minimos" played in his victory over the Muslims. Either that, or he was simply following in the footsteps of a long line of political propagandizers stretching back to the pharaohs of Ancient Egypt. For whatever reason, as a condition of their royal licence to practice in Spain, he insisted that their name be changed to the

Frailes de la Victoria, or the Friars of the Victory. They soon became known colloquially as *Victorianos*.

From friars to fried fish: Málaga's victorianos

The coastline around Málaga has always been exceptionally rich in anchovies. In his book *Málaga and its Anchovies*, the Spanish writer Manuel Hernández notes that during the peak of the annual anchovy season, fishermen caught more than they knew what to do with. The larger, more mature anchovies found buyers in the local markets. But the juveniles and young fry—the *minimo*—were a perennial problem, and all too often the fishermen simply left them on the beach to rot. Under the heat of the late summer's sun, the stench of these decaying *minimo* anchovies permeated the city with such force that an ordinance was passed to prohibit their dumping. But instead of laboriously hauling them back out to sea as the ordinance required, the fishermen simply gave the *minimo* to the friars as alms, effectively killing two birds with one stone.

For the friars, the arrival of these *minimo* anchovies at the *convento* was welcomed, as they helped to feed the steady stream of hungry pilgrims who arrived daily. Initially, the friars probably followed the local Moorish method of preparing the anchovies: the heads were removed, and then they were rinsed in water, dusted with salt, and dredged in flour before being fried in the region's excellent olive oil. They were known, rather generically, as "fried fish."

At some point, the friars added a unique twist to the traditional Muslim technique. Prior to being fried, three or four of the floured anchovies were arrayed like a fan. A flour paste was used to "glue" the tails together, before placing them on a wire rack and lowering them into hot oil for a minute or two until golden. It is not clear to what extent this was originally done for aesthetic reasons, or whether there was some Catholic symbolism associated with it, but over time, it became known as a "Catholic tradition." Nowadays, for the sake of expedience, the battered anchovies are deep-fried separately. But the roots of this tradition may help to explain why the newly arrived Catholics—who traditionally showed little interest in anchovies—came to embrace them so fully. As the popularity of the fan-shaped fried anchovies spread throughout the city, the association between the *minimo* anchovies and the *minimo* friars eventually led to both becoming known as *victorianos*. Associating anchovies with the friars and the patron saint of the city helped the local Catholics to overcome some of the negative stereotypes they had associated with anchovies.

Málaga and anchovies: a match made to last

Another factor contributing to the rise of Catholic anchovy consumption in Málaga is more bureaucratic and hierarchical: a medieval city ordinance. In the late fifteenth century, larger fish such as flounder, conger, and turbot were forbidden by city ordinance from being sold in public inns and taverns, as they were deemed too valuable for the lower classes that frequented such establishments. The wealthy wanted the best fish for themselves. Innkeepers were not only prohibited from selling them on their premises, but even prohibited from purchasing them in the market. In 1494, the city council of Málaga imposed a fine upon an innkeeper for selling a fish pie made with conger. As a result of this ordinance, only smaller fish could be sold to the general public. This would have helped to normalize the consumption of anchovies.

Málaga's affection for anchovies is now well established and is woven into the folkloric fabric of the city. Up until the mid-twentieth century, wandering fish sellers (known as *cenocheros*) were ubiquitous throughout the city, armed with cane baskets filled with fresh anchovies and sardines. They would sing their melodic *pregon*, prompting housewives to scurry downstairs to purchase the fresh-off-the-boat fish. In Málaga—in contrast to the rest of Spain—anchovies and sardines were always sold fresh, never salted. These scenes of fish sellers and housewives became part of the city's cultural and gastronomic identity. Fish sellers have become a symbol of Málaga and are featured on the city's statues and paintings.

By the late nineteenth century, Málaga's deep-fried *boquerónes* had caught the attention of Spain's emerging culinary crowd, though they all referred to them slightly differently. Northern writers did not refer to them as *victorianos*, as this term was region-specific. Angel Muro was quite complimentary about Málaga's deep-fried *anchoa* in his cookbook *El practicón* (1894), which is surprising as he tended to dismiss anchovies unless they were part of a French recipe. For outright praise of Málaga's *boquerónes*, we turn to Dionisio Pérez's *Guía del buen comer español* ("Good Spanish Cooking," 1929), in which he described anchovies arranged in a "graceful fan shape" as one of the most "delicate expressions of Spanish cuisine."[14] Pérez's *boquerónes* recipe departs from the traditional Catholic approach of serving them plain. It harkens back to the original *hut mu'affar* recipe, delicately marinating the anchovies in spices, lemon, and vinegar, but also departs from it, as Pérez's recipe is an escabeche, a sort of reverse-marination process where the cooked fish is soaked in a vinegar bath as the final stage before serving.

However they are prepared, anchovies are consumed in huge numbers by modern Malagueños. While statistics are practically non-existent for earlier periods, the Spanish writer Luis Bellón's *El boquerón y la sardina de Málaga* ("The Anchovy and Sardine of Málaga," 1950) details just how extensive anchovy consumption was in Málaga in the first half of the twentieth century. Almost 95 percent of the anchovies that were caught off the coast of Málaga—the fifth largest city in Spain—were sold fresh and consumed locally. Malagueños clearly did not share the rest of Spain's distaste for these umami-rich little fish.

Reflecting on the enduring popularity of Málaga's *boquerónes*, Bellón notes that they have been "for many years the main course in the diet of the modest classes."[15] He attributes this to the fact that they are "fried in an unsurpassable way."[16] While this may be mostly due to Andalusia's famed olive oil, one cannot help but think of their unique traditional "arrayed" presentation. To this day, an annual festival is held in honour of *Santa Maria de la Victoria*, filling the streets of Málaga with tens of thousands of people. As part of a grand procession, Ferdinand's original statue of the Virgin Mary is paraded through the streets to the Cathedral of Málaga, where it is worshipped in a *novena*, a sort of multi-day mass for the faithful. A glimpse of the *Santa Maria de la Victoria* feeds the festivalgoers' souls, while *victorianos* (or *boquerónes fritos*, as they are often now called), deep-fried and consumed in the millions, feed their stomachs.

Affordable fish: Juan Altamiras' Nuevo arte de cocina

After *Arte de cocina* was written for the royal court in 1611, not a single cookbook was published in Spain for another 134 years. This drought only ended with the publication of Juan Altamiras' *Nuevo arte de cocina* in 1745, which was addressed to an audience of modest means. Altamiras was a Franciscan friar and cook engaged in the charitable work of feeding the poor, and his cookbook contains many ingredients that could be grown in a common vegetable plot or procured from local markets. Dispensing with the usual aristocratic favorites, such as venison and wild boar, Altamiras focused on the cheaper cuts of meat and organs with which most Spaniards were familiar: lungs, kidneys, testicles, hearts, blood, and feet. In a similar manner, he began the Lent section not with a fancy fish like sturgeon, sea bass, or salmon, but with salt cod, a fish that the poor consistently ate. "Since it is my hope to teach you everything you need to know," he began, "I thought I would open with salt cod. At this point you may think it is of little substance."[17] He was acutely aware of how salt cod was perceived by the high and humble alike. But Altamiras had the culinary wisdom to look past its cultural baggage to its essence: umami.

Altamiras was the first to publish a salt cod recipe in Spain, and he included twelve of them for good measure: salt cod with garlic and parsley, salt cod in a green sauce, salt cod dumplings, and a salt cod tortilla, to name just a few. Curiously, for someone who sang the praises of salt cod and had recipes for salted tuna and salted hake, Altamiras included no salted anchovies in his recipes. The addition of salted fish recipes was a breakthrough in a Spanish cookery book, though the lack of an anchovy recipe reminds us that anchovies were still poorly perceived and excluded from the culinary conversation. But from this point forward, salt cod would become a regular addition to Spanish cookbooks as it was healthy, reasonably affordable, and contributed loads of flavor, despite being dismissed by elites.

The wait for anchovies to appear in another cookbook was long: 227 years, to be precise. The honors go to the chief baker to the court of kings Philip V and Ferdinand VI, Juan De La Mata, and his cookbook entitled *Arte de reposteria* ("Art of Pastry," 1747). While it is true that remarkably few cookbooks were published since anchovies last appeared in Ruperto de Nola's sixteenth-century cookbook, the fact that they were not mentioned once before De La Mata's book is telling.

So how did De La Mata reintroduce anchovies onto Spain's gastronomic stage? He slipped them into salads and soup.

Anchovies feature in two salads in his cookbook: *Ensalada real labrada*, which is a sort of salmagundi (a pan-European salad featuring cold cuts), and *Ensalada verdes de todos generos*, a leafy green salad with an Italian influence which calls for "anchovies or bottarga" (dried mullet roe). Anchovy bones (but oddly, no other part of the fish) are used to flavor the most common type of gazpacho, *Capón de galera*. Though anchovies played a rather minor role in De La Mata's cookbook, they started to move closer to center stage thereafter.

No longer overlooked by cooks: anchovy recipes by Louis-Eustache Audot

The first time that anchovies featured significantly in a cookbook published in Spain was in 1854, in *La cocinera del campo y de la ciudad; o, nueva cocinera económica*, "The Cook of the Country and the City; or, New Economic Cookbook." But in a twist entirely appropriate to our story, the recipes came courtesy of a Frenchman, as the cookbook is a Spanish translation of the thirty-fourth edition of the hugely successful French cookbook by Louis-Eustache Audot. In the original French version, Audot drew upon regional recipes from around France (and a much smaller number from neighboring countries), and we find anchovies used in a variety of dishes, from meats to fowl and sauces to salads. Of all his recipes, perhaps the most recognizable to modern readers is the "Leg of lamb provincial style," which involves roasting a leg of lamb stuffed with twelve cloves of garlic and twelve anchovy fillets. Audot's cookbook also features the French favorite, "Anchovy butter," which calls for salted anchovies to be rinsed, passed through a hair sieve, and then kneaded with an equal amount of butter. Audot even includes the old English standby "Anchovy essence," which, the author helpfully noted, could be kept in the kitchen to enliven a sauce or left permanently on the dining-room table, *à l'Anglaise.*

Of the thirty-three anchovy recipes in Audot's French cookbook, the Spanish publisher cut twenty-one. This conveys a great deal about the state of play for anchovies in the two countries. One recipe cut from the Spanish cookbook was for roasted partridge with anchovies. Interestingly, Audot took this recipe from Altamiras' 1745 cookbook, and the original version used sardines, not anchovies. In altering this key ingredient, Audot must have realized that anchovies would be more appealing to his French audience. Taking a different tack, the Spanish publisher decided that too many anchovies would have the opposite effect on Spanish readers and omitted the recipe altogether.

Audot's cookbook reflected the ongoing influence of French cooking upon the courtly cuisine of Spain. But originally, these roles were reversed. In the Middle Ages, Arab and Jewish ingredients and culinary techniques washed across the Iberian Peninsula, leaving behind a host of new flavors that the Christian rulers adopted. This new hybrid Spanish cuisine then spread to France and the French court in the fifteenth and sixteenth centuries. But the tide turned with the rise of French *haute cuisine* in the seventeenth century, and French cooking started to influence the Spanish court. The French culinary revolution was predicated, in part, on separating sweet from savory, and nowhere was this more evident than in their sauces. While sauce recipes from the medieval period combined sugar or dried fruit with savory ingredients—the so-called "mixture" approach—the publication of La Varenne's *Le Cuisinier françois* in 1651 inaugurated a shift that separated them out. Savory sauces were crafted with citrus juice, wine, and anchovies, an approach that came to full fruition in the eighteenth and nineteenth centuries. Audot's cookbook adopted this new approach and separated savory from sweet, a trend which also spread to Spain, England, and Italy.

Fighting French influence: efforts to build a Spanish national identity

Spanish elites, like elites everywhere, eagerly adopted French customs and traditions in most matters related to food. Dinner menus were even printed in French at the Spanish royal court. According to professor of Spanish studies Lara Anderson, two Spanish intellectuals spoke out against the "tyranny of French cuisine," emphasizing the need "for Spain to achieve cultural autonomy from France."[18] Writing under the assumed names of Dr. Thebussem and the King's Chef, they penned a series of letters which brought the debate to the public at a key moment, when many states in Europe were actively engaged in nation-building.

Published in 1876 under the title *La mesa moderna*, "The Modern Table," their exchange concerned the glaring failure of the Spanish Crown to promote Spanish food as an essential ingredient of national identity. They recognized that Spain was different from France in a crucial way: while Parisian food was deemed emblematic of national cuisine in France, any attempt to define Spanish national identity through food would need to recognize its regional diversity and culinary traditions. *La mesa moderna* sparked a national debate that was carried forward by several writers who grappled with the thorny issue of a Spanish national cuisine. Thorny, because at the same time, separatist movements were flourishing in the Basque country and Catalonia, both of which rejected the notion of "Spanish identity" in any form. Nonetheless, it was a pivotal moment in Spanish culinary history, one that prompted the royal court to start printing their menus in Spanish, not French.

One cookbook writer who carried forth the flag of Dr. Thebussem and the King's Chef (at least in his praise of Spanish cuisine) was the Spanish writer and chef Angel Muro, who published his cookbook *El practicón* in 1894. The book was a huge success and filled a tremendous gap in the market, ultimately going through thirty-four editions between 1894 and 1928. Similar to *Mrs. Beeton's Book of Household Management* in England (1861), Pellegrino's Artusi's *Science in the Kitchen and the Art of Eating Well* in Italy (1891), and Irma S. Rombauer's *Joy of Cooking* in America (1931), *El practicón* guided a generation of the aspirational middle class in Spain. Part of Muro's brilliance was that his recipes reflected the dominant French gastronomy that the upper classes consumed, but that the middle classes desired and wanted to emulate. While French gastronomy assumed pride of place, his praise of regional Spanish dishes set his work apart from the usual fare published in Spain. One indication of Muro's appreciation of regional cooking is his inclusion of thirty-one recipes for salt cod, which he considered a great delicacy. But despite its wealth of regional dishes, Muro's cookbook was eventually shunned, thirty-five years after publication, for its over-reliance on French recipes. By the early 1930s, it was out of print.

Muro seemed conflicted about anchovies. On the one hand, he recognized them as a critical ingredient in sophisticated French-influenced dishes, noting that "[a]nchovy butter is better than all other seafood flavored butters."[19] On the other hand, in a hierarchical list of fish, "[t]he anchovy and a few other insignificant [fish]" came last, after sardines.[20] In effect, Muro aligned with the bias against anchovies that was prevalent in Spain at the time: least desirable, smallest, and basically insignificant, unless they were used in *la tradition française*, at which point they are held in high esteem.

A TWIST IN THE TAIL

Lack of local interest: anchovies packed for export

From the fifteenth to the early nineteenth centuries, references to fishing, processing, or selling anchovies in Spain are few and far between. Anchovies were like a ghost, a presence felt but rarely seen, and nowhere was this more evident than in the far north of the country along the coast of the Bay of Biscay.

The rugged coastline of northern Spain extends for roughly 700 kilometers, from the Basque region to Cantabria, Asturias, and eventually Galicia. The sought-after fish in these regions were the moneymakers: sea bream, bonito, hake, sardines, mackerel, and mullet. Like their forefathers, fishermen targeted these species relentlessly and sold their catch locally at fish markets. However, most of the catch was pickled, brined, or salted for transportation on the arduous journey to the inland provinces.

Life was extremely hard in these remote and isolated ports. Contrary to popular belief, the Basque and Cantabrian coastlines are not particularly rich fishing grounds. Generations of fishermen and their families lived in a state of perpetual poverty, with fishing equipment and techniques little changed over the centuries. Each voyage into the unforgiving Bay of Biscay was dangerous, and almost every Cantabrian and Basque port has a monument to the fishermen who have lost their lives at sea. Even setting out to sea was a risky undertaking, as the rugged coastline offers few natural ports, making each departure and return fraught with peril. One particularly horrific storm in 1878 claimed the lives of over 200 Basque fishermen.

The precipitous coastline of northern Spain also hindered trade with inland communities. Transport links to most of the remote ports were poor, often little more than dirt tracks that had been used since medieval times. Until the twentieth century, trade with the inland provinces was undertaken by muleteers, whose long trains of over-loaded mules and ox-drawn carts were a ubiquitous sight in the countryside. Foreign travelers to Spain often romanticized the muleteers, comparing them to long trains of camels crossing the desert, but it was hard and dangerous work hauling the preserved fish inland and returning with wine, wheat, oil, and vinegar. Fresh fish were laboriously transported on foot to nearby villages by women, who often covered up to 40 kilometers in a day. "These female fish-sellers," writes Spanish historian María José Sevilla, "hauling their meagre catch over mountain roads to reach the villages of the interior, were romanticized in old folk songs, and their image accompanied numerous anchovy tins" (Fig. 4.4).[21]

The first cannery in Cantabria opened in 1857, and every kind of fish was soon being packed in a tin. Bonito was a favorite, though its high cost kept it out of reach for many Spaniards. Far more common in Spanish cupboards were tinned sardines, which were much cheaper. Anchovies were canned along the north coast as early as 1869, but there was not much interest in the product.

Fig. 4.4: The "Active" brand of the cannery "Sons of M. Garavilla" portrayed a traditional female fish seller setting off on her rounds to remote inland villages. In the background, the headquarters of Sons of M. Garavilla can be seen in the Basque port town of Lekeitio, where anchovies were seasonally processed in huge numbers. (*Courtesy of the Museo Marítimo Vasco, Diputación de Gipuzkoa, San Sebastián.*)

While the Spanish were still sorting out their conflicted feelings about anchovies, a group of foreigners arrived on the north coast of Spain and launched what would become the largest anchovy industry in Spanish history. As there was practically no domestic market for anchovies at that time, those caught as bycatch were typically used as bait for more profitable fish or dumped in the fields as fertilizer, as José Sevilla notes. Anchovies were little more than a trash fish, not worth hauling to market. But the Cantabrian Sea off the north coast of Spain was teeming with some of the finest anchovies on the planet, and the new arrivals created an enormous industry that transformed the small fishing villages along the entire coastline, from San Sebastián to Galicia. It was the start of Spain's great anchovy boom, and it was a group of Italians who set it all in motion.

Italians ride the Cantabrian anchovy wave

In Italy, salted anchovies were in high demand. Powerful northern Italian seafood processors and distributers were looking for new markets, as they were having problems maintaining sufficient stocks. Some have attributed the anchovy shortfall in Italy to overfishing in the Mediterranean Sea, particularly in the Ligurian Sea off the northwest of Italy and around the island of Sicily. Others have pointed to larger climatic changes throughout the Mediterranean basin that might have affected anchovy reproduction. While both may have played a role, Spanish historian Luis Javier Escudero Domínguez points to the ever-increasing export sector as the primary factor. As Sicilians and southern Italians emigrated abroad *en masse* to North and South America in search of a better life, they brought with them the recipes of their homeland, many of which called for salted anchovies.

It is not clear how Italian commercial seafood processors first learned of the bountiful anchovy stocks in the Bay of Biscay, but Domínguez recounts a story about an Italian diplomat who was visiting the Cantabrian coast and how he observed an abundance of anchovies "and the scarce interest of the natives in them."[22] It is presumed that this diplomat discussed his findings with several industrialists, including Angelo Parodi fu Bartolomeo, a seafood distributor with a fleet of merchant ships based in Naples. Bartolomeo promptly sent one of his ships to the Cantabrian coast to gauge the extent of the anchovy stocks, possibly as early as 1880. The rumors were true: anchovies were near and far and everywhere in between. And they could be purchased for next to nothing as there was practically no local market for them. For several weeks, the Italians acquired anchovies and processed them right on deck. With the hold filled with barrels of salted anchovies, the ship returned to Naples with its rich harvest. It was at this point that one of the most influential Italians on Spain's anchovy fishery entered the story.

Vella revolutionizes the anchovy fishery in Spain

If we were to locate the beginning of Catholic Spain's belated love affair with anchovies, then we would start with one man: Giovanni Vella. His genius, the invention that would change anchovy consumption in most of Europe and the Americas, was to create a new style of prepared anchovies: fillets packed in oil. No longer did you need to rinse, clean, and debone salted anchovies; they were ready to eat straight out of the tin, with no fuss or muss.

Vella's tale is not just about this small culinary revolution, but also one man's enduring tribute to the love of his life—Dolores Inestrillas of Santona. Upon their marriage, Vella built a fishing boat to catch anchovies and christened it *La Dolores*. After several successful seasons, he built a salting factory, also named "La Dolores." And when a daughter arrived? Dolores. He then invented a new kind of processed anchovy—oil-packed fillets—and sold it under the trademark "La Dolores." While we may tip our hat to his invention of the oil-packed anchovy, clearly, when it came to his true love, Giovanni Vella took his hat off to Dolores.

Christened Giovanni Vella Scatagliota in 1864, in the Sicilian town of Trapani, Vella's start in life was a humble one. Trapani was well known for its salt mines at that time, and salt, along with anchovies, would go on to play a critical role in Vella's life. As a young boy, he was undoubtedly exposed to the "salter's life" in the small family-run shops that specialized in salting fish for local consumption and export to the Italian mainland. Hoping for a more prosperous future, the young Vella left his Sicilian homeland for the north coast of Africa, where he engaged in fishing and salting in Algeria, most likely at the port of El Kala. Next, he turned up in Naples, working on the wharves with the merchant ships that unloaded their wares in port.

In his article, "Italianos en el Cantábrico: Identidades e histórica de una migración," Domínguez hypothesizes that it may have been in Naples that Vella met Bartolomeo, the Italian processor who played a key role in opening up what would become known as Spain's "anchovy coast."[23] Sicilians were known for creating superior-quality salted fish, and Bartolomeo may have recognized the talents of the young Vella. However they met, Vella was hired, and arrived in the Cantabrian region of Spain in 1889 as Bartolomeo's agent. He was a stranger in a strange land, looking to buy a seemingly worthless little fish that the locals called "bocarte," meaning "big-mouth," as anchovies swim with their mouths open wide while filter feeding.

Vella's arrival in Cantabria was timely, as three key factors soon aligned to create the perfect conditions for the exploitation of anchovies. Firstly, a trade agreement signed in 1888 between

Spain and Italy exempted anchovies from any trade tariffs, as, historically, anchovies had never amounted to any significant trade between the two countries. Given that Spain lacked a meaningful domestic market for anchovies—unlike Italy— anchovies could be purchased for next to nothing. Equally important for their long-term profitability, the Bay of Biscay was teeming with anchovies, as the virgin fishery had never been targeted. Just one year after Spain and Italy concluded their treaty, salted anchovies were leaving the Cantabrian ports of northern Spain bound for Italy.

The second factor favoring the exploitation of Cantabria's anchovies was that Sicilians lacked work in their homeland. After the unification of Italy in 1861, the southern part of the country and Sicily were plunged into economic ruin. Such were the catastrophic consequences of austerity measures and the poorly planned political unification (and its aftermath), that between 20 and 30 million Italians emigrated, mostly from southern Italy and Sicily. Men were out of work, women made do with next to nothing, and children went hungry. By the end of the nineteenth and beginning of the twentieth century, starving emigrants poured onto steamships bound for other parts of Europe and the New World, hoping for something better. Caught up in the Sicilian turmoil were the salters who were forced to work farther and farther away from their homeland, often along the north coast of Africa, elsewhere in Europe, or in the Americas. Of the Italian salters who landed in Cantabria, more than two thirds came from Sicily, and over 85 percent of those came from the city of Palermo.

Finally, concurrent with the problems in southern Italy, the entire Cantabrian and Basque fishery in Spain was in a state of stagnation. Fish catches had remained anemic for decades, with little capital to stimulate the coastal economy. Fishing gear, boats, and even techniques were all handed down from previous generations with little innovation. "Thus, with the fishing sector in a state of coma," writes Domínguez, "and unflattering prospects for the future," the appearance of the Italian processors and their Sicilian agents was a godsend and represented a welcome infusion of cash into an otherwise moribund fishery.[24] Fierce competition among the Sicilians for the coveted anchovy market led to a tripling in price in just a few short years. This in turn injected fresh capital into the lethargic economies of the coastal ports, allowing fishermen to replace their outdated fishing gear and upgrade their old sail-powered fishing boats to the far more efficient steam-powered vessels. Tariff-free trade, the availability of Sicilian salters, and a Cantabrian fishery ripe for change all helped to create a thriving new industry.

Remarkably, the Sicilian salters did not face the usual hostility and hatred from locals with which immigrants are typically confronted. The Sicilians set up small salting shops alongside the existing Spanish canneries and pickling factories. As they were not competing for the sea bream, bonito, or sardines on which the local Spanish factories depended, they were not viewed as a commercial threat. The local fishermen were particularly welcoming, as the Sicilians paid cold hard cash for a fish that nobody else wanted. Friction with the local fishermen was minimal, as an entirely new market based on anchovies was opening up to them. As the icing on the cake, the fishermen's wives and children found work in the salting factories, thereby adding another income stream for their families. From these humble beginnings, anchovies would come to dominate the entire fishery of the Cantabrian and Basque coastlines in just twenty years.

Vella's breakthrough: anchovies in oil

The demands of setting up salting factories in a new land required a diverse skill set: part entrepreneur, part salter, and part politician. Vella appears to have embodied all three, and during his early years on the Cantabrian coast he successfully bought, salted, and shipped anchovies back to Italy on behalf of Bartolomeo's company. Throughout this period, he cemented his relationship with Spanish fishermen and local vendors and expanded his business horizons by opening a barrel manufacturing plant. In 1907, Vella struck out on his own, setting himself up as an independent salter and cannery owner, with Bartolomeo agreeing to carry his "La Dolores" brand of salted anchovies on consignment.

Salted anchovies were in constant demand back in Italy. Each season, Vella's anchovy salting factories (by 1913, he had three operating in different ports) would work around the clock for a couple of months, awaiting the arrival of merchant ships in Santoña to haul the salted anchovies back to Italy.

One problem that vexed Vella was that his factories spent most of the year standing idle. Traditionally, the Sicilian salters in northern Spain would pack the salted anchovies in barrels and ship them off at the end of summer, and then their work was done. Santoña was just the first of several stops for the merchant ships, which also made port in Portugal and along the Mediterranean coastline, acquiring additional fish. During this extended voyage, Vella's anchovies would slowly mature below deck in their barrels, unrefrigerated. Upon arrival in Italy, they were fully, if not overly, ripe. Vella sought to come up with a system that allowed him to work through the winter in Spain. The labor was cheaper, and he could more closely oversee the entire maturing process himself, thereby increasing his share of the profits.

Another factor that likely encouraged Vella to find a new way of packaging anchovies, as Domínguez points out, was that World War I periodically disrupted shipping in the Bay of Biscay due to the German blockade. Salted anchovies are a perishable product, and Vella was only paid once they had sold in Italy. If the anchovies were held up on the docks in Spain or rotted in transit, the season's harvest was lost. Vella therefore became determined to unlock the dormant Spanish market, as Domínguez has documented through extensive oral histories. While Italy still paid top dollar, Spain, as a secondary market, could help offset any lost sales. Perhaps the Spanish would be more receptive to anchovies if they were not salted, but were potted in butter? Vella hired a chemist from the Catalan region, and they set about their first experiments.

One problem with butter is that it can go rancid, as the gluttonous Charles V had grudgingly acknowledged back in 1557. Vella's breakthrough came when he substituted olive oil for butter. Not only was the taste improved, but the anchovies lasted much longer. Now, at last, he had a product that could be sold in the Spanish market. "His fixation on the fillet was almost obsessive," writes Domínguez, "and he continuously innovated the processing stages in order to improve the product."[25] Even though salted anchovies were far more profitable than anchovies preserved in oil (which required additional labor, oil, and canning), Vella's faith in his new technique was unwavering. He would not live long enough to see his beloved anchovy fillets packed in oil become the preferred type of anchovy in most of Europe and all of the Americas. It would take another thirty years before sales would start to take off.

The anchovy gold rush lures a second wave of Italians

While Vella's oil-packed anchovies were struggling to find a market, sales of salt-packed anchovies were booming, which drew a steady stream of Italians—from both the south and the north—to Spain's anchovy coast. Brothers, cousins, uncles, and in-laws comprised the second wave of Italians to Spain. Unlike the pioneering Sicilian salters who were employees of the northern Italian processors, these second-generation arrivals were often self-financed, sometimes with their hard-earned nest eggs from America. The four brothers of the Billant family from Sant'Elia on the outskirts of Palermo, Sicily, typified this phenomenon. Each emigrated to the great economic engine that was America, made some money, and then, perhaps drawn by the magnetic pull of their homeland, cashed in and returned to Sicily. Calogero Billant acquired his capital working in the fruit industry in the central valley of California; Giuseppe worked as a foreman for a railroad company in Milwaukee before moving to Denver to manage a fruit and vegetable distribution warehouse; and Nunzio worked in Pittsburgh. Details of the American sojourn of the fourth Billant brother, Giovanni, are unclear.

As the Billant brothers trickled back to Sicily, one of their brothers-in-law, Antonio Dentici, informed them of the money to be made by salting anchovies in Spain. They each set off in turn for the anchovy coast. One common tactic for new arrivals was for each family member to set up shop in a different port— ideally one that the Italian parent companies had not already penetrated—so that they did not compete. The four Billant brothers adopted this approach: Calogero started his salting shop in the Basque port of Mutriku; Giovanni settled in the neighboring port of Ondarroa; Giuseppe joined Calogero in Mutriku; and Nunzio set up shop in the Cantabrian port of Castro Urdiales (Fig. 4.5).

The arrival of these second-generation Italians eager to pay cold hard cash for anchovies helped to fuel the ongoing economic boom along Spain's northern coast. Supporting industries continued to spring up in the ports and surrounding valleys: sawmills made timber for warehouses and factories, metal shops manufactured machine parts, and hotels opened their doors. More significantly, the high price paid for anchovies gave fisher-

Fig. 4.5: Like the Billant brothers, the extended Dentici family followed suit and had a son, brother, or cousin setting up shop in different ports. (*Courtesy of the Museo Marítimo Vasco, Diputación de Gipuzkoa, San Sebastián.*)

men the confidence to invest in new gear and boats. In 1898, the first steam-powered fishing boats arrived in the Bay of Biscay and immediately out-fished those still relying on the manpower of oars and sails. But these early steam-powered motors were a double-edged sword: even though catches increased, the boats were known as "widow makers" for their propensity to explode, killing all on board.

The introduction of internal combustion engines revolutionized the fishing industry. Compared with steam-powered motors, which required a specialized engineer to spend hours prior to departure bringing the temperamental boilers up to pressure, the new diesel motors were simpler, safer, and far more efficient. They also freed up valuable real estate on deck, as they did not require enormous boilers. Not only could the new internal combustion-powered boats catch and hold more fish, but the quality of the harvests also improved, as the time between the catch and return to port decreased dramatically.

All along the coast, Spanish fishermen and their families enjoyed immediate economic benefits from the Italian influx, but Spanish-owned canneries were effectively locked out of the new anchovy gold rush. With all the anchovies destined for the single market of Italy, the Italian distributors quickly consolidated control of the Cantabrian and Basque anchovy markets and set up a de facto monopoly. The mechanics of the monopoly played out each season. The first source for salted anchovies was always the distributors' own subsidiaries. Next in line were the Sicilians and northern Italians who had gone independent but had long-term relationships with the distributors. Last, and very much least, were the Spanish-owned canneries. Only after the Italian processors had exhausted all their contacts with their Italian brethren would they turn to the Spanish-owned canneries. This severely restricted the economic viability of the Spanish canneries, as they never knew whether they could ship their anchovies on consignment until after all the Italian products had been purchased. More than one Spanish cannery owner watched in horror as their salted anchovies rotted in the warehouse, never having left Spanish soil.

While this approach effectively shut the Spanish-owned canneries out of the salted anchovy business, life was not all that much better for the independent salters. The increasing catches of the 1920s, which should have been a boon to them, ironically forced many independents into bankruptcy. The heart of the problem was a textbook example of a mismatch between supply and demand. Too many salted anchovies were destined for Italy. The economics of supply and demand was rooted in the natural fluctuation cycles of anchovy reproduction in the Bay of Biscay—the same natural phenomenon that plagued Peruvian processors in the 1950s. In favorable environmental years, when anchovy reproduction spiked and catches were high, the corresponding glut caused their price to drop precipitously, forcing a number of salters into bankruptcy as their product sat on the wharfs of Genoa, Livorno, and Naples, unable to find a buyer at a profitable price.

Exports wane, with Spain to gain

The resolution of Spain's anchovy conundrum, whereby anchovies were largely ignored in Catholic Spain for nearly 500 years, was prompted by a series of tumultuous events that befell the country in the early twentieth century. An international trade war, the Great Depression, the Spanish Civil War, and World War II devastated Spain over three decades. Perversely, each of these cataclysmic events would nudge the door open for anchovies' eventual acceptance.

The development of improved transportation links throughout the country was the first step towards a greater embrace of anchovies. Commencing in the mid-1920s, a small but growing percentage of the anchovy catch along the Cantabrian and Basque coastlines was sold "fresh" in the interior of the country. Traditionally, only highly desired and costly fish merited the long and expensive journey to the interior, but for the first time, fresh anchovies could be transported cheaply and purchased for next to nothing in the interior provinces.

The Cantabrian port of Castro Urdiales is just one example of this phenomenon: up to 75 percent of its anchovy catch was shipped fresh to Madrid, Barcelona, and Zaragoza. This was prompted by the relocation in 1926 of roughly half of Castro Urdiales' Italian salting operations to the growing ports of Santoña and Laredo. Without the Italian buyers who paid top dollar, fishermen along the Cantabrian and Basque coastlines had little choice but to accept the cheaper price paid by domestic wholesalers, who then shipped the anchovies by truck and rail to the interior where they were sold for a song.

Much to the chagrin of the Italian salters on the north coast of Spain, it was not their cherished salted anchovies that led the march to increased consumption. Instead, it was fresh anchovies, from which they made no money. Determined Italian salters persisted in their quest to crack the Spanish market, often resulting in bankruptcy.

These early bankruptcies were a portent of events to come not just for the Italian salters, but also for Spanish canneries of all kinds of seafood. Across the Atlantic, storm clouds were gathering as increased tariffs and trade protection marked the election of Warren Harding to the presidency of the United States. As Europe started to recover from World War I, and agricultural production picked up again, US farmers saw their sales drop precipitously, resulting in the Emergency Tariff Act of 1921. What started as a simple bill to protect American farmers spiraled out of control, covering everything from steel and cotton to meat and fish. New amendments were continually added during the late 1920s, culminating in perhaps the greatest congressional economic blunder of the twentieth century: the Smoot–Hawley Tariff Act of 1930.

Over 20,000 imported goods were swept up in the madness of the Smoot–Hawley Tariff Act, including anchovies. The average tariff reached almost 60 percent, which effectively shut down the American market for Spain's seafood exporters. Italy also enacted a raft of tariffs which effectively slammed the door shut for the importation of Spain's salted anchovies. With international export markets greatly diminished, seafood processors turned to the only remaining viable market: the interior of the country.

The hunger years: thinking inside the box

In contrast to the situation just a few years earlier, when barely 10 percent of Galicia's seafood (Spain's largest seafood-producing region) was destined for the Spanish market, by the early 1930s over 50 percent was directed internally. While the most popular fish were sea bream, hake, bonito, and sardines, anchovy sales—whether canned (including those packed in oil, brine, or vinegar) or salted—also increased. However, economic historian Ernesto López Losa explains that anchovies were mostly sold at a loss, as the industry struggled to find buyers who could afford their product.[26]

Even darker storm clouds were looming over Spain, as the second half of the decade witnessed the outbreak of the Spanish Civil War, which plunged the country, and the anchovy processors, into crisis. The Spanish Civil War (1936–9) pitted a group of right-wing military generals, supported by conservative businessmen, monarchists, and the staunchly Catholic Carlists, against the left-leaning, democratically elected Republican government, a far more secular and diverse group, ranging from moderates to Marxists to anarchists. The Nationalist General Francisco Franco assumed power and proclaimed himself *Caudillo* of Spain, a fascist title equivalent to Hitler's *Führer* and Mussolini's *Il Duce*. While the atrocities of the Civil War often take center stage in any discussion of this period, it was a far more pedestrian problem that plagued Spain for over fifteen long and brutal years: hunger. This era became known for many—especially those who supported the losing Republicans—as "the hunger years" (*los años del hambre*) or simply "*la miseria*." "Escaping hunger," writes historian Miguel Ángel del Arco Blanco, "would be the main obsession of most people in the 1940s."[27]

One of the central economic policies put forth by Franco was autarky, or national self-sufficiency. As imports were curtailed or cut off, ration cards became the key mechanism by which the dwindling food supply was allocated. But the system was rife with corruption, which spawned a black market that ignited a firestorm of inflation, leaving ordinary wages wholly insufficient for even the most basic of foodstuffs. Life became unbearable, with everything from bread and oil to vegetables linked to one's ration card. Soon, even ration cards became useless as the most basic of supplies ran short: rice and sugar disappeared and could only be procured on the black market. Bread, when available, was baked with adulterated flour, and the dreaded lentils became known as "resistance pills." Meat and eggs were unheard-of luxuries.

In Spain's charged environment of food scarcity, anchovies would gain a new prominence by entering Spanish foodways, albeit tentatively, at both ends of the spectrum: high and low. On the one hand, fresh anchovies entered from the bottom as they were one of the most affordable, nutritious, and readily available sources of protein in the marketplace. Though driven by desperation rather than an appreciation of anchovies, this helped to shift the long-held narrative that deemed anchovies unacceptable. On the other hand, oil-preserved anchovies started to enter Spanish foodways at the top of the spectrum, becoming a marker of class and culinary sophistication alongside traditional elite favorites like truffles, *foie gras*, and caviar. Upscale hotels and restaurants in Europe and the United States kick-started this phenomenon, as anchovy fillets packed in oil presented themselves far more handsomely than the traditional salted fillets. This undoubtedly contributed to anchovies being served in a host of fancy French dishes that Spanish elites were emulating, from *hors d'oeuvres* to salads and mains. The famous Niçoise salad typified this change, adopting the sleek new oil-packed anchovy fillet over the comparatively drab-looking traditional salted anchovy.

Spanish cookbooks: barely a look-in for anchovies

While anchovy consumption in Spain was on the rise, anchovies were still a far cry from forming part of the culinary mainstream. Cookbooks reflected this clearly, as anchovies still barely merited a mention. What the cookbooks of this period did mirror were the grim gastronomic realities playing out in the central squares and marketplaces, where food had become an increasingly scarce commodity and adulteration and fraud were rampant. In the 1941 cookbook *Cocina de recursos: deseo mi comida* ("Resourceful Cooking: I Desire My Food") by Ignasi Doménech i Puigcerós, the author addresses Spain's food scarcities, albeit indirectly, in order to squeak past Franco's censors. An experienced chef, who had been employed by diplomats in Paris, London, Barcelona, and Madrid, Doménech was drawn to the plight of those who struggled to make satisfying meals with insufficient wartime rations. Part of the book's historical value lies in its resourceful recipes, which create an art form of ingredient substitution. Not a single recipe calls for milk or eggs, as the author knew that these were practically impossible to procure. Instead, he focused on creative ways to conjure up dishes that resembled their pre-war (and pre-famine) counterparts. The Spanish essayist and historian Maria Paz Moreno notes a few of these gastronomic doppelgängers:

> *Calamares fritos sin calamares* "Fried calamari without calamari"— basically fried onion rings, *Mayonesa falsa* "Fake mayonnaise", *Selecto café de guerra* "Select wartime coffee", made from carob beans and roasted peanut shells, *Girasoles rebozados fritos* "Fried sunflower heads", and *Chuletas de arroz* "Rice chops"—made by forming a paste of cooked rice that was then put into a mold in the shape of a pork chop, coated with breadcrumbs and fried.[28]

In this context, Doménech cautioned against eating meat in any restaurant: "Even though they call it beef or ox, I know that it came from horse, donkey, or mule."[29] Lest we have any doubts about this practice, every city seems to have had a restaurant cooking dubious cuts, and Ángel del Arco Blanco reports an incident from the city of Seville: "[I]t was discovered that a woman who supposedly cooked jackrabbits in her restaurant was in reality serving cats to unwary customers. In some villages and towns, cats and dogs 'disappeared mysteriously' in the hardest moments."[30]

While this should have elevated fresh anchovies to the fore-front of the nation's consciousness, old biases were surprisingly resilient. One cookbook underscored this problem head-on by devoting itself entirely to the next cheapest seafood protein after anchovies: sardines. Written by José Guardiola y Ortiz and published in 1938 in Alicante (which was under Republican control at that time), the cookbook targeted people of "modest means." It was titled *Platos de guerra: 60 recetas prácticas, acomodadas a las circunstancias, para la conservación y condimento de la sardina* ("War Dishes: 60 Practical Recipes, Adapted to the Circumstances, for the Preservation and Seasoning of the Sardine"). It seemed that Ortiz was making every attempt to dissuade people from stooping to the lowest fish in the seafood ranks: anchovies.

The anchovy/tapas hypothesis

While food scarcity accounted for only modest increases in anchovy consumption in Spain, another surprising factor that may have played a role is what could be termed "the anchovy/tapas hypothesis." This would help to explain how a country that never really showed much enthusiasm for anchovies went on to become the largest consumer of oil-preserved anchovies in the world.

At their most basic, Spanish tapas are small plates of food that can be served either hot or cold but are always offered with alcohol. Tapas are not served at home, nor are they considered part of a meal. "Tapas are not so much a kind of food as a Spanish way of eating," notes cookbook author and culinary historian Clifford A. Wright.[31] Roasted almonds with rosemary, smoked paprika, olive oil, and a sprinkle of salt are a type of tapas, as is the traditional *Pulpo a la Gallega*, Galician-style octopus served with a healthy dusting of paprika. Olives, whether served plain or stuffed with anchovies or peppers, are so popular that large glass jars of them feature prominently in many tapas bars throughout the country.

Over time, tapas have evolved into several regional variations. One of the most popular is known as *pinchos* (Basque: *pintxos*) from northern Spain. *Pinchos* are held together with a toothpick, and are often, but not always, anchored to a slice of bread. The toothpick not only holds it all together, but also serves as a convenient way for the bartender to add up your bill. One of the most famous non-bread *pinchos* is the "Gilda," named after Rita Hayworth and said to be inspired by her curves: on a toothpick, an anchovy sweeps around an olive and the outstretched arms of a green *guindilla* pepper—only three ingredients, each occupying its own real estate, yet collectively creating an entirely new flavor sensation that some say is nothing short of divine.

Tapas proved enormously popular throughout the country as it emerged from the devastating effects of three long years of civil war. "Food historians have noted how the Spanish Civil War marked a decisive 'before' and 'after' in the culinary history of Spain's capital," writes Maria Paz Moreno.[32] While many factors contributed to this phenomenon, one of the most significant was wartime rationing, which made securing sufficient food supplies a daunting task. Chicken might be available one day, then be impossible to source the next. Even vegetables made inconsistent appearances in the marketplaces, which made menu planning an almost impossible undertaking. The conclusion of the war brought improved food supply, and the opening of numerous restaurants and *tabernas* (taverns). With the improving economic climate of the late 1940s, *tabernas* became increasingly popular places to meet after work for tapas, especially for those who moonlighted on second jobs to make ends meet.

Anchovies are a perfect fit for *tabernas*, and this forms the first part of the anchovy hypothesis. Whether they are salted, oil-preserved, pickled in vinegar, or deep-fried as *boquerónes*, they are a welcome addition to tapas of all kinds. One could even go so far as to say that tapas were invented for anchovies to find a home. Equally important, anchovies are salty, and it is precisely this saltiness that stimulates the desire for more drink—manna from heaven for *taberna* owners. This explains why tapas were often served free of charge in the past. Most establishments now charge for them, as they are so popular that they have evolved into their own gastronomic niche.

The very first Spanish cookbook devoted entirely to tapas was published in 1944: *Tapas y aperitivos*, by José Sarrau. At a time when cookbook publishing had slowed considerably, devoting an entire cookbook to tapas was a testament to the growing popularity of these "small realities," as the author enthusiastically described them.[33] In his very *castizo* and witty style, the author delved into the world of tapas in the city of Madrid. His book is invaluable as it examines three different classes of establishment serving appetizers and tapas: elite bars, upscale *tabernas*, and the plain but always popular neighborhood *tabernas*.

At the top of the hierarchy are elite bars, where the "posh" and "gentlemen of good fortune" would meet in exclusive, club-like establishments.[34] These bars had comfortable seating, abundant fresh-cut flowers, and mirrors lining the walls to enable a surreptitious glimpse of one's fellow patrons. All this exclusivity and refinement was reflected in the prices, which meant their doors were closed to most Madrileños, as the city's inhabitants are known. Significantly, the small plates on the menu were all referred to as "appetizers" rather than "tapas," following the French fashion to which elites aspired. Most telling is the author's observation that they only served *anchoas*, and never *boquerónes*. The distinction was clear: *anchoas* belonged to the elite continental custom of eating oil-preserved anchovies, while deep-fried *boquerónes*, which arose in the south of the country, were for *tabernas* and their humbler patrons (Fig. 4.6).

From the lofty heights of anchovy canapés and labels written in French, the next rung down Madrid's culinary ladder brings us to the *colmado*, a sort of mid-range establishment that can be best described as an upscale *taberna*. As befitting an establishment that straddled the culinary and social divide, the menus featured both French-influenced "appetizers" and traditional Spanish "tapas." Part of the appeal of these upscale *tabernas*, as Sarrau notes, was that they afforded their customers the opportunity to discover "some new novel tapas that excite the palate."[35] Indicative of their mid-range price point, one could find both oil-preserved anchovies and deep-fried *boquerónes* on their menus. Even with all its cultural baggage denoting social class, salted cod also appeared on their menus, something that elite bars eschewed.

Fig. 4.6: Hoping to cash in on the culinary sophistication of France, one Spanish processor produced labels in French for the domestic market, circa 1950s. (*Courtesy of the Museo Marítimo Vasco, Diputación de Gipuzkoa, San Sebastián.*)

One popular type of tapas in these mid-range establishments featured an oil-preserved anchovy tightly wound in a circle with a vinegar-preserved caper in the middle. This was one of the first anchovy-based tapas that Giovanni Vella offered commercially. While their sales never took off in his lifetime, by the late 1950s these tapas were available "pre-packaged" in supermarkets in Spain. Another tapas found in *colmados* featured an oil-preserved anchovy fillet laid on a slice of ripe tomato; a simple yet powerful combination of two umami-rich ingredients.

Sarrau saved his greatest praise for the humble *taberna*. Part social institution, part watering hole, and part eating establishment, *tabernas* offered Madrileños of all classes a brief respite from their hectic and work-filled lives. *Tabernas* were particularly popular before lunch and dinner, with great crowds spilling out into the streets. Here one would find traditional Spanish tapas with few French or continental influences. With meats and poultry still expensive in the post-Civil War years, seafood became the default protein on offer at *tabernas*. Given their modest price in the wholesale markets, fresh anchovies deep fried in oil or served in a vinegar escabeche were plentiful at *tabernas* in the 1940s, but it was rare to find the more expensive oil-preserved anchovies. This would of course change in the coming decades, when all types of anchovies would be offered.

The first *boquerón* that Sarrau listed was Málaga's traditional deep-fried anchovies arrayed like a fan. While the symbolism of the arrayed anchovies undoubtedly escaped most Madrileños, their presence revealed how *boquerónes* had penetrated the heartland of the country (Madrid lies nearly 13 kilometers from the geographical center of Spain). *Boquerónes* are ideal tapas as they are a finger food, perfect for enjoying while standing at a crowded bar with a drink in hand. In addition to Málaga-style *boquerónes*, Sarrau's book was the first to mention a recipe for egg-battered *boquerónes*:

Breaded boquerónes

They are cleaned, head and spine removed, seasoned with salt and passed through flour. Next, they are bathed in a beaten egg and covered with breadcrumbs. In a frying pan, add a small amount of oil and fry, making sure that the oil barely covers them yet browns them on both sides. Remove them and set aside to drain off the excess oil. When serving, place a slice of lemon over the boquerónes.[36]

The second part of the anchovy/tapas hypothesis is linked to a rather peculiar phenomenon: the Spanish time zone. "Many travellers believe Spain's late mealtimes are a reflection of the country's laidback attitude," writes journalist Jessica Jones, "but that couldn't be further from the truth."[37] Put simply, the Spanish are living in the wrong time zone, and have been for almost eighty years. This has implications for everything, including anchovies.

The root of the problem goes back to Franco. In 1940, Franco ordered that Spain's clocks be changed from Greenwich Mean Time (GMT) to Central European Time (CET) as an act of solidarity with Hitler's Germany. This apparently innocuous change meant that Spain, which geographically aligns with England, Ireland, and Morocco, was now in the same time zone as Poland, Hungary, and Serbia, all of which are over 2,000 kilometers to the east. By advancing the clocks one hour, Spain's 1:00 p.m. lunch got bumped to 2:00 p.m., and dinners now began at 9 o'clock at night. To this day, much of Spain's prime-time television does not begin until 10:00 p.m.

Compounding the time zone problem, many Spaniards during the Franco era moonlighted on second jobs, which had a ripple effect on when they ate their meals. With their second shifts ending late in the evening, many did not sit down for their evening meal until 10:00 or 11:00 p.m. This still occurs to this day, much to the bewilderment of foreigners who are shocked to see Spanish restaurants packed at midnight.

"Although moonlighting is not common in today's society," notes a Spanish editorial, "dining late could be a vestige of a time when it was" (Fig. 4.7).[38]

With life lived in the wrong time zone and mealtimes pushed progressively later and later, there was an immediate need to offer quick bites of sustenance to hold people over until their proper sit-down meal. While cafés, cafeterias, and snack foods sold in supermarkets all helped people cope, *tabernas* arguably profited the most, with their doors open first thing in the morning until late at night. And it was the *tabernas* that offered anchovies a new lease on life, as they could be incorporated into an array of different tapas. Whether deep-fried as *boquerónes*, oil-preserved and draped across a small *pincho*, or preserved in vinegar and served as is, anchovies had at last found a way in.

Fig. 4.7: The Spanish artist Salvador Dalí's *The Persistence of Memory*, painted in 1931, is recognized as a surrealist masterpiece speaking to the fluidity of time. It is also prescient in a society that soon came to live life in the wrong time zone. (*M.Flynn/Alamy Stock Photo.*)

A TWIST IN THE TAIL

Improving fishery on the north coast

After years of poor catches and exports to Italy interrupted during both the Civil War and World War II, the anchovy fishery along the Cantabrian and Basque coastlines started climbing out of a nearly two-decade period of stagnation. By 1951, it finally reached a level of production not seen since 1935. The increasing anchovy catches could be partly linked to a group of Spanish technocrats who liberalized Franco's autarkic economic policies, reinvigorated the fishery through credits and loans, and allowed the fleet to modernize. New and larger boats equipped with powerful motors, the latest advancements in navigation, fish-finding sonars, hydraulic pumps, and nylon nets (versus the traditional hemp) vastly improved productivity and led to huge increases in the anchovy harvest. By mid-decade, the fishery entered what was known as the "golden season," a nearly ten-year period of record-breaking anchovy harvests.

The increasing anchovy harvests of the 1950s prompted many locals in port towns to set up small-time operations to make extra money. Any spare room, hallway, or basement could be converted into an anchovy operation: all that was needed were a couple of wooden barrels, a few sacks of salt, and fresh anchovies. At the end of each season, these "preserved" (i.e. "salted") anchovies would be sold to the larger commercial companies. The Spanish canneries incorporated these "free riders" into their own production lines, as did the Italians. So many small-time operations sprang up that many coastal towns started to smell like one giant anchovy-processing plant, with the briny aroma of salted anchovies wafting down every street, seeping into houses, and permeating furniture, clothes, and hair. It was the smell of money, money that afforded more meat in the locals' diets, new shoes and schoolbooks for their children, and an occasional indulgence like a visit to a *taberna* after years of soul-numbing and gut-wrenching austerity.

Increasing anchovy harvests fed both the recovering export market and the growing internal demand in Spain. Almost 25 percent of anchovy exports were destined for the United States, with roughly one quarter of these preserved in oil. Unlike the salted-anchovy export market (which the Italians had locked up), the oil-preserved market was still developing, and both Spanish and Italian processors competed for the burgeoning business on the continent and in the Americas. Alongside these processed anchovies, internal Spanish demand for fresh anchovies was continuing to grow, both from the public who consumed them at home and from *tabernas* that sold them as *boquerónes*.

The excellent anchovy harvests of the mid-1950s were followed by some truly exceptional years, culminating in the all-time record harvest of 1960. According to statistics from the Cofradía de Pescadores, at the end of 1960, a total of 11.1 million kilograms of anchovies had been caught and auctioned in Santoña, an amount that would never be equaled again (Fig. 4.8).

The following year, the fishery collapsed. For the fishermen of Spain's northern coast, no sooner had the "golden season" arrived than the "great decline" began. In retrospect, this downfall was inevitable: a lack of fishing regulations and catch limits, coupled with technological advancements on the boats, quite simply decimated anchovy stocks in the Bay of Biscay. With the anchovy fishery in free fall, canneries started closing left and right. The price of increasingly scarce anchovies in the wholesale markets increased dramatically to the point that it was no longer profitable to sell them salted. Many Italian processors switched over to oil-preserved anchovies, as they had a greater added value. By 1968, the production of oil-preserved anchovies surpassed that of salted anchovies for the first time in the export market, a trend that would dramatically increase in the coming years. Countries that had traditionally depended upon Cantabrian and Basque salted

Fig. 4.8: Women working in the Ignacio Villarías factory, 1932. During the "golden season," every available set of hands was recruited to work in the factories. Workers were bussed in free of charge from surrounding cities, and groups of semi-nomadic Roma were signed up to meet the immediate need for help.

anchovies now turned to other sources to meet their needs at a lower cost, such as Morocco, Greece, and Argentina.

Shift to oil-preserved anchovies

As the popularity of oil-preserved anchovies increased in the 1970s and 1980s, production along the north coast continued to shift from large factories, with their emphasis on salted anchovies, to family-run operations that packed anchovies in oil. Many of these smaller-scale artisanal operations were run by Spanish families or the offspring of Italians who had intermarried with locals. They successfully tapped into a growing niche market for high-quality (and high-priced) oil-preserved anchovies, both domestically and internationally.

Oil-preserved anchovies were also given an indirect boost from the emergence of the *nouvelle cuisine* movement in France. Although the direct influence of *la nouvelle cuisine* across Spain was minimal, it did spark a regional movement that came to be known as Basque *nueva cocina*. Chefs like Luis Irízar and Juan Mari Arzak innovated new recipes, exploring simpler but more profound flavor combinations that revolutionized Basque cuisine. While the Basque *nueva cocina* was a hit in chic restaurants, attracting the attention of an elite international audience in the city of San Sebastián, it was in the humble *tabernas* and tapas bars of the city that anchovies benefited the most. Chefs began to experiment with more elaborate and unique kinds of *pintxos* that paired anchovies with a myriad of new ingredients. Gradually, a host of more daring and innovative Basque-style *pintxos* started to appear throughout Spain, with anchovies often the star of the show.

By the time Spain entered the new millennium, anchovies had firmly established themselves in the country's *tabernas* and tapas bars. But, curiously, salt-cured anchovies were—and still are to this day—divisive in Spain. And there are still people who dislike them in any form. For many of these, their dislike of preserved anchovies is so profound that they do not even "see" them. A recent culinary history of Madrid does not mention anchovies once throughout the entire book, despite anchovies having been present in the city's *tabernas* since the early part of the twentieth century.

From a scorned fish to an adored dish

The history of anchovies in Spain is a curious tale. At the turn of the twentieth century, anchovies were left out of discussions on Spanish identity and the country's gastronomic traditions. Yet many in modern Spain assume that they have always been eaten. As one Cantabrian gentleman remarked in a *taberna* recently, "Anchovies are in our blood, and always have been."[39] Not really. Perhaps nothing captures the British historian Eric Hobsbawm's phrase, "inventing traditions," in gastronomic terms quite as aptly in Spain as anchovies, those long-scorned little fish that only in the late twentieth century became instrumentally associated with tapas and *pintxos*.[40]

While anchovies are appreciated to varying degrees in other countries, Spaniards have embraced them as part of their culinary identity. So great is modern Spain's love affair with oil-preserved anchovies that Spaniards are now the largest consumers of them in the world, with an average consumption of 2.69 kilograms per year. If one factors in that a good proportion of the population nonetheless disdains them, then the actual figure for those who do eat them is probably much, much higher. And this figure excludes fresh *boquerónes*. If these are added into the mix (along with vinegar-preserved anchovies and the occasional salted anchovy), then Spanish consumption is truly extraordinary.

For an anchovy aficionado, perhaps no city on earth can match San Sebastián. San Sebastián is the anchovy equivalent of Rome, Jerusalem, or Mecca for the more spiritually minded. Tucked away in small alleyways in the old city is a slew of tapas bars, and beneath their gleaming glass countertops lie a dazzling array of artfully arranged anchovies paired with unique ingredients. If *boquerónes* are your pleasure, then perhaps a deep-fried anchovy coupled with a slice of green "Gernika" pepper and a few drops of lemon juice will call out to you. Or maybe it will be the anchovies that have been marinated for hours and then covered with fried garlic and chili peppers that will tempt you. Or perhaps you will succumb to an oil-preserved anchovy on toasted bread with cured ham or smoked salmon, possibly topped with a vinaigrette or dollop of mayonnaise.

Basque *pintxos* have proven so irresistible that caution needs to be exercised upon entering any tapas bar in San Sebastián. These tasty and artistic bites seduce the eye and tantalize the tastebuds, prompting yet another round of drinks. Before you know it, you have tried them all, from salted cod simmered in tomatoes and orange juice, to oil-preserved anchovies skewered with smoked salmon, hard-boiled eggs, prawns, and vinaigrette. *¡Buen provecho!* (Fig. 4.9).

Fig. 4.9: Dapper and delighted, this anchovy logo from the 1950s portrays a little fish with big flavor, dressed to impress on the gastronomic stage. (*Courtesy of the Museo Marítimo Vasco, Diputación de Gipuzkoa, San Sebastián.*)

To Canterbury, England

Lausanne
Lake Geneva
St. Maurice
Geneva   Great St. Bernard Pass
Aosta
Milan
Po   River   Mantua   Venice
Turin
Bassura   Genoa   Ravenna
Francigena
Ligurian Sea   Florence
Livorno
Siena   Tiber River
Ascoli Piceno
Giglio   Viterbo   Adriatic Sea
Island
Civitavecchia   Rome   ITALY

Naples
Cetara

Tyrrhenian
Sea

Palermo

Mediterranean Sea

N
0   25   50 miles
0   25   50 km

5

THE ITALIAN ANCHOVY

FOREVER A FAVORED, FLAVORFUL FISH

Italy has had a long and glorious tradition of cooking with anchovies. At any point in Italian history, you can be certain that at least some members of society were eating anchovies. In contrast to the other countries in Europe that we have explored, anchovies have never gone out of style in Italy, although some detractors did exist. We begin our story of the Italian anchovy with the rediscovery of the world's first cookery book, Apicius, *after it lay dormant for centuries. While this Roman-era cookery book has only a walk-on role, it sets the stage for later events when Italians began to embrace anchovies wholeheartedly in their cooking. The rediscovery of* Apicius *owes much to the aspirations of a particular Pope and the humanist scholar he recruited to stock his library.*

Enoch d'Ascoli and the quest for humanist texts

Enoch d'Ascoli had every reason to be optimistic in the year 1447 CE, as Pope Nicholas V had just made him the first official librarian of the Vatican. Even more promising, the Pope had tasked him with a mission of utmost importance, one that was likely to set him up financially for the rest of his life. Enoch d'Ascoli was about to go book hunting. Little did he know that his journey would lead to the rediscovery of the mysterious *Apicius*, a long-lost manuscript and the first true cookery book ever written. It would also lead to his financial ruin.

Pope Nicholas V was an ardent bibliophile and humanist, versed in classical thought and languages. He hoped that by reading ancient manuscripts he would come to understand the world in a new way—one that might help feed the hungry, cure the sick, and further the glory of God. He needed someone to scour monasteries in northern Europe for ancient manuscripts long since forgotten, to acquire the originals (or have copies made), and return them to Rome to stock the Vatican's new library.

The decision to hire Enoch d'Ascoli was not made lightly, as the mission required a special skill set. First, to determine which manuscripts were of value, he would need to be fluent in both Greek and Latin. Second, he would need to be a diplomat, able to negotiate with abbots in far-flung monasteries—church officials, that is, who may not have known the value of the books in their possession but were probably clever enough to know something was up. Third, the right candidate would have to be street-smart and able-footed, comfortable crossing high mountain passes and navigating his way to monasteries in isolated valleys where banditry was rife. In short, he needed a man like Enoch d'Ascoli.

Enoch d'Ascoli was born around 1400 in the city of Ascoli Piceno, about 150 kilometers east of Rome, just inland from the Adriatic Sea. Aside from a few biographical details, little is known about him. After studying humanities in Florence, he began teaching rhetoric and poetry, possibly in Perugia. He must have been a talented scholar, for he soon caught the attention of one of the wealthiest men in Italy, Cosimo di Giovanni de' Medici of Florence, and he landed the plum gig of tutoring Cosimo's two sons. When the eldest was sent to Rome to enter the *curia* (the Vatican bureaucracy), Enoch d'Ascoli accompanied him. He must have crossed paths with the Pope, for when we hear of him next, Nicholas V had made him the first official librarian of the Vatican.

Enoch d'Ascoli departed from Rome in the late spring or early summer of 1451 CE. After several days traversing the Tuscan plain he arrived in Livorno, the "warehouse of Italy" and its main port for salted fish.[1] Salted fish was big business in Livorno, and it was distributed to the wealthy cities of Pisa, Siena, and Florence. Much of the salted fish that wound up in Tuscany was caught in the rich fishing grounds off Sicily. As far back as the Roman era, legendary amounts of bluefin tuna, mackerel, sardines, and anchovies had been caught along the Sicilian coast. One ship's manifest, dated to January 11, 1388, records a cargo of 100 barrels of salted sardines, 50 barrels of salted tuna, and 25 barrels of salted anchovies, all destined for Livorno.

During the same period, salted fish also arrived in Livorno from ports in other countries. Clever merchants in Barcelona conducted a thriving trade redistributing salted sardines and anchovies from southern Spain (Cadiz, Málaga) to Livorno. English ships bound for Livorno were loaded to the gunwales with salmon, caviar, and pilchards, returning home with barrels of bottarga and salted anchovies. Even herring caught in the Baltic Sea were shipped to Tuscany at that time. A merchant manual written by Saminato del Ricci in 1396 details how demand for salted herring in Tuscany made it a highly profitable commodity to import.

During his journey, Enoch d'Ascoli would have encountered anchovies on offer in Tuscany, whether they were pickled, salted, or fresh. Pickled anchovy recipes featured in cookery books over the next several hundred years, indicating their popularity at the time. Although the anonymously written *Neapolitan Recipe Collection*, dated to the second half of the fifteenth century, was from a different region and later period, it provides a rough idea of how anchovies may have been prepared. One of its salad recipes could not be any simpler (or tastier): dress marinated anchovy fillets—probably cured in vinegar—with olive oil, vinegar, and oregano. Accompanied by some bread and a little watered-down wine, this would have made a light and refreshing bite to eat under the hot Tuscan sun.

If Enoch d'Ascoli was feeling a tad peckish in Tuscany but did not want to stop for a sit-down meal, he might have eaten a few salted anchovies with bread on the go. If the day was finished, and the nightly repast was calling out, a number of more elaborate anchovy recipes could have presented themselves. If *Liber de coquina*, an anonymous early fourteenth-century recipe collection, is any guide, he may have eaten a regional variation of fresh anchovies in a red wine broth with saffron, or fresh anchovies pan-fried and seasoned with marjoram, rosemary, and sage, along with a touch of bitter orange juice.*

As our intrepid book hunter crossed the Po Valley and started to climb the foothills of the Alps, he would have encountered the first real test of his journey: the Great Saint Bernard Pass. As far back as the Bronze Age, this pass was utilized to cross the western Alps, which formed a seemingly impenetrable barrier separating northern Europe from Italy. The plateau at the top of the pass was dominated by the forbidding peaks of Mont Mort

---

* Although lemons had been introduced by the Arabs to the western Mediterranean world around 1000 CE, the first significant cultivation did not occur until the mid-fifteenth century in Genoa, which helps explain why most recipe collections up to this point usually call for bitter oranges for their acid component.

(Death Mountain) and the Grande Chenalette. At one point, Enoch d'Ascoli would have glimpsed the reassuring sight of the Saint Bernard Hospice. As he approached, he would have been confronted by a peculiar smell, something completely unexpected at a height of 2,400 meters: the briny aroma of salted fish.

The great French writer Maguelonne Toussaint-Samat recounts how "the Saint-Maurice customs post on the Saint Bernard Pass was imbued with the stench of the stacks of salt fish traveling over the pass in both directions. Storing sardines, anchovies and above all herring in bond was then forbidden."[2] But the best efforts of the customs house to stop this practice were in vain, and salted fish continued to find temporary lodging in every nook and cranny of the building. Over 300 years later, as Napoleon was marching his army over the pass *en route* to invading Italy, the problem had still not been resolved, and one of his commissioned officers wrote a letter to his wife complaining that the hospice stank of salted fish.

We can hazard a guess as to where all this salted fish was headed. The salted sardines and anchovies were most likely being transported northwards from the Italian Peninsula to Switzerland and onwards to France. There, they would have been one of the cheapest salted fish in the marketplace. Conversely, the herring would be heading south, where they fetched good coin in the marketplaces of Italy. With almost a third of the Christian calendar year being designated "meatless days"—which often allowed for fish—this helps to account for why preserved fish were constantly on the move in Europe, from Scandinavia to Sicily.

The subsequent stopovers on Enoch d'Ascoli's journey are uncertain, though his likely next destination was the Abbey of Saint Maurice in the Rhône Valley. He then may have continued on the Via Francigena westwards across Switzerland, past Lausanne, and over the Jura Mountains into France. Alternatively, he could have departed the pilgrim route somewhere after

Montreux and headed northwards, winding his way through central Switzerland until he reached the Rhine River and crossing into present-day Germany. Little is known of this part of his journey, but he did spend some time in a Danish monastery where he acquired a copy of Tacitus' *Annals*, a key source of information about Roman history in the first century CE. He also spent time in Norway, possibly as far north as Bergen.

Long-lost manuscript found: the mysterious Apicius

Four long years after his departure from Rome, Enoch d'Ascoli eventually arrived at the Abbey of Fulda in what is now central Germany. This was exactly the kind of monastery he was seeking. Founded in 744 CE, the Benedictine Abbey of Fulda was established by Saint Boniface to consolidate Christianity's hold on power in central Germany. The abbey gained additional prominence with the death of Saint Boniface, whose burial at the monastery turned it into a site of religious pilgrimage. A concerted effort was made to acquire more holy relics, and the fame of the monastery grew with each additional fragment of hair, bone, or sliver of wood. At its peak, the library held over 2,000 manuscripts, making it the largest in northern Europe.

By the time Enoch d'Ascoli passed through its gates in 1455, the monastery of Fulda had been reduced to a faint echo of its former self. And what exactly was Enoch d'Ascoli looking for? At the top of his list would have been a complete copy, or at least the missing sections, of Livy's monumental history of ancient Rome, *Ab urbe condita*. While a quarter of this work had already been recovered, fame and fortune awaited the man who discovered the rest. However, Enoch d'Ascoli did not find any of Livy's missing manuscripts (nor did anyone else in the ensuing 500 years). Instead, he retrieved several important works, some of which were invaluable in reconstructing the history of Rome. For our purposes, however, the most interesting text acquired was a copy of the Roman recipe collection, *Apicius*.

At first, Enoch d'Ascoli thought he had recovered a major medical text of historical importance. The confusion arose from a letter written by the Italian Renaissance humanist Niccolò de' Niccoli, which had specifically mentioned the *Apicius* manuscript as containing "excellent medical knowledge."[3] As if to confirm its medical pedigree, the *Apicius* manuscript was found rolled up in the same codex as the medical treatise *De observatione ciborum*, written by the Greek-trained doctor Anthimus—the very person who condemned *garum*, as noted in the medieval anchovy chapter of the current volume (Chapter 1). Enoch d'Ascoli did not have the *Apicius* manuscript copied: he purchased the original outright from the abbey. Despite his optimism, had he reviewed the *Apicius* manuscript in detail while at Fulda, he would have discovered a collection of recipes concerned purely with cooking. Of the 459 recipes devoted to gastronomy, only 13 reference anything remotely therapeutic or medical.

At this point, a new wrinkle arose in Enoch d'Ascoli's manuscript hunting in northern Europe: his benefactor, Pope Nicholas V, suddenly fell deathly ill. Enoch d'Ascoli hightailed it back to Rome. The death of Pope Nicholas V could jeopardize everything: his quest for humanist texts in northern Europe, his job at the Vatican library, and crucially, his financial future. When he finally made it back to Rome, it was too late: the Pope was already dead, as was Enoch d'Ascoli's career.

The new Pope Callixtus III, born Alfonso de Borgia, was hostile to humanism. Living up to his family's infamous reputation, he promptly shut down all the humanist projects of his predecessor, including the library. What is more, the Pope was preparing for a new crusade against the Turks, who had recently conquered Constantinople and were knocking on Europe's back door. In addition to halting all costly urban regeneration projects in Rome, Pope Callixtus III sold a number of Vatican properties to raise funds for his army. At a time when every penny counted for the Pope's war chest, he would likely have ignored previous papal agreements and declined to make any significant payments to Enoch d'Ascoli. Apparently, Pope Callixtus III accepted a few manuscripts from Enoch d'Ascoli, but rejected everything else, including the *Apicius* manuscript. Presumably, he let Enoch d'Ascoli keep it in lieu of direct financial compensation for his work. This was a devastating blow to the scholar. He decided that selling the *Apicius* manuscript to a collector would be his best shot at salvaging his financial future. Despite his best efforts, a buyer never materialized, and Enoch d'Ascoli died a poor man.

While the tale of Enoch d'Ascoli came to a rather tragic end, the *Apicius* manuscript would live on to see brighter days. To understand how this came to be, and why it is important to our story, it is necessary to delve into Renaissance humanism and what this movement hoped to achieve.

From disinterest to intrigue: Apicius *and Renaissance humanism*

Renaissance humanism arose in the early fourteenth century. Its birth as a movement was loosely based on the scholar and poet Petrarch's increasing dissatisfaction with life as he saw it unfolding around him. Francesco Petrarch (1304–1374) inspired Renaissance humanists to pursue a notion that human beings should think and understand moral and spiritual questions critically—that they should side-step the God-centered dogma of medieval scholars and turn instead to classical Roman and Greek texts as inspiration for living a richer cultural life and embracing Christianity more fully.

With such pressing topics on their plate, one can imagine these humanists' excitement when Enoch d'Ascoli returned to

Rome with *Apicius* in tow. But alas, their eyes fell on a simple list of recipes with instructions that were disappointingly formulaic and brief. Nothing was mentioned on how to live, which plants were ideal for restoring health, or even how to adjust bodily humors through food. All that our humanists could glean from *Apicius* was how to cook a rabbit. This was the first strike against *Apicius*.

The second strike was that—at least philosophically—some of these humanists were suspicious of what the book really stood for. In their understanding of the world, derived from classical teachings, prudence and moderation were the keys to virtuous conduct, especially when it came to food and drink. In the 1300s, Petrarch had already dismissed everything to do with the Apician lifestyle: "I have [...] led a happier existence with plain living and ordinary fare than all the followers of *Apicius*, with their elaborate dainties."[4] His condemnation was the most damning of all, as Petrarch was looked up to as the father of humanism.

As early as the fifth and sixth centuries CE, we start finding references that speak of Apicius as an insatiable individual, a sort of gastronomic Caligula. It appears that over time, Apicius had evolved into a semi-mythical character of unconstrained decadence. He was described as "a greedy fellow"[5] and the "exemplar of a glutton,"[6] with his food perceived as an obscene perversion: "Away with the seasoners of sauces, away with the wiles of cooks, away with the dishes of Apicius."[7] A tenth-century text gets right to the point: "Apicius is the proper name for a glutton."[8] Petrarch and the humanists who followed in his footsteps simply could not reconcile *Apicius* with parsimony and restraint.

The final strike against *Apicius* was purely gastronomic: nearly every recipe featured *garum*, the ancient fish sauce often made with anchovies. Some humanists were baffled by *garum*, as the condiment had fallen out of favor nearly a thousand years earlier. If any of them had managed to sample some *garum*, they would have likely viewed it in the negative, equating the briny elixir with decay.

For all their disdain towards *Apicius*, a funny thing happened on the way to the forum. Over just a few years, a sort of changing of the guard occurred in humanist circles, and *Apicius* went from being derided to becoming an object of fascination. The informal leader of this new breed of humanists was Pomponio Leto (born Giulio Sanseverino), who around the year 1460 founded the Roman Academy in his home. For Leto and his like-minded brethren, such as Platina (born Bartolomeo Sacchi), everything connected to ancient Greece and Rome was embraced with a newfound fervor. Leto's house became the site of elaborate garden parties with banquets staged *alla antiqua*, Latin poetry readings, and young boys—probably Leto's pupils—adding an element of sexual frisson (at least for the older guests). Wine flowed freely, and the gatherings were considered slightly transgressive as guests discussed pagan rites that rubbed the church up the wrong way.* Many humanists were so committed that they adopted Greek and Latin names and often wore togas. Reportedly, Leto went so far as to wear a toga around town, which is the fashion equivalent of a twenty-first-century man wearing a Renaissance tunic, hose, and codpiece into a neighborhood Starbucks to order a macchiato.

In contrast to the more modest aspirations of earlier humanists, Pomponio Leto and his colleagues were determined to recreate

---

* Leto, Platina, and several other humanists would eventually get arrested and thrown in the dungeon at the Castel Sant'Angelo for a rumored conspiracy to assassinate Pope Paul II, among other dubious charges. While being held in the clink, Platina was relentlessly interrogated by agents of the Pope and they nearly succeeded in having his head. Only through the benevolence of his benefactors did Platina eventually walk out alive. The next eminence, Pope Sixtus IV, adored Platina (and humanism), and gave him a comfy job in the Vatican library.

the glory of ancient Greece and Rome in all its cultural splendor. This included the food they ate. The Italian Renaissance scholar Damiano Acciarino argues that Leto was so interested in *Apicius* that he may even have translated a copy himself.[9] As Leto and his colleagues read about ancient Romans and their love of mushrooms, they reconsidered the value of *Apicius*. "The text [*Apicius*] was often cited by Platina and his friends in the Roman Academy in their discussions of what it would mean to live 'in the ancient style,'" writes the historian Susan Pinkard. "Interestingly," she continues, "truffles, porcini, and other mushrooms—all of which were prominently featured in *Apicius*' recipe collection—did have something of a comeback in the Renaissance. This revival may be the specific result of *Apicius*' influence."[10] Not only are mushrooms frequently mentioned in *Apicius*, but also vegetables of every kind. Indeed, an entire chapter of *Apicius* is devoted exclusively to vegetables, and another to pulses. Given that the ancient Romans deemed vegetables worthy of their table, the humanists decided that they (as successors of the Romans) ought to embrace them as well.

The growing acceptance of vegetables among elites who had traditionally viewed them as beneath their station, also came into focus with a cookbook by Maestro Martino, who was linked to the humanists through Bartolomeo Platina. *De arte coquinaria* ("The Art of Cooking") has been called "The first modern cookery book," and its author, the first celebrity chef.[11] Recognizing its indispensable role in the evolution of cookery, the scholar of medieval Italian literature Luigi Ballerini writes, "*The Art of Cooking* is to the Renaissance what Auguste Escoffier's *Le guide culinaire* (1903) is to contemporary French cuisine."[12] Aside from the clear and detailed cooking instructions provided by Maestro Martino, the inclusion of vegetables in his recipes is what really stands out. All kinds of chard, lettuce, broccoli, cauliflower, turnip, fennel, mushroom, celery, onion, and garlic feature prominently in his recipes.

It is this commingling of elite and non-elite gastronomy that Massimo Montanari sees as fundamental to the creation of Renaissance cuisine, a style of cooking that would form the foundation of Italian cookery in the years to come. The inclusion of vegetables rounded out Italian cuisine. In its own small way, *Apicius* may have contributed to this development. Italian cookery was about to come into its own, as were anchovies.

Anchovies straddle the social divide

As the Renaissance gained momentum, so did anchovies. They were eaten across the entire social spectrum, from the poorest of the poor living in rural hovels to successful merchants and artisans, right up to high-ranking church members and the aristocrats who patronized them. Every social class was eating anchovies, but how they ate them varied enormously. While the impoverished would eat as many as they could get, the rich were warned to consume them with restraint, as anchovies were best left to those with "rough constitutions."

For most folks living on the Italian Peninsula during the Renaissance (circa 1350–1600), life was a daily struggle. Poverty was generational; there was never enough to eat, and most were lucky to scrounge a scrap or two of protein per week. Animal feet, ankles, noses, and ears were all eagerly consumed. Alongside these appendages, a small piece of anchovy was a godsend, as it could add a smidgen of flavor to otherwise plain polenta, unadorned gruel, or stewed roots. Anchovies were such an effective way to introduce some yearned-for flavor, that in the far north of the country, they even made their way inland to remote valleys where one might be surprised to find them.

Around the middle of the Renaissance (circa 1450), there arose a band of loosely affiliated anchovy traders in northern Italy who came to be known as *acciugai*. These itinerant anchovy peddlers arrived in the port city of Genoa each autumn to acquire anchovies from salt fish merchants. With their mule trains fully loaded, they departed over the Apennine Mountains on the ancient *Via del Sale* ("The Salt Road"). Salt, or "white gold" as it was sometimes called, had been transported along these smuggling trails since the early medieval period, and anchovy peddlers simply piggy-backed on clandestine routes over the mountains. Their destination was the inland region of Piedmont and even as far east as Lombardy.

The life of an itinerant anchovy seller was brutal and thankless, requiring months on the road and nights spent under the stars. Curiously, the trade of anchovy peddling was dominated by the inhabitants of a few rustic hamlets located in the Alpine valley of Cuneo. For these impoverished young men, selling anchovies was one of the few ways to save enough money to buy some land, and, God willing, procure a wife. Housewives eagerly awaited the peddlers' return from Genoa, having depleted their stocks of anchovies from the previous year. Piero Raina notes that one anchovy seller, a certain Gicao from the village of Bassura, had his own special song to announce his arrival in each village: "Anchovies of Malaga, of Setabal, buy them, eat them, and they will keep you warm all winter!" (Fig. 5.1).[13]

Thanks to the early trade of salted anchovies in the fifteenth and sixteenth centuries, the inhabitants of the Piedmont region created their own anchovy-infused dipping sauce called *bagna càuda*. While its exact origins are still debated, some argue that the dipping sauce was created to make the limited supply of winter vegetables more appetizing. The name of the dip captures its essence perfectly, as *bagna* refers to "dip" or "sauce" and *càuda* to "hot." To a hot bath of olive oil and butter, one adds sliced garlic and anchovies. As the flavorsome anchovies and garlic meld together into a soul-warming wave of umami, one can dip some

Fig. 5.1: Selling gastronomic goodness, one anchovy at a time. Early twentieth-century anchovy seller in the foothills of the Alps. (*Courtesy of www.invalmaira.it and the Anchovy Museum of Celle di Macra, Italy.*)

sliced, raw vegetables into it, such as fennel, celery, radishes, cauliflower, or cardoons (artichoke thistles).

Moving an immense distance up the social ladder, anchovies were also found in the merchant and successful artisan classes. Increased financial resources meant that anchovies were not merely used as a flavoring agent in gruels and stews, but could also be enjoyed on their own, perhaps accompanied by some decent bread. A simple grocery list found among the papers of the Renaissance artist Michelangelo offers us an intimate glimpse into the genius who created some of the most iconic works of art in human history, including the ceiling of the Sistine Chapel, the monumental *David*, and the heartbreak of *La Pietà*. What did the man who many consider the greatest artist of all time include on his grocery list? Anchovies (Fig. 5.2).

The anchovies on Michelangelo's list would likely have been salted, or possibly brined or preserved in vinegar. The naturally high oil content of fresh anchovies would have made them deteriorate too rapidly to withstand the long trek from the coast to the inland city of Florence, where this list was written in 1518. Food historian Gillian Riley proposes that Michelangelo's grocery

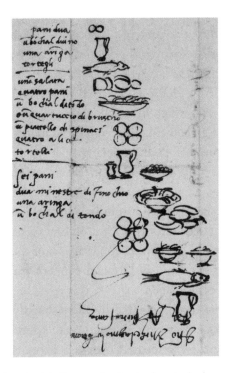

Fig. 5.2: The bowl with four anchovies is the ninth down from the top. While seemingly just a quick sketch, care was taken to distinguish the rims of every bowl. In this way, Michelangelo provided visual clues to his illiterate helper who did his shopping. (*Courtesy of the Casa Buonarroti Museum, Florence.*)

list is for a Lenten or "lean day" meal, as no meat or dairy are mentioned. She also observes that as simple as the list may appear to our modern eyes, it indicates a person of financial means, one who would have been well off enough to indulge in good wine, decent bread, herrings (imported from the North or Baltic Seas), and anchovies.[14]

For those at the very top of the social hierarchy, a wide range of possibilities awaited their anchovies. Cristoforo di Messisbugo was a *majordomo*, or chief steward (a position that ranked far above a cook in the Renaissance), for Duke Alfonso d'Este and his son, Cardinal Ippolito. Messisbugo produced a series of banquets that formed the basis of his cookbook, *Banchetti, composizioni di vivande e apparecchio generale* ("Banquets, Composition of Dishes and General Presentation," 1549). At one of his banquets in 1528, fifty-four guests started with a cold course served from the *credenza*, which included an asparagus salad, marzipan biscuits, a leafy-green field salad, cold sliced mullet, little pastries stuffed with sturgeon, and an anchovy salad.

What is intriguing about this starter course is that an anchovy salad was placed alongside a dish featuring the fabled sturgeon, perhaps the highest-ranked fish in Italy in the sixteenth century. Massimo Montanari cites this kind of "unexpected proximity" between high- and low-ranked foods as one of the unique characteristics that distinguished Italian cookery from the rest of western European cuisine.[15]

Banquets like those prepared by Messisbugo were often the setting for discussions on international relations. In 1536, Cardinal Lorenzo Campeggio hosted a banquet in Rome in honor of Emperor Charles V, in an attempt to smooth over relations with his arch-enemy King François I of France (who just happened to be married to Charles V's sister, Eleanor of Austria). Diplomatically speaking, the dinner did not quite work out as hoped, as shortly thereafter, Charles V marched his army onto French soil. In terms of the food, on the other hand, it was a success, thanks to the illustrious chef Bartolomeo Scappi. Nestled among 200-plus dishes was this little anchovy-based gem: "Alici acconcie con olio, aceto, et origano." Probably served as a light salad, the anchovies were most likely marinated in vinegar and then finished with a drizzle of olive oil and a sprinkling of oregano, a traditional dish widely enjoyed in the Italian Peninsula and Sicily.

Scrap the cookbooks of the past: Scappi's Opera *is here*

Bartolomeo Scappi was the most acclaimed chef of the era, and his dishes eclipsed those prepared in Europe's other royal kitchens. Born into a humble family in Lombardy, Scappi managed to work his way up through the kitchen hierarchy until he became the head cook to several cardinals. Eventually, Scappi graduated to the big house, where he found work in the Vatican kitchen. Over time, he became head cook to Popes Pius IV and Pius V. His fame was solidified in 1570 with the publication of his monumental cookery book, *Opera* ("Work"). Containing over a thousand recipes, *Opera* was the most complete cookery book the world had ever known.

What made *Opera* so exceptional was that, for the first time, a chef who fully understood what makes good food great was able to translate that knowledge to the written page. This stood in contrast to Cristoforo di Messisbugo and Maestro Martino, both of whom crafted fine food with their recipes, but offered little practical help when it came to executing them. Every cookery book up until *Opera* functioned more or less as an aide-mémoire for an experienced chef, or as an archive documenting the "Lifestyles of the Rich & Famous," so-to-speak, for future generations. This is exactly what Messisbugo's cookbook aspired to be: a tribute to the greatness of his benefactor the Grand Duke Alfonso d'Este and his son Cardinal Ippolito. Scappi's *Opera*, by contrast, provides both lists of ingredients and step-by-step instructions, a first for a European cookery book.

While Scappi could craft an ostentatious banquet unmatched by any other, what he stressed over and over in *Opera* was the importance of taste. This allowed him to sidestep the negative cultural baggage that clung to certain kinds of foods, especially fish. "Turbot, John Dory, lampreys, eels, and oysters," writes Gillian Riley, "receive the same attention [in *Opera*] as minor fish and seafood such as sardines, anchovies, sea slugs, and clams."[16] Controversially, Scappi even claimed that fishermen could prepare the best fish. How could a lowly fisherman bring forth better-tasting fish than a professional chef with a pantry full of spices at his disposal? "The fish prepared by fishermen are better than those prepared by chefs," wrote Scappi, "simply because they are fresher."[17]

Scappi elevated seemingly ordinary foods to a new realm of flavor. One example was his recipe for an anchovy pie. To set the stage, let us compare Scappi's recipe with an earlier medieval fish pie recipe. Compiled anonymously and written in the Tuscan dialect, the latter came to us from the *Libro della cocina* ("The Book of Cooking"), which drew inspiration (and recipes) from the earlier Latin recipe collection, *Liber de coquina*:

Fish pie, *Libro della cocina* (circa late 1300s)

Make some hard dough [with flour and warm water] and mould it in the trout's shape or in a round shape. Gut, scale, wash and salt the trout, place it in the dough mould and put ground spices, oil, and saffron on it. Close the mould following the shape of the trout, and make horns at each end, like a boat. Make two small holes in the dough, at each end, or make just one in the middle. Cook it in the oven, or in between testi [hot stones]. When it is well cooked, pour rose water or the juices of oranges or citrangole [a variety of orange with a stronger taste that was appreciated for its medicinal qualities]. During the times of year when meat is allowed, put some melted lard in it instead of oil. You can make similar pies with other fish: sardines, anchovies, red mullet and others.[18]

Anchovy pie, Bartolomeo Scappi's *Opera* (1570)

To prepare pies of large sardines and anchovies *en croûte* [meaning wrapped in pastry and baked].

Get one of the above-mentioned fish, wash it in wine, split it down the middle, removing its bones and sprinkle the halves with sugar, pepper, cinnamon, cloves and nutmeg. Put them into a small pastry shell interspersed with raisins and beaten fine herbs, and a little butter or oil. Cover the pie over and bake it. When it is half done, through the hole on top you can put in a sauce made of raisins and ground *mostaccioli* [a spiced cookie], moistened with orange juice and malmsey, and sugar. When it is baked, serve it hot. You can also do it with spring onions, prunes and dried visciola cherries the way the one above for salted tuna belly is done.[19]

While both recipes drive towards the same culinary destination, they vary in the routes they take. Scappi did not reinvent the fish pie so much as refine it. This was the trick of his trade: he brought culinary coherence to existing recipes by spelling out the specific ingredients and techniques required. For instance, instead of the generic "ground spices" listed in the *Libro della cocina*, Scappi announced each Renaissance all-star by name: sugar, pepper, cinnamon, cloves, and nutmeg. Scappi also used more refined techniques in his recipe, such as adding the sauce when the pie is half-cooked rather than at the end; adding multiple layers of sweetness, rather than just rose water; using fresh herbs; and drawing on both Sicilian and older Arab traditions with the addition of dried cherries, prunes, and raisins.

While Scappi was justifiably famous for his lavish banquets—it is how he made his name, after all—his cookery book is nonetheless full of much simpler fare. For instance, his recipe for caviar on toast could not be more straightforward: "It [caviar] is served on a warm slice of toast with orange juice and pepper on it."[20] Scappi freely juxtaposed dishes of elegant simplicity with highly complex Renaissance flavors, with their echoes of medieval spicing. Another simple recipe is for an anchovy salad, in which anchovies are "dressed with oil, pepper, vinegar, and oregano."[21] And that's it.

This kind of simple fare appealed to Popes Pius IV and Pius V, both of whom Scappi cooked for. Neither pontiff required Scappi to flex his culinary muscles, as both were living in an austere era, brought about in large part by those pesky Protestants in the north. The ceaseless demands for papal reform had a negative effect upon Rome's banqueting culture, and the long tables, heaped with an array of tantalizing dishes, were replaced with more humble fare. The days and nights of decadent parties attended by cardinals and bishops and lithe young bodies in various states of undress were no longer acceptable. Rome's cultural pendulum had swung from the warm embrace of Renaissance excess to the cold and austere ways of an institution that was under attack. Anything with even a hint of impropriety was now subject to the harsh glare of the Inquisition. Even Michelangelo's famed Sistine Chapel was deemed too immodest and suffered the indignity of painted loincloths and fig leaves to cover its depictions of human anatomy.

Taste versus class: who chose anchovies from 1600–1800?

In a number of contemporary histories of Italian cuisine, the 1600s fly by in a blur. Blink, and you will miss the 1700s as well. A few anecdotes, a brief mention of a cookbook or two, and then we are off to the greener pastures of La Varenne's *Le Cuisinier françois* and the French culinary revolution that would reorient most of the elite gastronomic landscape of western Europe. The separation of sweet from savory in *Le Cuisinier françois* is simply too tempting when it comes to telling the story of what European elites ate and why (everyone else's diet remained largely unchanged). And yet, despite the revolution that started in northern France and then spread to the rest of Europe, Italy remained enthralled with its Renaissance flavor profiles, and—some would say rather snidely—stuck in a culinary cul-de-sac. After hitting a peak with Scappi and being in the vanguard of western European gastronomy, Italian food lost its innovative zeal and became somewhat dated and out of style.

Nonetheless, Italian cuisine between 1600 and 1800 was filled with wonderful food, and much of it included anchovies. This begs the question of who was eating all these anchovies. Italian cookery books are filled with them, and their recipes reveal how the elites were consuming them in everything, from salads to main courses to sauces and garnishes. Fancy a royal salad with anchovies, bottarga, radishes, olives, and capers? Or perhaps some sea bass with an anchovy sauce? But missing from these cookery books is what the other 90 percent of society did with anchovies. How important were anchovies to the poor? How much did they cost relative to other fish in the market? While we may not know *how* the poor were eating their anchovies, we know that they were eating them—and quite a lot of them—by looking at fish landings in Italian ports.

Records from the port of Ancona on the Adriatic Sea reveal that in 1557, the price difference between the cheapest and the most expensive salted fish was only 150 percent—a relatively minor figure by historical standards. And the price difference between salted anchovies and salted sardines? A mere 50 percent. By contrast, during the same period in southern Spain, salted sardines often sold for up to 500 percent more than salted anchovies, indicating the disdain in which anchovies were held.

Drawing on records obtained at the port of Ancona and historical sources close to the church, the Italian historian Maria Lucia de Nicolò posits that anchovies were an extremely important food source in Italy at that time, "especially for the poor."[22]

The poor were also eating a lot of anchovies on the opposite side of the Italian Peninsula, and the volume traded at the port of Civitavecchia outside Rome is equally revealing. While records between 1590 and 1596 are somewhat incomplete and should be considered with caution (figures for cod are absent, and those for tuna are suspiciously low), it is nonetheless fascinating that the second highest number of boat landings carried anchovies. Whereas records from Ancona indicate that salted anchovies were priced right alongside other salted fish, the figures from Civitavecchia tell us that far more anchovies were arriving in port than any other similarly priced fish. Clearly, there was a huge demand for salted anchovies, and people living on both sides of the Italian Peninsula ate a lot of them at that time. While the elite undoubtedly had first dibs on the choicest ones arriving at Civitavecchia, there is every reason to suspect that the vast majority of anchovies were destined for the poor.

Another indication of the social class of those eating anchovies stems from the Sumptuary laws passed in 1661, which the Jewish population living in Rome was forced to follow. These laws restricted the kinds of food that commoners could eat, thereby preventing them from putting on airs and acting above their station. For the Jewish community, this meant that they were restricted to bluefish, like anchovies and sardines. This gave rise to the Jewish-Roman specialty called "aliciotti con l'indivia," a tasty but simple dish of two main ingredients: anchovies and curly endive. Fresh anchovies and curly endive were arranged in alternating layers, seasoned with salt, pepper, and a few drops of oil, and then baked.

Customs records from Civitavecchia a hundred years later indicate that demand for anchovies was as strong as ever. To meet the need, a far-ranging network was in play, stretching across the Mediterranean Sea and possibly out into the Atlantic Ocean. Salted anchovies were imported from Cefalù (Sicily), Calabria (southern Italy), Giglio Island (off the Tuscany coast), Corsica, and the port of Genoa. Genoa is of particular interest as it functioned as a trans-shipment center, and some of the anchovies found there are likely to have come from as far away as Málaga and Catalonia in eastern Spain, as well as the Atlantic coast of Portugal (Table 2).

Table 2: Fish landings at Civitavecchia between November 1696 and October 1697

Pesce (fish)	Weight in lbs	Percentage
Merluzzo (salted cod)	844.799	29.5
Tonnina (preserved tuna in oil)	550.387	19.2
Alici (preserved anchovies)	470.107	16.4
Saracche (herring or other bluefish)	313.818	11
Aringhe (preserved herring)	260.483	9.3
Sorra (bluefish)	139.165	4.8
Caviale (caviar)	47.637	1.66
Neroli marinati (designation unclear)	40.254	1.4
Tonno (fresh tuna)	28.133	0.99
Sarde (sardines)	24.786	0.86
Pesci (fish)	24.098	0.84
Moscimano (preserved tuna)	20.850	0.72
Sgombro (mackerel)	13.801	0.48
Sugherelli (preserved Atlantic mackerel)	12.955	0.45

Volpe marinata (marinated Atlantic thresher)	18.143	0.63
Anguille (eels)	17.644	0.61
Ostriche (oysters)	9.979	0.34
Stoccafisso (air-dried cod)	9.892	0.34
Altri (others)	13.764	0.48
Totale	2,860.695	100.00

That salted cod occupies the premier position is not surprising, as during the seventeenth and eighteenth centuries it flooded the market in Europe. More surprising is the dramatic drop in sardine numbers, as just a hundred years earlier they were dominant.[23]

While most of these anchovies were being consumed by the poor, cookery books from this period reveal that aristocrats were consuming them as well. By the late sixteenth and early seventeenth centuries, however, a new kind of class prejudice took hold, with implications for anchovies. Although food hierarchies had always been active in elite circles, many popular ingredients were now shunned with a newfound fervor—beans, pasta, and alliums being the most conspicuous. Salted meat and fish also acquired a negative veneer, deemed inappropriate for the delicate and refined constitutions of aristocrats. Salted anchovies were swept up in the mania.

Galenic doctors came to believe that salted fish in general, and salted anchovies in particular, were potentially harmful, as their over-consumption could result in one becoming excessively "dry." The Italian doctor Giovanni Filippo Ingrassia (1510–1580) noted that salted anchovies could be enjoyed on occasion, "as long as you don't fill the whole meal with [them] as the poor usually do."[24] Another Italian doctor, Alessandro Petronio, noted in 1592 that the rich could enjoy good quality, fresh fish, but that salted sardines, "food known by all and therefore not worth talking about," as well as salted anchovies, "very frequent for family use," were best left for the poor. Petronio articulated the growing suspicions about anchovies when he wrote that they were "food for the poor" and "food for rough people, accustomed to exertion."[25]

While doctors advised against salted anchovies on medical grounds, some stewards started objecting to them on aesthetic grounds. Cesare Evitascandolo, a *scalco* (a Latin term meaning "steward" or "feast maker") and author of the cookery book *Dialogo del trenciante* ("Conversation with a Meat Carver," 1609), noted that it is never a good idea "to place in the midst of a banquet table onions, scallions, anchovies, and similar things, though it may seem to some a pretty invention, it will not however be honorable, for besides the stink they bear, they will suggest that the diners are rustics."[26] In other words, only the uncouth would dress their banquet table with such obvious symbols of poverty. Anchovies, onions, and leeks were all fine when combined with other ingredients to create a well-balanced meal, but in and of themselves, they were food for the poor.

Despite Evitascandolo's objections, prevailing medical wisdom, and anchovies' increasing associations with the poor, the rich were nonetheless eating an awful lot of them. One explanation for the ambiguous space that anchovies came to occupy during this period can be attributed to the gulf between humoral theory and actual food practices in the Renaissance. Just as doctors' dietary advice often goes unheeded in today's world, elites continued to walk on the wild side and eat salted anchovies, regardless of what their doctor or *scalco* said. The simplest explanation is that the rich, just like the poor, genuinely liked anchovies. A crusty piece of bread with a salty preserved anchovy or a salad of fresh anchovy fillets marinated in vinegar was just as tasty in the Renaissance as it is today.

A TWIST IN THE TAIL

Cooking with anchovies, seventeenth-century style

In 1634, Giovanni Battista Crisci published *Lucerna de corteggiani* ("Lantern for Courtiers"), a cookery book devoted to the gastronomic heritage of Naples and southern Italy. While many have debated whether Crisci was a *scalco* (steward) or cook, his obsession with etiquette, court officials, name-dropping, and endless lists of menus, all point towards a steward of some standing. Crisci organized his parade of menus into three categories: daily cooking, Sunday cooking, and banquet cooking. His recipes reveal the late Renaissance/Baroque obsession with sugar. From meat to fowl, and even anchovy salads, sugar was Crisci's go-to seasoning.

At the beginning of the seventeenth century, delicate salads were the very height of culinary sophistication, especially those filled with field greens and lightly dressed with oil, vinegar, lemon juice, salt, and pepper. Crisci's book is full of such leafy green salads. He often enhanced them with blue borage flowers, which added a splash of color and emitted a faintly sweet, honey-like aroma.* Elites clamored for these delightful salads dappled with flowers. Perhaps in a nod to Naples' soul-crushing summer heat, Crisci included over twenty-five variations of an anchovy salad. The differences between Crisci's anchovy salads often consist of a single ingredient:

Anchovy salad with lemon
Anchovy salad with lemon and pepper
Anchovy salad with lemon, pepper, and oregano
Anchovy salad with lemon, oil, and pepper

---

* Edible borage flowers are currently back in vogue and probably here to stay. Contemporary chefs working in fine dining covet these flowers for the same reason as their seventeenth-century counterparts: they add a colorful dash of whimsy and imbue a hint of sweet opulence.

Anchovy salad with oil, vinegar, oregano, and pepper
Anchovy salad with lemon and sugar

And so on and so forth. *Scalchi* like Crisci were funny characters, and Crisci's endless lists of menus speak not only to what people ate or the magnificence of the host, but also stand as records of how to eat correctly. Choosing which dishes went together and the best order in which to eat them, and above all, knowing the humoral temperament of the master of the house so that all the dishes could be spiced accordingly, were important aspects of a *scalco's* role. Whether one was served an anchovy salad with lemon, or an anchovy salad with lemon and pepper, spoke to the wisdom and mysterious arts of a *scalco*.

Thirteen years later, in 1647, another *scalco* named Giovanni Francesco Vasselli published *L'Apicio overo il maestro de'conviti* ("Apicius; or, The Master of Banquets"). His endive salad is a Baroque marvel built upon the sweet-sour flavor combination that had defined gastronomy for the previous thousand years. Every note for a successful salad is present: the vinegar and pomegranate seeds lend a sour taste, while the treasured sweetness comes from sugar and cinnamon. Anchovies provide the all-essential umami. Salads like these came into their own during this period, and as Alberto Capatti and Massimo Montanari point out, they drifted from simply being served as an appetizer to assuming the more respected position of a side dish or an accompaniment: what Italians nowadays call *contorni*.[27]

Of particular interest is Vasselli's anchovy sauce, a condiment that was highly favored in the seventeenth century. Vasselli noted that his anchovy sauce was intended for all kinds of "fish dishes." While there was a long tradition of anchovy-like sauces in Italy, Vasselli updated his version by contrasting the sour note of vinegar with cinnamon, cloves, and—in a nod to Baroque sensibilities—candied orange zest. Pepper, *mostaccioli* (a type of spiced cookie crumbled into dishes), and salted anchovies completed the sauce. Such was the popularity of this sauce that around fifty years later, Antonio Latini lifted the recipe in its entirety for his own cookery book.

Hot on Vasselli's Baroque heels was Bartolomeo Stefani's *L'arte di ben cucinare et instruire* ("The Art of Fine Cooking," 1662). Stefani was another cook who was enthralled with sugar, candied citrus, pastries, creams, and anything hinting of culinary excess. In his thirty-odd recipes that include anchovies, one finds them combined with meat, fowl, all kinds of fish, and even crustaceans (spider crabs). But rather curiously, anchovies are not included in a single salad.

Judged by our standards today, most of Stefani's recipes are simply too much of a good thing: too much sugar, too much rose water, too many perfumed scents (ambergris! musk!). Like much of the Baroque period itself, many of his dishes appear slightly overwrought, such as his "Grilled sturgeon with a salsa bastarda" made with amber (fossilized tree resin) and anchovies. Amber was highly valued during the Renaissance (and earlier periods), not just for jewelry but also for its ability to bring good luck, protection, and healing. Amber was also incorporated into aristocratic recipes, perhaps as much for its health benefits as its faint fragrance. So why did Stefani concoct a dish that pairs the noble sturgeon with a sauce containing amber and then call it "salsa bastarda"? Despite enhancing the dish and adding to its overall flavor, might the humble anchovy have been held to a different standard, like a bastard son who is acknowledged but not recognized as a legitimate member of the family?

Stefani's cookery book also features a recipe for anchovy sauce. His version is in the same Baroque school as Vasselli's, though it differs in its addition of butter, oil, and capers. This reflects an awareness of the new style of cookery that was emanating out of northern France. In terms of spices, however, both Vasselli and

Stefani relied on a model of spicing that stretched back to the medieval period, with cinnamon, cloves, and a sweetener doing the gastronomic heavy lifting. When we compare this with the French chef La Varenne's anchovy sauce, we see that he jettisoned these heavy spices and replaced them with butter, egg yolks, and nutmeg, each of which contribute to creating a rich, creamy, and more subtle base. Though only a few simple steps separate each of these recipes, they are worlds apart in terms of flavor, texture, and consistency.

Antonio Latini: sweet-tooth and scalco to the stars

Antonio Latini was everything we would expect from a great Renaissance *scalco*: a gourmand, an astute political animal, and somewhat of a petty snob. Latini came from a dirt-poor background, but his drive and ambition propelled him out of the poverty-stricken countryside and towards the alluring lights of Rome, where, at the age of sixteen, he found work as a kitchen helper in a wealthy household. Latini rose rapidly through the ranks and eventually landed the coveted position of chief steward to Cardinal Antonio Barberini, nephew of Pope Urban VIII. He must have charmed the socks off Urban VIII, as he was awarded the prestigious title of "Knight of the Golden Spur."

Near the end of his life, Latini published his massive two-volume cookery book in Naples, *Lo scalco alla moderna* ("The Modern Steward," 1692–4), a masterpiece of late Renaissance Baroque cooking. While Latini's cookery book was published on the cusp of a new culinary epoch, its recipes were nonetheless the product of Scappi and Messisbugo's era, with complex spices used generously to balance the humoral qualities of his dishes. Latini's additional not-so-secret weapon was to heap generous amounts of sugar into practically everything. His love of sugar is reminiscent of Martino, Stefani, and Crisci. But alongside his sweetly seasoned recipes, Latini threw in an occasional recipe of such startling simplicity that it stops you in your tracks. This ability to straddle two different gastronomic realms makes his cookery book a bit of a Rorschach test: many praise his work as the pinnacle of Baroque cookery, while others shake their heads in disbelief at the sugary madness of it all. One thing is certain: Latini's work was the last hurrah of Baroque cookery before the northern French influence took its hold on the Italian Peninsula.

Latini knew that times were changing in the culinary world, as he titled a chapter of his cookery book, "How to season without spices." However, this was more of a token acknowledgement of the gastronomic changes afoot than any meaningful commitment to seasoning dishes in the new French style. Aside from a couple of paragraphs about seasoning with herbs, not a single recipe is presented, and he quickly returned to recipes spiced in the traditional style. Almost everything else in his cookery book epitomizes an old-school Neapolitan approach, which makes sense given that Latini was a *scalco* to some of the brightest lights of his day. *Scalchi* like Latini were focused on pleasing the taste buds of their benefactors, as well as maintaining traditions, etiquette, and everything else that was required to project the power of an aristocrat (Fig. 5.3).

One tradition that went back millennia in Naples was eating fresh anchovies, so it is not surprising that Latini listed several recipes for them. One recipe calls for fresh anchovies to be dusted with ground coriander, grilled, and then served with lemon wedges. A more elaborate version calls for fresh anchovies to be tossed together with aromatic herbs, raisins (the Arab influence is never far away in southern Italy), pine nuts, crushed garlic, and lemon juice, and then cooked on the grill. He also included a recipe for anchovies pan-fried with oil, onions, aromatic herbs, spices, pine nut milk, and grapes, served with lemon

Fig. 5.3: The charming frontispiece to Antonio Latini's *Lo scalco alla moderna* ("The Modern Steward," 1692–4), is a tribute to Baroque excess, much like his recipes. The richly laden grapevine with a contented cow sitting atop a pile of pewter plates dotted with an assortment of edible birds, all speak to nature's bounty (at least for well-fed aristocrats). The plates serve to remind us of the endless array of dishes that could be cooked up from such Renaissance abundance. (*Published with the permission of the Società Napoletana di Storia Patria. Further reproduction prohibited.*)

wedges. In addition to his recipes for fresh anchovies, Latini also noted that their salted brethren make excellent sauces. While salted tuna belly, mullet roe, or caviar can also be used for a sauce, "the best among them is that made with anchovies."[28]

His praise of anchovies is tempered by the name of one of his anchovy sauces, however, that professor of history Tommaso Astarita translates as the "Little sassy one." In Latini's original recipe, the title contains the Neapolitan word "*sfacciatella*," which does indeed refer to "sassy" or even "impertinent." It also carries an additional meaning, which can be translated as "little tart," or a woman that sleeps around—a meaning Latini would have likely understood during his multi-decade stay in Naples. As the Neapolitan name of Latini's recipe suggests, this sauce can "get on" with any kind of fish—hence, it is a *sfacciatella*. This kind of association between an anchovy and a loose woman is akin to another Neapolitan sauce containing anchovies, *la puttanesca* ("whore-style"), which is commonly enjoyed with pasta to this day. By titling his sauce in such a pejorative manner, Latini captured the ambiguous status of anchovies that often followed them throughout history: flavorful, but rather common and loose.

Vincenzo Corrado: clever cook, inventive style

Vincenzo Corrado was a man of many talents: a Benedictine monk, scholar, and philosopher, but above all, a talented cook who cleverly applied French culinary techniques to Naples's regional cookery. In the process, he also crafted a new, highly inventive, hybrid style. Between the eighteenth and nineteenth centuries, no other cook was more acclaimed in Italy or had a greater impact upon the direction of elite gastronomy. Corrado's love of food was nurtured from a young age in a Celestine monastery in Naples where he studied mathematics, languages, sciences, and, in a practical turn that would pay big dividends later in life, cookery. Upon leaving the monastery in his early thirties, he earned his most consistent income by teaching French and Spanish to the aristocratic offspring of Naples's elites. Both languages would come in handy in the cosmopolitan kitchens of the Prince of Francavilla's Cellamare Palace in Naples, where he would later produce a series of lavish banquets.

One of the things that made Corrado so exceptional was that he did not surrender to French culinary tastes in a wholesale manner. He chose instead to cherry-pick and incorporate their flavor profiles and techniques into his own regional style of cookery. The result was a series of recipes that feel surprisingly modern in their execution and include everything that we think of as quintessentially Italian. "Tomatoes are for pleasure," proclaimed Corrado with his typical enthusiasm in his cookery book, *Il cuoco galante* ("The Gallant Cook," 1773).[29] His recipe for *Pomidori alla Napolitana*, what we would call "tomatoes *au gratin*," looks surprisingly contemporary, as if it has stepped off the pages of *Bon Appétit* magazine:

> After cleaning the tomatoes of their skins and cutting them in half, you will remove their seeds and place them on a sheet of paper greased with oil in a baking tray. You will fill the tomato halves with anchovies, parsley, oregano, and garlic, all finely chopped and seasoned with salt and pepper. Having covered the tomatoes with bread crumbs, you will bake them in the oven, and serve them.[30]

Corrado's enthusiasm extended to vegetables of all sorts, and if he felt the need to punch up their flavor, he often served them with a zingy sauce, usually built on a foundation of lemon juice and anchovies. Following the French fashion, he added aromatic herbs, and showed restraint with regard to spices. In fact, one can distinctly discern the French influence in his use of sauces and *coulis*. For instance, Corrado included a sauce for fish that would be right at home in any French cookery book: white wine, capers, anchovies, mushrooms, thyme, mint, butter, and Parmesan cheese. In a similar manner, his recipe for "Fennel with anchovies" consists of raw fennel marinated in a paste of anchovies, aromatic herbs, and traditional Italian spices, then fried in oil and simmered in a decidedly French prawn *coulis*. Interestingly, the one sauce that is un-French in every respect and can be traced back to his predecessors Latini, Crisci, and Vasselli is his anchovy sauce. It seems that anchovy sauce had achieved a sort of "classic" status in Italy, a standard part of the culinary repertoire of taste expectations. Each chef would only make minor adjustments to it to suit their desired intentions.

Corrado's taste for anchovies led him to include them in an impressive 111 recipes, more than any other Italian chef in the past. In the intriguing recipe titled "Hen with anchovies," the bird is boiled with salt, bay leaf, "green lemon" zest, and pepper, then plated cold with a pistachio and anchovy sauce. Another inventive dish, *Al torna gusto* ("Back to taste again") presents a striking marinade for olives made with green peppers, fresh fennel (including seeds), garlic, mint, oregano, lemon juice, oil, and anchovies. Corrado loved adding anchovies to vegetables, something modern cooks would be well advised to consider. "Cauliflower with anchovies," "Asparagus with anchovies," and "Mushrooms with anchovies" are just a few of the vegetable side dishes that Corrado elevated to new heights of flavor with anchovies.

There was one particular guest at one of Corrado's lavish banquets who appreciated anchovies almost as much as he did. Giacomo Casanova, better known to history simply as Casanova, knew many ways to women's hearts, but one of the most surefire involved the humble anchovy. In his autobiography, *L'Histoire de ma vie*, begun in 1791, Casanova recounted the time when he fell in love with a nun of startling beauty on one of the Murano islands in the Venetian Lagoon. Surreptitiously visiting her at the convent, he charmed her with his wit, style, and grace, and she agreed to a secret *rendezvous* in Venice. Everything needed to be perfect for Casanova's planned seduction. He rented a fully furnished apartment for his hoped-for tryst, complete with a Las Vegas–style mirrored ceiling and an "English style water closet."[31] It was, reflected Casanova, the perfect lair to seduce this woman of God.

Leaving nothing to chance, the most notorious womanizer in the western world insisted on a trial run-through of the dinner with his cook, tasting every dish and sampling all the wines and champagne. Food was critical to Casanova's whole approach, as it was often at the dinner table where his seduction began in earnest. As the cook brought each dish to the table during their practice run, Casanova nodded in approval. Wild game, sturgeon, truffles, oysters: each was deemed superb, setting the stage for his conquest. At the end of the taste test, however, Casanova gave his feedback: everything was perfect, except for one thing. To seal the deal with his intended, it was imperative that they add an anchovy salad to the following night's dinner menu.

And the dinner with the nun? A resounding success. Later that night found them entwined in bed. As Casanova confided, "She was astonished to find herself receptive to so much pleasure, for I showed her many things she had considered fictions. I did things to her that she did not feel she could ask me to do."[32] And so on, and so forth, all night long. Clearly, both Casanova and Corrado—each in their own way—appreciated the immense possibilities of the humble anchovy.

A high point for anchovies: Francesco Leonardi and The Modern Apicius

Another cookery book author, Francesco Leonardi, embraced the French culinary aesthetic even more passionately than Corrado. Perhaps this is why he is not always looked upon as favorably. However, Leonardi was cooking in an era when French food dominated elite cuisine in all of Europe. In fact, French cuisine played an important role in shaping what we think of today as "Italian" food. The British historian John Dickie cuts to the quick when he writes: "Italian food would not be Italian food without the French."[33]

Leonardi learned the *métier* of French cookery in the stately Parisian home of Louis-François-Armand de Vignerot du Plessis, 3rd Duke de Richelieu. A key diplomat and statesman for the French government, the duke employed a large kitchen staff and entertained on a lavish scale. His family line was impeccable, one of his ancestors being Cardinal Richelieu, who had dominated every facet of French political and religious life in the early seventeenth century. Despite his distinguished pedigree, the Duke de Richelieu lacked any discernible morals and was rumored to have slept with half of Paris' *mesdames*. So successful was his womanizing that he was thought to have slept with the Duchess de Berry, her sister Charlotte Aglaé d'Orléans, and their cousin, Louise Anne de Bourbon. Nothing like shaking every branch of the family tree.

Working in the household of the Duke de Richelieu exposed Leonardi to the very highest rungs of Europe's political dynasties. He soon moved on and started working for the French King Louis XV, whom he accompanied on several campaigns. Military life must have agreed with Leonardi, as he next hitched his horse to General Ivan Ivanovic Shouvaloff, Grand Chamberlain of Russia. Departing Paris, Leonardi arrived in Saint Petersburg in 1778, where he became head chef to Prince Grigorij Grigoryevich Orloff. A rising star in the Russian military, Orloff had already caught the eye of the future Catherine the Great when she was still a princess. He had even assisted Catherine in leading a *coup d'état* against her husband. Playing his cards right and seasoning his dishes to French perfection, Leonardi was soon installed in the royal kitchen of Catherine herself. Russian nobility had a weakness for French-trained chefs, a tradition that would be cemented around forty years later when Carême was lured to Russia by Tsar Alexander I.

The harsh Russian winters eventually took their toll on Leonardi, who returned to his hometown of Rome where he published his masterwork, *L'Apicio moderno* ("The Modern Apicius") in 1790. As far as European cookery books go, this encyclopaedic six-volume tome is a standout for anchovies. Almost 250 recipes contain this distinctive fish, making *L'Apicio moderno* a high point for anchovies that has never been matched since. While Leonardi is well known as the first to print a recipe for pasta with tomato sauce, *inter alia*, for our purposes, it is his unwavering appreciation of anchovies that makes him such a prominent figure in the Italian culinary world.

Leonardi began his collection with the most elemental aspect of French cuisine: broths. This sets the stage for sauces, at which point anchovies come into play in a big way. In book five, anchovies are present in nearly a quarter of his sauces, from caper to endive, sorrel, and spinach. Leonardi's "Anchovy sauce" is a radical departure from the past. It is hard not to admire a cook with the confidence to walk past so much tradition and completely restructure a time-tested sauce. In his version, not a spice is in sight, nor is there any added sugar. Simmered onions, parsley, garlic, anchovies, vegetable *coulis*, and a dash of lemon juice round out his thoroughly French-style sauce. Aware of the anchovy's unique ability to perk up lackluster dishes at a moment's notice, Leonardi even included a recipe for anchovy paste that can be stored in the pantry and used "when needed."[34]

Leonardi's enthusiastic embrace of anchovies is on full display throughout his cookery books. Nearly a quarter of his soup recipes are graced with our humble fish, including onion, zucchini, fennel, vermicelli, and rice. Over half of his ragù recipes—a thick tomato and/or ground meat-based sauce—feature anchovies. What is more, it seems that Leonardi never came across a piece of seafood that could not be enhanced by an anchovy: cod, hake, tuna, herring, red mullet, cuttlefish, octopus, and squid, to name a few. In his "Salmon Livoniese," onions, shallots, parsley, truffles, mushrooms, garlic, and basil are simmered with eight anchovies and then allowed to cool. The salmon fillets are dressed with the cold sauce and then placed on freshly minced herbs, before being wrapped in paper and slow-cooked to perfection in a warm oven. A sprinkle of lemon juice ramps up the acid right before serving.

A unified country, united in hunger

The unification of Italy played a surprising and curious role in shaping the future of Italian food. Up to the second half of the nineteenth century, the Italian Peninsula was little more than a patchwork of competing states, fiefdoms, principalities, and constantly shifting territories that toggled between the latest power struggles. On March 17, 1861, the Kingdom of Italy was proclaimed under the watchful eye of King Victor Emmanuel II of Savoy. Its capital was Turin in northern Italy. While the mythology of the Italian state presents its founding as being achieved by a "generation of giants" who yearned for unification and freedom from foreign rule, the devil is in the detail, as usual.[35] The British historian David Gilmour characterizes the formation of the Italian state as simply "a war of expansion conducted by one Italian state against another."[36]

After unification, life in the south grew increasingly untenable, and the already meager diet of the poor worsened dramatically. Their basic diet consisted of healthy foods but lacked sufficient quantity and variety. Lentils, fava beans, and chickpeas were all highly nutritious, but needed to be consumed in sufficient quantities and supplemented with grains, vegetables, and fruits to ensure a balanced and healthy diet. Wheat became increasingly expensive for the poor throughout Italy, and many had to undertake work-arounds. In the cookery book *La cuciniera genovese* by Giovanni Battista Ratto, first published in 1863, bread rolls are cleverly made from chickpea flour and stuffed with sautéed anchovies, capers, celery, onions, and ideally a bit of pork belly. The availability of the latter was far from guaranteed; obtaining meat was practically unheard of and it was only consumed on rare occasions. When it did grace a dish, it was often an exceedingly small amount of what was known as the *quinto quarto* (the fifth quarter), the stray odds and ends left over after quartering: tails, knuckles, intestines, tripe, and lungs. Another simple recipe in Ratto's collection, *Broccoli trascinati colle acciughe salate* ("Broccoli dragged through salted anchovies"), is bare-bones basic but tasty nonetheless: salted anchovies are sautéed with a smidgen of oil, and then cooked broccoli is dragged (mixed) through it. Dishes like these brought a little flavorful relief to the chronically poor.

While Italy was almost entirely unified by 1870, the poor across the country were *morti di fame* (dying of hunger) and plagued by disease. "Bread" was often made with chickpeas or wild lentils combined with onions, broth, and wild herbs. Wild chicory scavenged from the countryside was the main vegetable consumed in many one-room hovels. Living standards, especially in the rural south, were rudimentary. Most "homes" in the rural countryside consisted of an open-plan layout, where the majority of the first floor was dedicated to sheltering livestock, such as a mule, a goat, or a smattering of chickens. A primitive woodstove for cooking might have occupied a corner, while the family slept in a loft, accessible by a ladder. A simple hole dug in the fields sufficed for a toilet. Running water was rare, and health issues were rife. A simple ailment or tooth infection could spiral out of control and lead to a life-threatening illness.

A TWIST IN THE TAIL

Lean cuisine and anchovies: a match made in heaven

As the poor navigated the dire economic world of post-unification Italy, a friar of the Order of Minims—the same order that King Ferdinand of Spain in the late fifteenth century blithely rebranded as *Victorianos*—published a cookbook that sought to highlight a "Lenten way of life." The diminutive anchovy, needless to say, was featured throughout the book—an astonishing 192 recipes included them, just over 40 percent. The author was Father Gaspare Delle Piane, and the recipe collection, bearing the title *Cucina di strettissimo magro* (Strictly Lean Cuisine), was first published in 1880.

Most Catholic orders embrace poverty, obedience, and chastity as their guiding principles. The founder of the Minims, Saint Francis of Paola (1416–1507), added a fourth: a perpetual Lenten life without meat, eggs, or dairy. The name "Minims" was chosen by Saint Francis to signify that they were even more modest than the "Minors," the friars who followed Saint Francis of Assisi. Only vegetables and seafood—Lenten foods—were deemed appropriate for those who followed *il minimo dei minimi*, as Francis of Paola referred to himself. Amidst such plain living and humbleness, it is no wonder that the Minims embraced anchovies so wholeheartedly.

Father Delle Piane's cookbook was aimed squarely at the affluent classes. Fine cuts of fish, calamari, shrimp, eel, and squid feature throughout its recipes, and delicate risottos are flavored with sea bream or truffles. But Father Delle Piane's cookbook also lists a number of simpler vegetable recipes that often rounded out Lenten meals. It is these basic vegetable recipes that provide an insight into how Italy's poor, who could rarely afford fresh fish, are likely to have eaten. His recipe for *frittelle di cavolfiore* (cauliflower fritters) demonstrates how a simple vegetable, enlivened with just a single anchovy, can go from ordinary to extraordinary:

Frittelle di cavolfiore

Boil cauliflower in salted water. When it is cooked, take it out, drain it, and pound it in a mortar with a salted anchovy and half a clove of garlic. Combine it with the batter in recipe 254 and fry it by the spoonful.[37]

The batter is made with flour, minced parsley, and a pinch of saffron moistened with white wine. This mixture is combined with the cauliflower paste and then fried to create tasty little fritters. The saffron adds an extra touch of elegance that lifts this otherwise humble dish, unexpected from a Minim who would likely have eschewed most spices.

Another simple recipe in Father Delle Piane's cookbook is for *zuppa agli spinaci*: spinach soup:

For six servings

4 onions

4 salted anchovies

1 bunch celery & parsley

1 carrot

6 grams dried mushrooms

10 grams tomato paste

4 tomatoes

60 grams almonds

4 bunches spinach

6 spoons oil

Water and salt as needed[38]

Dried mushrooms have the highest levels of umami of all vege-tables, dried or fresh. Combined with the two salted anchovies, they create an umami-rich foundation for the soup. The almonds add a little nuttiness, act as a thickener, and bring a little protein to the mix. Father Delle Piane rarely used spices in his recipes (apart from the occasional imported clove, saffron, or nutmeg), and none feature here. Being a friar of the Order of Minims, he likely deemed spices an unnecessary luxury. Local herbs were a different matter, but even then, they were mostly limited to parsley, thyme, and a bay leaf or two.

This spinach soup recipe is part of Father Delle Piane's "summer soup" section in which almost all the recipes contain anchovies. He follows the spinach soup recipe with what he calls *zuppa economica*. It is a basic vegetable soup featuring cabbage and root vegetables, but notably, this recipe, intended for those on desperately tight budgets, omits both the salted anchovies and dried mushrooms. For the truly destitute, even an anchovy or two was beyond their means.

Divided by difference, united by food

One cookbook whose sales skyrocketed during this period—published just a decade after Father Delle Piane's—was Pellegrino Artusi's *La scienza in cucina e l'arte di mangiar bene* ("Science in the Kitchen and the Art of Eating Well," 1891). It became a veritable Italian blockbuster and is said to have come second only to the Bible in every bourgeois household.

By the time Artusi published his cookbook, several decades had passed since the formation of the Italian state. And yet, the dream of a unified country with a shared culture seemed more out of reach than ever. The patchwork of different regions in Italy, each with its own language, history, and traditions, led the inhabitants of the new state to view each other as little more than strangers who had just happened, through a quirk of politics, to now find themselves living in a land called "Italy." For most of these "Italians," unification had only made their lives worse. As a result, the end of the nineteenth and beginning of the twentieth century marked a period of deep suspicion of the state. Culinary historian Karima Moyer-Nocchi recalls one common expression of the time: *fidarsi è bene, ma non fidarsi è meglio* (trusting is good, but not trusting is better).[39]

As newly baptized Italians were sorting out what it meant to be Italian, Artusi published his epoch-defining cookbook on Italian gastronomy. By including recipes from across Italy, Artusi helped Italians realize that they all had one thing in common: food. Regardless of which political party one supported or in which region one lived, food was fundamental to everyone, something for which every Italian shared a great love. *Science in the Kitchen*, or *L'Artusi*, as Italians affectionately refer to it, is considered the most influential cookbook of modern Italy, an essential part of Italy's "culinary canon."[40]

What made *L'Artusi* so special was that it was written in a convivial style that spoke to middle-class housewives and the world in which they lived. "With my manual," Artusi wrote, "... one need only know how to hold a wooden spoon to work something out."[41] Artusi adopted the tone of a favorite uncle or best friend whose enthusiasm for food was contagious. Gently but firmly—with a wooden spoon in hand—Artusi guided his readers forward. This approach was something that no previous cookbook author in Italy had successfully managed to do. By comparison, England by this time had a full-blown tradition of cookbooks geared towards housewives, culminating in the Victorian-era bestseller, *Mrs. Beeton's Book of Household Management*. France, too, had published a number of cookbooks with simplified recipes directed towards housewives. But Italy, owing in part to its paltry middle class, had not until that time produced a cookbook that ignited passions (and sales).

Artusi self-published an initial print run of 1,000 copies of *Science in the Kitchen*. It took four years to sell them all, but after that, sales took off. Artusi made food fun: with a wink and a nod, he walked the reader through Italy's glorious gastronomic past right up to the present day. Drawing on the works of previous generations of Italian cooks, Artusi paid tribute to Bartolomeo Stefani (1662) by including one of his soup recipes, which he titled "Zuppa alla Stefani." But in a nod to the present, Artusi modified Stefani's recipe for a modern audience:

> At [Stefani's] time, much use and abuse was made of all manner of seasonings and spices, and sugar and cinnamon were used in broth, as well as in making boiled or roasted meats. Omitting some of his instructions for this soup, I shall limit myself, aromatically speaking, to a bit of parsley and basil. And if the ancient Bolognese cook [meaning Stefani], meeting me in the afterworld, scolds me for it, I shall defend myself by explaining that tastes have changed *for the better* [original emphasis]. As with all things, however, we go from one extreme to the other, and we are now beginning to exaggerate in the opposite direction, going so far as to exclude herbs and spices from dishes that require them. And I shall tell him as well of the ladies who, at my table, have made gruesome faces when confronted with a bit of nutmeg.[42]

Capatti and Montanari emphasize that Artusi's goal was not to impose a sort of pan-Italian cuisine upon well-to-do housewives by forcing everyone to sit at the same table. Rather, he wanted housewives to recognize the diversity of Italian cuisine and explore dishes from regions as distinct as Venice, Bologna, and Naples. He handled each regional variation like a piece in a puzzle. Once completed, the jigsaw would portray "Italian food" as we know it today. But there is some truth to the argument that in the process of compiling his compendium, Artusi contributed to the homogenization of Italian cuisine, as all his recipes represented a certain class of cookery. He largely ignored southern culinary traditions and only included three dishes from Sicily.

Artusi was also overly reliant on French-inspired fare, so it is not surprising that anchovies are largely sidelined in many of his recipes. If we want to find out where Artusi hid his anchovies, we need to turn to his sauces. "The best sauce you can offer your guests," wrote Artusi with his typical enthusiasm, "is a happy expression on your face and heartfelt hospitality."[43] The first sauce listed in *L'Artusi* is a "Salsa verde with anchovies." Its basic ingredients have scarcely changed for centuries:

Salsa verde

To prepare green sauce, squeeze the brine out of some capers and then, using a mezzaluna, finely chop them together with an anchovy, a little onion, and very little garlic. Mash the mixture with a knife blade to make it into a fine paste which you will place in a gravy dish. Add a fair amount of parsley chopped with a few basil leaves. Blend everything in fine olive oil and lemon juice. This sauce goes well with boiled chicken, cold fish, hard-boiled eggs or poached eggs. If you have no capers, brine-cured peppers may be used instead.[44]

Artusi also presented a stripped-down anchovy sauce built on a foundation of capers, anchovies, olive oil, and some butter, the last to be added "sparingly":

Caper and anchovy sauce

This sauce is rather hard on delicate stomachs. It is ordinarily used with steak. Take a pinch of sweetened capers, squeeze out the brine and finely chop with a mezzaluna along with an anchovy from which you have removed the scales and spine. Heat this in olive oil and pour it over a beef steak that you have grilled and then seasoned with salt and pepper and some butter. Use the butter sparingly, however, otherwise it will clash, in the stomach, with the vinegar from the capers.[45]

By stating that anchovies could be hard on those with delicate stomachs, Artusi perpetuated a myth that stretched back to sixteenth-century doctors who deemed anchovies best suited to the poor. Despite everything anchovies brought to the table on the cusp of the twentieth century, the public was still being warned to treat them with caution.

Futurist cooking: disruptive, theatrical, political (and welcoming of anchovies)

Have you ever been to a dinner party where all the guests are dressed in pyjamas, and everything you thought you knew about food is turned on its head? A dinner where the tyranny of taste is cut down to size by elevating the role of touch, smell, sight, and sound? An evening where waiters waltz around the room, spraying perfume onto the nape of your neck as you listen to jazz and nibble at "Chicken stuffed with ball bearings" or "Blood clots in broth"? If you are unsure of what this all means, whether it is absurdist theatre, something vaguely political, or some kind of practical joke, then welcome to a Futurist dinner.

Filippo Tommaso Marinetti was the founder of the Italian Futurist movement and is best known as the author of *La cucina futurista* ("The Futurist Cookbook," 1932). Like many Italians, Marinetti was immensely frustrated with the shortcomings of unification, which had failed to deliver on its promises. Northern and southern Italy were further apart than ever, and Italy as a whole was still shackled to its past. This conundrum vexed Marinetti: why could Italy not move beyond its past and embrace the future? It did not take Marinetti long to pinpoint whom he perceived to be the culprits: the bourgeoisie. It was the conservatives and their love of *L'Artusi* who had a stranglehold on Italy.

To Marinetti and his like-minded Futurists, *L'Artusi* epitomized everything that had gone wrong with food *and* Italy. The last thing Marinetti was interested in was Artusi's wooden spoon, a symbol that (in his mind) bound Italy to its past. He wanted to dive straight into a future filled with modern technology like fast cars and sleek airplanes. "Artusi's day is over," wrote Marinetti with his typical bravado.[46]

Italian Futurists wholeheartedly embraced anchovies, largely in recognition of their shock value when combined with contradictory ingredients—like pineapple. This was all part of their greater goal of disrupting Italian foodways, and in the process, remaking the state itself. What better way to tip Italian culinary customs upside down than by elevating the humble anchovy to new prominence in Italian cuisine?

Anchovies even feature in a number of Futurist cocktails, such as the aptly named "Great Waters." With equal amounts of grappa, gin, kümmel (distilled from aniseed and cumin), and anise liquor, the drink is garnished with a small, floating wafer topped with a layer of anchovy paste. Perhaps it was meant to tingle the taste buds and infuse one with the possibilities of the future? Or perhaps not. That is the thing with Futurists; you could never be sure if they were hinting at some larger ideal, or if the joke was on you.

The Futurist Cookbook presents itself as an absurd joke, a charade meant to shake up staid bourgeois society during the Fascist and interwar period. But behind its whimsical recipes and flights of fancy lies a bedrock of more sinister ideals. There were two sides to Marinetti: the man intoxicated with absurdity and artistic expression, and the man infatuated with war and violence, which spoke to him of new possibilities for the Italian state. Only with the benefit of hindsight does it become evident that *The Futurist Cookbook* was closely aligned with a darker vision for the future, one linked to Benito Mussolini and Fascism. The goals of Futurism were sometimes even tucked away inside obscure dishes, as in this recipe for a Futurist antipasto:

Intuitive Antipasto

(formula by Signora Colombo-Fillìa)

Hollow out an orange to form a little basket in which are placed different kinds of salami, some butter, some pickled mushrooms, anchovies and green peppers. The basket perfumes the various elements with orange. Inside the peppers are hidden little cards printed with a Futurist phrase or surprising saying (for example: "Futurism is an anti-historical movement"—"Live dangerously"—"With Futurist cooking, doctors, pharmacists and grave diggers will be out of work," etc.).[47]

Professor Carol Helstosky writes eloquently about the different trajectories of Artusi and Marinetti and their impacts upon Italian cuisine. Artusi went on to become a beloved figure in Italy, a man whose cookbook could be found in every kitchen and who came to be considered the father of traditional Italian cuisine. "Marinetti, on the other hand," she points out, "died alone and forgotten in Bellagio in 1944."[48]

In and out of favor: flavor-filled anchovies in twentieth-century Italy

Italy in the twentieth century was something of a rollercoaster for anchovies. For the first half of the century, anchovies were incorporated enthusiastically into a host of dishes across all social classes, but as the country became more prosperous, anchovies were sidelined in favor of meat, dairy, and the convenience of prepackaged foods. But just when all seemed lost, and anchovies were on the verge of falling off the culinary radar, Italy rediscovered its "traditional" ingredients, and anchovies found their way back into kitchen cupboards.

The beginning of the anchovy's carnival ride commenced with the rise of Italy's National Fascist Party and Mussolini's iron grip on all levers of government. While most Italians had managed to scrape through World War I with just enough food on the table, the interwar and World War II periods saw them going to bed hungry every night. Under Mussolini and his misguided policies, Italy prioritized territorial expansion over domestic needs, and the country slid into economic ruin and food scarcity. Enter the anchovy, the magical ingredient that could inject a rare spark of flavor into otherwise bland and monotonous meals. Take chickpeas, for example. While many had no choice but to eat them plain, perhaps seasoned with a little salt, garlic, and oil, those who could slip an anchovy into the mix were treated to a far tastier dish. Anchovies similarly added some spark to the diets of fieldworkers in the southern region of Potenza, who would snack on dried peppers stuffed with small pieces of anchovy and fried in a smidgen of oil.

In more bourgeois circles, Ada Boni's *Il talismano della felicità* ("The Talisman of Happiness," 1929) provides a snapshot of Italy's diverse regional dishes. "Eggs Florentine style," "Eels Genoa style," and "Pork chops Modena style"—all of which contain anchovies—helped to stitch the country together through food. Some of Boni's anchovy recipes can be traced back to earlier eras. Her "Stuffed tomatoes with breadcrumbs," for example, is nearly identical to Vincenzo Corrado's recipe, written over 150 years earlier. Boni's version calls for a stuffing of anchovies, basil, parsley, garlic, olive oil, bread, salt, pepper, and a quarter teaspoon of sugar. Aside from substituting basil for Corrado's oregano (basil was a relatively late addition to the Italian culinary canon) and adding sugar, they are fundamentally the same recipe.

Boni included over seventy-five recipes with anchovies in her cookery book, sometimes in novel ways. Her recipe for "Filet of cod devil style" calls for a fillet of cod to be smeared with an entire tube of anchovy paste, left to marinate for an hour, rolled up and secured with a toothpick, and then fried in oil. This is one of the earliest recipes to use anchovy paste in a tube, a leisure option that speaks to a certain class.

Despite Boni's extravagant use of anchovy paste, most Italians made do with far less. With the advent of World War II, as food became increasingly hard to source, many relied on the black market. It was a disorientating time, and as David Gilmour notes, the joke within and outside Italy was that "on 25 July 1943—the day Mussolini was arrested by the king—the Italian people had gone to bed as fascists and woken up as anti-fascists."[49] Regardless of political orientation, the war was indiscriminate in cleaning out Italy's cupboards. In the wake of Mussolini's removal, the Italian government surrendered, and the Allies eventually drove the Germans out of the country. To keep Italy within the Allies' sphere of influence and curtail the ambitions of the Soviet Union within Europe, huge amounts of aid were funneled to Italy via the American funding initiative known as the Marshall Plan.

Anchovies doomed as economy booms

With a new system of governance in place and funds flowing in from the West, the following decade saw the economy positively explode. It became known as *Il miracolo economico*—the Italian economic miracle. By the late 1950s, the country had transformed from a stagnating, mostly rural nation into an industrial powerhouse. The Canadian historian David Gentilcore illustrates the transformation with reference to refrigerator manufacturing. "In 1951, Italy produced just 18,500," he writes, "but six years later the figure was 370,000, and by 1967 Italy was producing 32 million, making Italy the third largest producer of refrigerators, after the United States and Japan."[50] Most of the industrialization occurred in the north of the country, which triggered a multi-decade-long mass migration, as poor southerners decamped for the greener fields (and industrial factories) of the Po Valley. Wages in the north and in urban centers were double what could be made on a farm.

The publication of *Il cucchiaio d'argento* ("The Silver Spoon") in 1950 was timed perfectly to coincide with the emergence of a middle class that could occasionally partake in more ambitious culinary fare. The title of the book played upon their aspirations, as one of the most expensive gifts a bride could hope to receive on her wedding day was a spoon made of pure silver. Alberto Capatti and Massimo Montanari call it "the first important cookbook of the postwar years," and its eleven editions render it Italy's equivalent of the American cookery bible, Irma S. Rombauer's *The Joy of Cooking*.[51] While *Il cucchiaio d'argento* was ostensibly about moving past subsistence and into the realm of affluence, many of its recipes were quite simple and drawn from two earlier cookbooks produced by the same publisher. By incorporating a range of modest middle-class recipes and coupling them with more extravagant fare, the publisher hit the culinary jackpot: a coveted cookbook that every new bride hoped to receive.

One dish that had been around the block—both Artusi and Ada Boni included recipes for it—was the Piedmontese speciality *Vitello Tonnato* (veal with a tuna sauce). The pairing of milk-fed veal with tuna and anchovies mixed into a sort of mayonnaise-style sauce, makes little sense on paper but is quite extraordinary on the plate. *Vitello Tonnato* was traditionally eaten by those with means, as its ingredients kept it out of reach for most. But with its publication in *Il cucchiaio d'argento*, it reached a wider audience. Another dish with more aspirational airs is sturgeon with an anchovy sauce, variations of which go all the way back to the Renaissance.

Some of the simpler recipes in *Il cucchiaio d'argento* also reach back into Italy's past. One recipe, for example, adds a little garlic and chili pepper to Giovanni Battista Ratto's 1863 instructions for "Broccoli dragged through salted anchovies," thereby transforming the dish at very little cost. Another simple recipe with deep roots in the past is "Scorzonera [black salsify] with anchovies." This gnarled, charcoal-colored root is native to southern Europe, where is has been consumed since the Roman era. It has a wonderfully gothic appearance—sure to appeal to surly teenagers and curmudgeons of all ages—but when peeled, it reveals a creamy white stalk that pairs perfectly with the briny zing of anchovies. Olive oil, capers, white wine, vinegar, and the all-critical anchovy are sautéed and then poured over the boiled stalks for an immensely satisfying side dish.

Explosive economic growth after the war led to changing consumption patterns, with consequences for anchovies. With more disposable income at the end of each week, Italians could now afford a little more to eat, and one of the first things they bought was meat, a cherished source of umami that everyone lusted after. From the post-World War II period to the 1980s, Italian meat consumption increased by a staggering 400 percent per capita. During the same period, sales of dairy products also rose dramatically, with cheese leading the way, followed by milk. Sugar became a national obsession, and its consumption rose over 300 percent. Portion sizes also increased; never had so much food been served on so many different tables. By the end of the 1960s, the average caloric intake had increased by over one third. This matched the rest of Europe, an astounding feat for a country that was traditionally in last place.

As Italians of all stripes reveled in the riches of meat, dairy, and other earthly delights, they also started to pull back from those foods that reminded them of darker times. In his article "Temporal Trends in Wine and Food Consumption in Italy," Francesco Cipriani notes a substantial decrease in the consumption of traditionally low-ranked foods in the 1970s. Onions, cabbages, potatoes, legumes, brown breads, and, most importantly for our discussion, dried fish like anchovies, had sustained the poor for generations. "Even if the available details are insufficient," Cipriani writes, "one can easily hypothesize that during the change towards Metropolitan lifestyles during the 1950s and 1960s, as well as abandoning their cold farmsteads without running water ... there was also a strong temptation to abandon the 'poor' flavours of food items that were all too familiar."[52] In this context, it is easy to see how anchovies had worn out their welcome, as they were commonly associated with hardship. As soon as folks started making more money, they looked for a new dance partner. Meat and fowl, as well as butter and cream, were just a few of the long-desired ingredients that caught their eye.

Another thing that caught their eye was pizza.

Would you like anchovies on that?

From its lofty perch as one of the most beloved fast foods around the world, it is surprising to learn that for most of its history pizza was a scorned dish, deemed suitable only for the poverty-stricken hordes that lived in the city of Naples. Neapolitans did not "invent" pizza, as flat breads with toppings go all the way back to the Romans, Greeks, and arguably the Egyptians and Mesopotamians. However, Neapolitans still deserve some credit as they brought about significant changes in the types of toppings, the various combinations of them, and how the dough was shaped.

The earliest version of Neapolitan pizza consisted of flat bread topped with small amounts of garlic, lard, and salt. These bare bones "pizzas" proved immensely popular among the poor, most of whom lacked proper kitchen facilities. By the early 1600s, pizza was being sold all over the city by vendors with portable carts, and the poor flocked to them. It was survival food that tasted great, regularly eaten for breakfast, lunch, and dinner. If they could afford to splurge, they might purchase a pizza smeared across the top with tiny fish in their larval stage of development. These juvenile fish, known as *cecenietti*, were the cheapest fish in the marketplace, but they brought heaps of flavor and a little protein to an otherwise dreary diet. It was these flat breads covered with immature fish that likely served as the forerunner to what eventually became the anchovy pizza.

By the early 1700s, pizza was thoroughly established in Naples, with new toppings like cheese and tomato becoming huge hits. Pizzerias sprang up in shopfronts and became immensely popular at this time, and they even managed to entice some of the merchant classes to their premises. Thinly sliced pieces of dried meat sparingly sprinkled on top proved irresistible for those with deeper pockets. But most of the urban poor could only dream of such meaty decadence.

Despite the enthusiastic embrace of pizza by Neapolitans, it was either unknown or completely rejected by their fellow countrymen from other regions, as it was by travelers who spent time in the city. Visiting in 1831, Samuel Morse (of later Morse code and telegraph fame), wrote derisively that pizza was "nauseating" and that it "was covered over with slices of pomodoro [tomatoes] and sprinkled with little fish and black pepper and I know not what other ingredients, it altogether looks like a piece of bread that had been taken reeking out of the sewer."[53]

In 1886, another author also had it in for pizza, but this time, anchovies were specifically part of the problem. He is most well known for writing *The Adventures of Pinocchio* under the pseudonym Carlo Collodi, but Carlo Lorenzini's scorn for pizza would certainly have given him a second career as an angry restaurant critic: "The blackened aspect of the toasted crust, the whitish sheen of garlic and anchovy, the greenish-yellow tint of the oil and fried herbs, and the bits of red from the tomato here and there give pizza the appearance of complicated filth that matches the dirt of the vendor."[54]

Despite the ridicule heaped upon it by travelers and Naples' upper classes, the poor embraced pizza with a degree of enthusiasm that is truly astonishing. It would take another 150 years, however, before the rest of Italy finally "discovered" pizza. Everything changed in the mid-twentieth century when the massive postwar migration of southern Italians to the rest of the country in search of work kicked into high gear. In the past, when a *pizzaiolo* attempted to open a pizzeria in central or northern Italy, they failed miserably. None of the locals were interested, and customers from the south were few and far between. With huge increases in migration from the south, however, more and more pizzerias were opened in northern Italy. These simple trattorias were magnets for southerners who were hankering for their treasured pizza. Before long, pizzerias sprang up all over the country, and curious locals watched with bemusement as the recent arrivals lined up to buy them. Eventually, the locals dipped their toes in the water, and lo and behold, they too fell under pizza's spell.

Pizza was also nudged into wider acceptance in Italy from a far more indirect route: tourists from America. Pizza had made its way to New York with the early waves of southern Italian immigrants to the New World. As Americans visited Italy in the postwar years, restaurant owners were baffled as one tourist after another kept asking for pizza, a strange southern dish they knew little about. For restaurateurs, pizza was plebeian fare, not something you would spend good money on in a restaurant. However, as requests continued to pour in from enthusiastic tourists with fat wallets, pizza found its way onto more menus. As Karima Moyer-Nocchi notes, "Suddenly, there was money to be made from the pizza trade. A lot of money, in fact."[55]

This phenomenon led to the "pizza effect" that helped once reluctant Italians to open up and give it a go. The "pizza effect" refers to the process of "re-enculturation," whereby a once poorly regarded product is exported to the world at large, finds success, and is then reintroduced back home with a brand new, elevated status.[56] When pizza eventually achieved acceptance in the United States, Italians back home took notice. And one of the pizzas they started eating from one end of the country to the other was the classic from Naples—anchovy pizza.

Fast food like pizza was just one indication of Italy's changing foodways. By the 1960s and early 1970s, preprepared and processed food transformed Italy into a very different country than even just a generation before. On the plus side, industrial agriculture produced huge increases in crop yields, and for the first time the country had enough food to feed all its citizens. Profits also increased, thanks to the commodification of the food supply at the hand of multinational food conglomerates. With so much money at stake, marketing departments kicked into overdrive and repackaged Italy's culinary past, emphasizing authenticity and abundance. Food labels became rife with references to "tradition," while advertising campaigns featured dinner tables piled high with a veritable cornucopia of fruit, meat, fish, and vegetables.

Nostalgia for an imaginary past proved highly lucrative, as Moyer-Nocchi points out, and everyone got in on the act.[57] Restaurateurs revised their menus to emphasize their "time-honored" recipes and "genuine" cooking. Diners wanted a traditionally cooked meal, especially one prepared just like *nonna* did back in the day (even if *nonna* could never have afforded half the ingredients with which these dishes were now prepared). Almost every facet of Italy's culinary past was mythologized and painted in the rosy glow of tradition. Picture elderly *nonnas* lovingly crafting meals from scratch for their extended families, while rural workers on bucolic farms pick vine-ripened produce to be transported to a traditional "Antica Osteria." It is a wonderful image, even if in reality *nonna* is napping in the back room with the television blaring, the fields are regularly sprayed with fertilizers and pesticides, the farm workers are mostly eastern European (in the north) or African (in the south), and the restaurant cooks are just as likely to be from Bangladesh as Italy.

Still, all this mythologizing and nostalgia meant that traditional peasant fare was accorded a new degree of respect. Recipes that once called for only a few ingredients out of necessity, like beans with a sprig of wild rosemary, a pinch of salt, and a little piece of anchovy, were now celebrated as representing an authentic taste of the past. Scrapbooks that consisted of a few meager recipes and only a line or two of spartan directions were dutifully handed down from mother to daughter. Such simple and rustic dishes came to be regarded as unique aspects of one's heritage. Over time, even the humblest polenta acquired a patina of distinction.

All this nostalgia boded well for anchovies. One dish from the past that enjoyed a revival was the traditional Roman favorite, "Spring lamb with anchovies," cooked *alla cacciatora* and seasoned with just a few simple herbs like rosemary and sage. Journalist and cookbook author Katie Parla notes that the dish is a reminder of an earlier era when shepherds tended their flocks not just in the foothills surrounding Rome, but also on the streets that ran through the city center.[58] In a similar manner, "bagna càuda" transports us to an earlier era when the warm dip was served to workers on cold mornings before they headed out to the fields. Nowadays, it is more often eaten in the evenings, perhaps accompanied by a glass of wine before dinner. But the memories linger, as do the robust flavors of anchovies, garlic, butter, and olive oil.

Anchovies also made a comeback in more upscale dishes. In northern Italy, around Milan, one hugely popular dish was "Ossobuco alla Milanese" prepared with anchovies. To create this age-old favorite, veal shanks are slowly braised in beef stock and wine and then topped with a vibrant sauce, reminiscent of dishes that have been popular in Italy since the Renaissance. Called "Gremolada alla Milanese," the sauce consists of garlic, parsley, lemon zest, and anchovies. Another recipe with deep roots that found a new audience was "Rabbit stew with anchovies." Each city and region in Italy has its own version, but Liguria's is one of the most elaborate. It starts off with a sofrito of carrots, onions, and celery, to which pine nuts, walnuts, sometimes almonds, and even occasionally hazelnuts are added, along with anchovies, capers, black olives, rabbit, and a few other odds and ends. This is a rich, almost courtly dish, which reminds us that anchovies have long been mixing it up with meat in Italy.

During the 1990s, anchovies were also awarded the seal of approval of Slow Food, a hugely influential organization that was the brainchild of Carlo Petrini. Outraged at the unchecked spread of fast-food culture in Italy (including the opening of a McDonald's restaurant in the historic district of Rome), Petrini founded Slow Food in the late 1980s in an attempt to preserve Italy's traditional foodways. By advocating artisanal as opposed to industrially produced food, the Slow Food movement is dedicated to reinvigorating traditional farming practices, with the goal of recognizing that food is more than just a mere commodity. Petrini argues that food is a way of life, bringing important questions to the conversation about the relationship of food to identity, nutrition, and economics. In his opinion, food is political, and eating is a political act. Petrini is right, of course, but critics point out that there seems to be a disconnect between the organization's lofty goals and the more pedestrian concerns of roughly half the world's population who do not have enough to eat. When artisanal Italian lentils cost up to five times the price of their industrially grown counterparts, the politics of food meets the pocketbook.

Criticisms aside, the Slow Food movement was instrumental in bringing back an awareness of how artisanal products can express a sense of place, of *terroir*, and how that in turn contributes to the well-being of society and the planet. And what could be more artisanal, more traditional, than slow-cured anchovies? The Slow Food movement champions anchovies from the Amalfi Coast, especially those from the village of Cetara, where the ancient fishing technique known as "*menaica*" is still practiced. These anchovies are hand-caught in traditional nets each evening, and by dawn, are sold to artisanal producers who batch cure them for up to nine months at a time. Along with cheese, wine, and some dried meats, anchovies put the "slow" into Slow Food. On the Slow Food website, one of the more intriguing recipes is "Sicilian anchovies in lettuce" (*mesculine'na lattuga*). Boiled lettuce leaves are combined with anchovies, garlic, breadcrumbs, capers, almonds, pecorino cheese, and lemon zest. You can almost taste the vibrant flavors just by reading the recipe.

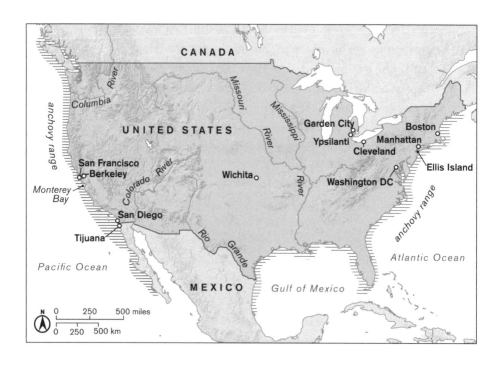

6

THE AMERICAN ANCHOVY

INCHING TOWARDS ACCEPTANCE

This epic dive into the history of anchovies has so far explored their journey through several European countries, but anchovies did not stop there. As immigrants began to populate the New World, they brought their gastronomic traditions with them. For some, anchovies became a comforting reminder of home. Yet curiously, aside from a few pockets of mostly southern European immigrants, Anglo-Americans in the eighteenth and nineteenth centuries never took a shine to anchovies—a story of America's abundance and missed opportunities. Upmarket gastronomic trends in the twentieth century brought anchovies some favor with the public, but even to this day, Americans do not consume them with the same enthusiasm as their European counterparts. Fortunately, today the tide is turning. As more Americans are looking to challenge their palates and eat more sustainably, the humble anchovy has started to get the recognition it rightfully deserves.

French food: fashionable or too fiddly?

At the turn of the twentieth century, the United States was the preeminent economic power in the world. The Spanish–American War of 1898, which Secretary of State John Milton Hay referred to as a "splendid little war," positioned the United States for what would become known as the "American Century."[1] Cities like New York were expanding at an unprecedented pace, with skyscrapers reaching unimaginable heights, fueled by waves of immigrant labor and unbridled optimism. With the price of real estate rising and the stock market starting to shake off decades of inactivity, the rich were suddenly getting a whole lot richer. But for all their newfound wealth, many New Yorkers were still a tad insecure when it came to taste and manners. No matter how thick their purses, many still felt like country bumpkins at heart: financially rich but culturally poor. Paris, the "City of Light," came to represent all things refined and civilized: manners, fashion, and especially food.

The best French restaurant in New York City at the turn of the century was Delmonico's. Originally opened in 1837, Delmonico's was widely considered to be the first restaurant to hit the high-water mark of fine dining in America. Its menu drew heavily on all the French favorites: a *fricandeau of veal with spinach* could be had for 80 cents; a *terrine of de foie-gras* cost $1; and a *vol-au-vent*, first perfected by Antonin Carême, would set you back $1.75. Duck was the most popular roasted meat on the menu in 1898, in five different forms, while lamb, beef, and mutton were also well represented. In addition to these more substantial offerings, one could begin a meal with "Anchovies on toast" for the hefty sum of 40 cents. *Hors d'oeuvres* like anchovy toast were trendy and upper crust, both things that New Yorkers (and Americans) desperately wanted to be at the dawn of the twentieth century (Fig. 6.1).

Fig. 6.1: Delmonico's, at the intersection of Beaver and William Streets in downtown New York City, circa 1893. At what was considered one of the swankiest restaurants in North America, the start of a grand meal often commenced with a stiff drink and an anchovy toast.

While many urban elites (mostly white, Anglo-Saxon, and Christian) first encountered anchovy toast in upscale restaurants like Delmonico's, for the middling classes (and those aspiring to them), their first exposure was more likely to have been through a cookbook. One that was enormously influential was *The Boston Cooking-School Cook Book* (1896) by Fannie Farmer. Considered to be the first of its kind in America, with clear directions and precise measurements, it was an instant success that introduced a generation of American housewives to the anchovy *canapé* (a fancy way of saying anchovy toast). Farmer often borrowed from the best, and her anchovy *canapé* recipe comes courtesy of Escoffier. Escoffier put anchovy butter directly on top of bread, and then added anchovy fillets and chopped egg whites and yolk. Farmer followed suit, but in an act of culinary daring, she also piped a border of anchovy butter around the edge.

While this is a classic-style *canapé*, some of the recipes in Farmer's cookbook are more elaborate, such as "Mock crab canapés" (taken from *Mrs. Curtis's Cookbook* of 1909). When blended with other ingredients, anchovies often functioned as a fishy stand-in to replace or "mock" more costly seafoods:

Mock Crab Canapés
½ cup grated cheese
4 tbsp creamed butter
½ tsp salt
½ tsp paprika
½ tsp mustard
1 tsp anchovy paste
1 tsp vinegar
2 tbsp chopped olives
To cheese add butter, salt, paprika, mustard, paste, vinegar, and chopped olives. Spread between rounds of white bread.[2]

The canapé *from cocktail party to Prohibition … and back again*

Anchovies had a platform, but what really launched them in America was the cocktail party. Even though the origins of this social gathering are hotly debated, one thing is clear: Americans took to it with a vengeance. While cocktail parties relieved hostesses of the burden of preparing a formal meal, they were not completely off the hook. All those cocktails made with eighty-proof alcohol required some sustenance to get the revelers through the rest of evening. *Hors d'oeuvres* were the obvious answer, and for every crazy new cocktail there was an equally exotic new *hors d'oeuvre*. The convenience of anchovy fillets packed in oil meant that hostesses no longer had to soak, debone, and clean anchovies prior to serving. All they had to do was open a tin, and they were good to go. What started as an elite affair was quickly adopted lower down the social strata. As the 5 o'clock tipple became standard, so did the accompanying *hors d'oeuvres*. *Canapés* were particularly popular with practical-minded Americans, because one hand could hold the toast-and-topping while the other held the drink, a no-nonsense, two-fisted approach to socializing whose popularity has never waned.

Just as the cocktail party with its fancy anchovy *canapés* was gaining momentum, the arrival of Prohibition in 1920 threatened to derail it. Yet, in a curious twist that undermined the intentions of the prohibitionists, making alcohol illegal backfired. What could be more alluring than the clandestine consumption of a forbidden substance? Production of spirits skyrocketed, and speakeasies cropped up like a pox. Located in basements and tucked far away from the prying eyes of the law, speakeasies for the most part were improvised bars that could pop up overnight and be gone by the weekend. Whether it was cocktail party drinks in an elegant salon, or bootleg booze hastily swilled in a seedy bar, people required nibbles to keep them from getting flat-out hammered. Once again, *hors d'oeuvres* were the solution. Anchovy *canapés* were particularly beloved by speakeasy owners, as their salty bite kept customers coming back for more liquid refreshment. The more they drank, the more *canapés* were offered, until everyone was well into their cups, to use a favored term of the era.

While speakeasy patrons were drinking and listening to the latest craze called "jazz," at the "dry" end of society anchovies were served to Calvin Coolidge, the thirtieth president of the United States, at a dinner held in his honor at the Waldorf

Astoria Hotel, Manhattan, on February 12, 1924. The menu began with anchovy *canapés* and the ubiquitous fresh celery and olives—two "must-haves" at any social gathering. Interestingly, the most notable dish served that night was the Waldorf salad, a particularly American concoction consisting of fresh celery, green apples, and walnuts, all dressed in mayonnaise. The creator of the Waldorf salad was not a chef but the legendary *maître d'hôtel* of the Waldorf Astoria, Oscar Tschirky.

Tschirky had capitalized on his association with the hotel by publishing a massive 900-page cookbook titled *The Cookbook by "Oscar" of the Waldorf* in 1896, that contained not only his famed "Waldorf salad" but also a variety of different *hors d'oeuvres* and *canapés* featuring anchovies, a nod to their growing popularity in the United States. He championed bold flavors in his *canapés*, pairing anchovies with other salt-cured foods like capers, olives, or even their old rival, sardines. He not only used them as co-stars, but also as the main feature, as in his dainty anchovy butter sandwiches. Perhaps unsurprisingly, anchovies featured most prominently in his salads, such as "Anchovy salad," "Chicken salad," "Dutch salad," "French salad," "Japanese salad," "Russian salad," "Salmon salad," and "Truffle salad." By cleverly sneaking an anchovy or two into these recipes, Tschirky ramped up their flavor without anyone being the wiser.

By the time Prohibition ended in 1933, *hors d'oeuvres* were practically mainstream in both good and bad ways. Some of the *hors d'oeuvres* in Irma S. Rombauer's *The Joy of Cooking* (1931) illustrate how a practical American approach, eschewing any fancy footwork, could sometimes lead to peculiar flavor combinations:

Anchovy pickles

Wrap:

Small pickles

with:

Anchovies[3]

While the haiku-like efficiency of Rombauer's directions is praise-worthy, from a practical perspective, it leaves one hanging: sweet or sour pickles? To be fair, it is unlikely to have really mattered, as anything that provided a modicum of sustenance after the second or third Martini would have been a success. No less curious is her recipe for "Peanut butter and bacon rolls," a finger food presumably designed for an inebriated crowd. Rombauer, too, used anchovies to spice up her salad recipes. For example, her "Anchovy and beet dressing" includes chopped beets, hard-boiled eggs, bitter greens like Belgian endive, and anchovies combined with French dressing. She also included an "Anchovy sauce for spaghetti," a basic tomato-based sauce with anchovies. It was these kinds of simple, economical, and delicious meals that made her cookbook a beloved mainstay of the American kitchen.

By 1940, Americans had long recovered from the Prohibition, and cocktail parties once again became an American institution. In the words of chef and cookbook author James Beard, the cocktail party "brings forth the best, and sometimes the worst, in all of us."[4] In his book, *Hors D'Oeuvre and Canapés* (1940), Beard guided the reader through the art of a cocktail party, presenting a vast assortment of tasty finger foods. Fifteen of those recipes rely on anchovies. They range from the well-known "Anchovy allumettes" and "Anchovy canapés," to the more laborious and obscure "Anchovied chicken liver." However, a true gourmand like Beard knew that an uncomplicated *hors d'oeuvre* is sometimes best:

> With our simple drinks in front of the fire, there is always a tray with a choice morsel of cheese, perhaps, and some anchovies fresh from the can or bottle, some fresh, green, crisp tidbit such as the first green onions of the season, or a bit of succulent fenuchi [fennel?], or some superb celery ... Each morsel is delicious and stimulating to the appetite, for it is flavored with good will and love and understanding.[5]

When *Gourmet* magazine came out with *The Gourmet Cookbook* Volume I (1950) and Volume II (1957), it seemed that anchovies had secured their place in the American food scene. But as culinary history would show, it was their swansong for the next three decades. Volume I of *The Gourmet Cookbook* was a massive undertaking, with over 2,000 recipes, 93 technicolor photographs, and perhaps the most enthusiastic, elegant writing ever to grace an American cookbook. Much of this enthusiasm was geared towards France, which, as the publisher underscored, was home to "probably the greatest national cuisine the world has ever known."[6] While contemporary audiences may beg to differ, French food completely dominated fine-dining discourse in 1950s America. Journalist Emily Green notes that owning *The Gourmet Cookbook* defined you "as a person of great sophistication," and that they "promised a kind of fine mischief, beckoning us from familiar foods into worlds of untold glamour." The chapter on *hors d'oeuvres* "opens with the lip-smacking declaration: 'To begin at the beginning, note this: every meal deserves a good start.'"[7] And what better way to start a sophisticated meal than with one of the twenty-two different anchovy *hors d'oeuvres*, such as the seductively named "Anchovy cocktail kisses"?

Ketchup in America: nothing fishy, something sweet

Curiously, Americans have never taken to cured anchovies or anchovy-based ketchup and condiments quite like the British. We can hazard a guess as to why, and it centers around the particular food pathways that anchovies occupied in Britain and how they carried over to America. In Britain, whole salted anchovies were always an imported food from the Mediterranean and the Bay of Biscay, and as such, they carried a certain cachet. For those who could afford the occasional treat, eating whole salted anchovies accompanied by a pint or two of ale was something to look forward to. One is reminded of Samuel Pepys who eagerly consumed them at every opportunity. For those who could rarely afford meat or fowl, an anchovy or two added to a ketchup, porridge, or soup was a cost-effective way to introduce a little umami into an otherwise drab meal.

While British immigrants to America in the eighteenth and nineteenth centuries took many culinary cues from their homeland, in America they were able to consume meat and fish in proportions that were unimaginable back home. Part of America's allure was the dream of eating meat and fish on a regular basis. Why bother with a costly and imported salted anchovy when American meat and fish were plentiful and cheap and provided all the umami that was needed? Historian Roger Horowitz notes that immigrants were continually stunned at how much meat was available in America, and he cites one letter written in 1840 to relatives back in the British Isles that read, "I eat meat every day," to which the response back to him was: "It can't be true."[8]

The abundance of affordable fresh meat, fowl, and all kinds of large fish in American markets left little need for the diminutive anchovy as a flavor enhancer. Also, as an imported food, salted anchovies were expensive and hard to source outside of big cities. Ketchup was one casualty of the American indifference towards anchovies. In her wildly successful cookbook, *The Virginia House-Wife* (1824), Mary Randolph lists five different kinds of ketchup—mushroom, walnut, oyster, and two kinds of tomato—with not a single anchovy in sight. Of her fifteen recipes for sauces, the only one that contains anchovies is the familiar sounding "Fish sauce to keep a year." In fact, it is the only recipe in the entire cookbook to feature anchovies. Rather tellingly, it was lifted, practically verbatim, from Charlotte Mason's *The Lady's Assistant* of 1777.

While anchovy-based ketchup failed to take hold in the United States, tomato-based versions proved all the rage. The earliest printed recipe for a tomato ketchup was written by the American James Mease, and no anchovies were included. Mary Randolph also left anchovies out of the mix, with only tomatoes, salt, onions, mace, and black pepper gracing her recipe. This ketchup differed markedly from its fishier British cousins across the Atlantic.

American-style tomato ketchup continued to evolve into a thicker, sweeter, and tangier sauce, thanks to the addition of copious amounts of molasses and vinegar. As the linguist Dan Jurafsky notes, by the 1850s, anchovies had practically disappeared from every kind of ketchup produced in America.[9] The H. J. Heinz Company exemplified this trend in 1876 with their now world-famous brand of ketchup, which lacks any anchovies. By adding ample amounts of sweeteners, the shift from savory to sweet ketchup was complete, and the company created a condiment that dominated the market. In time, it would become the national condiment, as American as apple pie.

Italians in America: adapting old cuisine to new conditions

The story of the Italian anchovy's emergence in America at the turn of the twentieth century is like that of a late blooming child: while the potential for success was there all along, it took far longer than anyone anticipated. Although well-to-do Americans were happily eating anchovies as *hors d'oeuvres* at cocktail parties and fancy French restaurants, decades would pass before Italian American cuisine lured Americans into its wonderful world of anchovies. We pick up the story at the turn of the twentieth century, when hundreds of Italian migrants were arriving at Ellis Island every day. For most of these unskilled Italian laborers, the surest way of making a buck in America was to enter the food industry. Since they worked for less pay than many Americans were willing to accept, most immigrants eventually found work, however unsavory or backbreaking it may have been.

Regardless of which part of Italy they came from, one thing that all Italian immigrants had in common was their love of regional dishes from their homeland. While immigrants in diasporas everywhere are emotionally attached to traditional foodways, Italians are often reputed to be even more so. Ironically, for many Italians in this wave of immigration, this was the first time they had the buying power to partake in the traditions of their country fully and regularly, and thus the Italian American table became famous for its abundance—a demonstration that they were living the dream. Traditional dishes also started to change shape, due to the interweaving of Italian regional styles, additions and substitutions based on the availability of foodstuffs, and the influence of American and other cuisines.

One product of this new Italian American cuisine was tomato sauce. As the writer June Sohn notes, Italian American tomato sauces had a completely different character from those made back in Italy.[10] When a poor *paesano* made a tomato sauce in southern Italy, for instance, the plum tomato was king. Its thin skin and minimal seeds were critical in a land where firewood was scarce, and cooking times were short. Tomato sauces made from plum tomatoes required little more than a dash of salt, perhaps a little onion or garlic, and a quick sauté to reach their destination. By contrast, in the late nineteenth and early twentieth centuries on the East Coast of the United States, the most popular tomato varieties were the Paragon and Acme, both of which were considered the most flavorful tomatoes of their day. But these bad boys had super thick skins and were full of seeds, characteristics that required extensive cooking to break them down. Another difference concerned the quantities of ingredients. Now that

Italians had access to all of America's abundance, sugar, salt, oregano, onion, garlic, olive oil, and perhaps even some celery, were all regularly added in amounts that would have made a *nonna* back in the old country roll her eyes in disbelief.

Italian Americans came to embrace these so-called "red sauces" to a degree that Italians back in Italy would have found mystifying. In the "land of plenty," everything was fair game for a lusty red sauce. Whether it was meat, fowl, fish, or vegetables, a heaped ladleful of red sauce was thought to complete all kinds of dishes. Red sauce was so popular that it was even thought—only half in jest—to improve one's love life. One iconic dish created during this period was "spaghetti and meatballs," swimming in a sea of red sauce. While a similar dish may have already existed in some parts of Italy, the way it was smothered in red sauce was very Italian American. For recent arrivals who had fantasized about meat and pasta for years, this dish was nothing short of heaven on earth. Even better, if they lacked a wife (which most men did), "spaghetti and meatballs" could be found in any tavern on Bleecker Street.

Anchovies enter restricted waters

Reviewing newspaper articles and restaurant menus from the early twentieth century, one is hard-pressed to find mention of an anchovy. There are loads of references to all kinds of meat, fowl, fish, and seafood, but anchovies are practically non-existent. This can be explained in part by looking at the evolution of Italian American restaurants. As these became more successful in the 1920s, their food and décor were upgraded to entice the well-heeled restaurant-goer. Many of these upscale Americans were attracted to the hearty Italian American fare that was served in generous portions and had been doctored to appeal to their cautious, mainstream tastes. Anchovies would have been too distinct and assertive for their palates. Nonetheless, the one place anchovies were still welcome was on an antipasto platter, in keeping with the ongoing trend in French *hors d'oeuvres*.

Just as the anchovy was finding itself restricted on Italian American restaurant menus, it miraculously found a new home in the Caesar salad. The origins of this dish are nearly as opaque as its dressing, but most agree that it was invented by the Italian American Caesar Cardini in 1924. Like countless immigrants before him, Caesar first set foot in America at Ellis Island. Arriving on May 1, 1913, he visited several cities before eventually settling in San Diego, where he opened a restaurant. As Prohibition drained his French-inspired restaurant of its customers (Caesar astutely followed the money, which led him to open a French restaurant), he decided to move his eatery to Tijuana to capitalize on all the Hollywood boozers who flocked south to enjoy a tipple or two. As the legend goes, one night at closing, a group of hungry Americans arrived, but the kitchen cupboards were bare. Caesar improvised with what was available, and *presto*, the Caesar salad was born. While the original recipe was not written down (hence the debate as to its ingredients), it supposedly consisted of romaine lettuce and croutons hand-mixed with a dressing made from a raw egg, Worcestershire Sauce, garlic, olive oil, Dijon mustard, Parmesan cheese, black pepper, and (depending upon the version of the story) the all-critical anchovy. As one enthusiast wrote, a Caesar salad is nearly "impossible to dislike."[11]

While the Caesar salad was slowly gaining wider acceptance, by the 1930s, Italian American restaurants had been thoroughly commodified for their mainstream clientele. Antipasti platters grew to epic proportions, as Americans expected everything to be "big." Waiters sang off key and flirted with wives, adding to the novelty of an exotic dining experience. Even the décor evolved, with evocative murals painted on the walls depicting the streets of Naples with Mount Vesuvius gently percolating, or perhaps a cherub peeing into a pond, featured in every dining room. Success begat imitators, and soon every Italian restaurant in America was following a similar formula offering the Italian experience. Perhaps the biggest drawback was that every restaurant was now serving the same repertoire of dishes. As a restaurant guide from the 1930s pointed out, New York was "full of Italian restaurants—good, bad, and indifferent—all serving the same courses of minestrone, spaghetti, ravioli, scaloppine and tortoni."[12] Writing a couple of decades later, a reviewer for *Gourmet* magazine laid the blame for the monotonous menus squarely on the shoulders of restaurant owners: "The typical Italian restaurateur," Jay Jacobs wrote, "is overly concerned with his own conception of what will and will not appeal to American tastes and what will and won't sell."[13]

Many critiques of Italian American restaurants from this era lamented how their proprietors thought they knew what white Americans wanted to eat. As the argument assumed, white Americans would have been happy to eat more interesting dishes *if only* the menu had afforded them that opportunity. But this fails to recognize what most Americans looked for in a night out at an Italian restaurant. As author and journalist John F. Mariani astutely points out, "The fact is that most Americans who went out for Italian food expected it and *wanted* it to be those entrenched clichés of Italian Americana ... all serving variations of the same dozen dishes [original emphasis]."[14] Most Americans were not looking for obscure Italian dishes with "interesting" ingredients just yet. What they wanted were the greatest hits—the fan favorites—and no one cared whether they were traditionally Italian or a hybrid creation like "veal parmigiana with a red sauce."

THE AMERICAN ANCHOVY

Industrialization leaves no place for anchovies

As America emerged from the Great Depression and entered the 1930s and 1940s, the industrialization of the food supply started to influence what housewives bought and prepared for dinner each night. This trend accelerated with the end of World War II, as mass-produced and ready-made meals became widely available, reasonably priced, and above all, were convenient. In fact, convenience was sold as one of the great benefits of modernization: a new way to purchase food (supermarkets!), prepare it (straight out of a can!), and consume it (TV dinners eaten on fold-out trays while watching your favorite show!).

Unfortunately, all this convenience and standardization did not leave much room for anchovies, which fell out of fashion and became a dated, misunderstood little fish. For middle-class housewives, why bother with a messy and strong-tasting anchovy fillet when nothing could beat the mild taste and convenience of a processed cheese ball rolled in chopped walnuts? Campbell's soup swept the nation, as did Shake 'n Bake for chicken, and the drink of every aspiring astronaut, Tang. In whatever form it came—canned, frozen, or freeze-dried—convenience and economy were central to consumer choices.

Even celery and olives got swept up in these changing consumer preferences. Hilary Sargent, writing in the *Boston Globe*, notes that for almost 200 years, celery and olives "were absolute must-haves on every traditional Thanksgiving menu."[15] They were so popular that they were featured on the menus of the finest restaurants in America. "Until," writes Sargent, "all of a sudden, they weren't."[16] With the industrialization of the American food supply, celery was no longer an exotic vegetable reserved for special occasions, as it was now available all year round. Like anchovies, it had lost its cachet.

Industrialization and standardization homogenized the flavor of food that Americans ate, and nowhere was this more apparent than with Chef Boyardee. After a successful career as head chef at the Plaza Hotel in New York City, the Italian-born immigrant Ettore Boiardi opened his own restaurant, Il Giardino d'Italia, in Cleveland, Ohio, in 1924. Diners raved about his spaghetti dinner served with his signature tomato sauce. As compliments turned into requests for the recipe, Boiardi started to sell the sauce in recycled milk bottles as a side hustle, in which anchovies were nowhere to be found. Sales took off, and in 1928, Boiardi opened a factory to produce his tomato sauce full time. He renamed his line "Chef Boyardee" so that non-Italians could pronounce "Boiardi" correctly.

While Chef Boyardee's heat-and-eat meals were a hit with housewives, what really launched his company to fame and fortune was the distribution of his precooked meals as rations for the troops during World War II. All four branches of the armed services placed huge orders for Chef Boyardee products. To keep up with the enormous demand, Boiardi's factory ran 24–7. At the peak of production, a staggering 250,000 cans rolled off the production line each day. Once the war was over, millions of troops returned home with a taste for the mildly seasoned Chef Boyardee meals. In no time at all, housewives across America were including cans of "Spaghetti and meatballs" and "Beefaroni" on their weekly shopping lists. Italian American housewives would have balked at purchasing anything in the overly bland product line. However, as Mariani points out, for most other Americans, this *was* authentic Italian food.

One mass-produced pasta "kit" that helped to sever the link between anchovies and pasta in America was Kraft's "Macaroni & Cheese." Almost immediately, it became a family favorite that was eagerly embraced in the culinarily conservative English-speaking world, from Canada to the United Kingdom to Australia. It was the perfect dish for Anglo-Americans, as it was highly processed, convenient, and marketed with the slogan,

"Make a meal for four in nine minutes."[17] Its flavor has since been likened to crack for children.

Although cookbook author Maria Gentile noted in 1919 that anchovies ranked as the third most popular ingredient in pasta sauces, by the mid-twentieth century anchovies were practically out of the game. Thanks to Kraft's "Macaroni & Cheese," Chef Boyardee, and their competitors' pasta kits and canned products, a certain conception of what pasta was all about took hold in mainstream America. Commercial food processors limited their pasta sauces to three specific kinds—cheese, tomato, or meat—with no hint of anchovies. Anchovies were deemed too "ethnic," not fit for modern Americans and their preference for mild flavors and subdued aromas. By the end of World War II, very few non-Italian Americans had even heard of an anchovy sauce, let alone eaten one with pasta.

Italian American cookbooks (or a lack thereof)

While restaurants and mass-produced pastas almost never featured anchovies, the one place you would expect to find them would be in Italian American cookbooks. But even here we are out of luck. The main problem, as Professor Donna R. Gabaccia notes, is that unlike the German, Finnish, Jewish, and Chinese immigrant groups, there were almost no cookbooks published by or for Italian immigrants in America until the 1950s. The culinary traditions of Italian immigrants were mostly transmitted orally rather than via the written word. "Most of the immigrant cooks who came to the United States regardless of their background," writes Gabaccia, "brought their recipes with them in their heads."[18]

Despite the dearth of anchovies in cookbooks and cooking pamphlets in the early twentieth century, we know that Italian Americans were eating anchovies, and lots of them. Indeed, they were sold in every Italian American corner store and could be found in every Italian American home kitchen. We also know where many of these anchovies were coming from. According to data from the Santoña customs office in Cantabria in northern Spain, in 1929 almost one third of exported anchovies were destined for the United States.* Sales to the United States were so robust in 1929 that Domenico Cefalù, a member of one of the most prominent Italian anchovy-salting families operating in northern Spain, moved to New York to capitalize on the steadily increasing market. Exports to America continued to grow, and between 1948 and 1951, they surged to an average of 30,921 kilograms of finished product per year.

Another Cefalù family operation was run by Giuseppe Cefalù Tarantino and his son Antonino, who began exporting anchovies from Spain to the United States in 1931. While almost all the anchovies exported to Italy were salted, those going to America were mostly packed in oil. Anchovies in oil were more convenient, and despite their higher price point, they were eagerly embraced by Italian Americans who could afford to pay a couple of pennies more. In Italy, salted anchovies were preferred, perhaps as much for their long tradition as for their lower cost. Housewives on a shoestring budget could purchase one or two salted anchovies at a time at their local market, as opposed to having to buy a whole tin. Not surprisingly, of the anchovies directed to the American market, the vast majority were sold to Italian Americans, with a much smaller percentage winding up in the Greek American community. Sales to Anglo-Americans were practically non-existent, apart from those to the fancy French restaurants and households that served *hors d'oeuvres*.

Giuseppe Cefalù Tarantino and Antonino decided to focus all their exports on the lucrative American market. Some of their

---

* Most of the remaining anchovies were exported to Italy.

anchovies were jointly marketed in the United States with
Antonio Cefalù—yet another member of the prolific Cefalù family—under the brand name "The Mayflower" (Fig. 6.2).

Not until the publishing boom of the 1950s did all these
Cantabrian anchovies make an appearance in cookbook recipes.
The audience for these cookbooks was somewhat surprising, and
three of these books merit a closer look. Rose L. Sorce's *The
Complete Italian Cookbook* (1953) is a combination of Italian
American and traditional Italian recipes, that lends the book a
somewhat uneven quality. One of her intentions was to show
both Italian Americans and others that despite the dismal state
of food offered in Italian American restaurants, another gustatory

Fig. 6.2: While many Italian anchovy brands marketed in the United
States appealed to Italian nationalism, like the "Garibaldi" brand that
linked itself to Italian unification, Giuseppe Cefalù Tarantino chose the
name "The Mayflower," perhaps to signal an association with the first
immigrants to America, the English pilgrims who settled in 1620. One
thing every immigrant to America had in common at that time was that
they all came by boat.[19]

world awaited them with the recipes in her book. In the foreword to the cookbook, John Ciardi elaborated:

> Unfortunately for many Americans who know Italian cookery only through the common run of Italian restaurants, this joy in a good table is not an ingredient that lends itself readily to commercial success. Thus for every Italian restaurant worthy of the name, scores of so-called Italian restaurants continue to serve boiled flour and sour tomatoes as "spaghetti," or something very like boiled cardboard and limp cheese as "pizza." The good Italian restaurant is a joy indeed, but one is not always easy to find. And unless you do find one, there is only one way to get a good Italian meal—you have to prepare it at your own or someone else's home.[20]

From this promising beginning, some of her recipes, especially the Italian American hybrids, were clearly influenced by Americans' new obsession with convenience. Worcestershire Sauce and bouillon cubes sneak into a number of them. Then, there are recipes like "Chicken supreme" whose cornflake topping appears to be directed towards the sliced-white-bread, Betty Crocker crowd. Despite these missteps, a total of thirty-two recipes in *The Complete Italian Cookbook* contain anchovies, and these are some of her most interesting. Sorce's recipes for "Spaghetti with anchovies," "Spaghetti with cauliflower," and "Spaghetti with fresh fennel" all contain anchovies and were probably served regularly in Italian American households from one end of the country to the other. But several of her recipes also show strong links to historical Italian recipes. "Mixed salad with an anchovy dressing," for example, speaks to another era, with its combination of wild herbs, dandelion greens, fennel root, vegetables, and a tangy anchovy dressing. And her recipe for "Stuffed tomatoes" is not far from Vincenzo Corrado's 1773 version: while she replaced Corrado's breadcrumb topping with rice cooked in broth, both recipes contain tomatoes, anchovies, garlic, and herbs.

Ada Boni's *The Talisman Italian Cook Book* (1950), a direct translation of the Italian version first published in 1929 in Rome, is considered one of the classic Italian cookbooks of the twentieth century. Originally intended for bourgeois housewives, it is a fascinating compendium of Italy's regional cuisines, that introduced American housewives to an entirely new kind of Old World cooking. Anchovies are sprinkled throughout the 800-plus recipes, often in unusual and interesting places. They are paired with clams in Boni's recipes for "Clam soup" and "Spaghetti vongole" and are used to enhance the flavor of every kind of vegetable, including artichokes, chicory, eggplant, mushrooms, peas, peppers, potatoes, and tomatoes. Anchovies feature in her "Bagna càuda" recipe, along with all the usual suspects (butter, olive oil, and garlic), but she also added a nice twist: thinly sliced truffles.

While *The Talisman* introduced a whole generation to authentic Italian cooking from the old country, Maria Luisa Taglienti's *The Italian Cookbook* (1955) is filled with Italian recipes modified for an Anglo-audience. It followed on the heels of Elizabeth David's highly successful and authoritative cookbooks: *A Book of Mediterranean Food* (1950), *French Country Cooking* (1951), and *Italian Food* (1954). In the first chapter of Taglienti's cookbook, titled "Hors d'oeuvres" (with "antipasti" written in parenthesis below), we find anchovies added to traditionally French dishes, such as deviled eggs, stuffed eggs, and snails. Taglienti even included French-inspired recipes such as "Maître d'hôtel butter" and "Brown chaufroid sauce," in case we are unclear which way the wind is blowing. Though clinging to the security inherent in French cuisine, Taglienti nonetheless included a number of interesting regional Italian dishes, thirty-two of which contain anchovies.

Julia Child exiles anchovies

While Italian food was struggling to gain wider acceptance, the fervor for French cuisine continued to grow, and Americans wanted more. *Mastering the Art of French Cooking* (1961), by Julia Child, Louisette Bertholle, and Simone Beck, was a timely publication that quickly became the go-to Bible for upwardly mobile middle-class Americans eager to expand their culinary horizons. Although Child and her co-authors were not the first to simplify French cooking for an American audience, they were by far the most successful at breaking down the seemingly impenetrable thicket of French terms and techniques that stymied previous cookbooks and left readers bewildered. All too often, cooking directions required an arsenal of copper pots, pans, and specialized utensils that most middle-class Americans did not possess— not to mention the fresh tarragon and obscure herbs that could not be found in local supermarkets. Within three years, not only was *Mastering the Art of French Cooking* the most successful cookbook across the country; one might even say that it integrated French food into the American foodscape.

Book sales of *Mastering the Art of French Cooking* were helped along in 1963 by Child's ground-breaking public television cooking show, *The French Chef*, which introduced the tall 6′ 2″ Californian with a patrician bearing and a mid-Atlantic accent to living rooms around the country. Between her book and her television show, Child was embraced like a long-lost relative from the good side of the family, someone with money and education. Her timing was impeccable, as French food had never been more popular; the entire country gazed in awe at the White House, where John F. Kennedy and his wife Jacqueline Kennedy (née Bouvier) dined on French food prepared by their very own French chef. America was in the midst of a French food craze, which spoke to housewives of a life beyond canned soup, frozen vegetables, and grilled steaks. Even if most middle-class men preferred their backyard barbecue and a can of beer, their wives were ready for a culinary adventure into the exotic possibilities of *boeuf bourguignon*, potatoes *au gratin*, and *vin rouge* (Fig. 6.3).

Child learned to cook at the prestigious Le Cordon Bleu cooking school in Paris in the early 1950s, just catching the last gasps of *la cuisine classique*. There she came to embrace the teachings of Escoffier and Carême, whose legacies cast a long shadow across the French gastronomic landscape. Thanks to this influential pair, *haute cuisine* had become increasingly rigid, with little room for improvisation or innovation. Escoffier in particular was regarded as the authority of *la cuisine classique*, and his recipes were treated as though they had been written in stone and carried down Mount Sinai by Moses himself. Chefs consulted his *Le Guide culinaire* like a bible, and a well-worn, dog-eared copy could be found in the kitchen of every high-end restaurant in France. But the gastronomic revolution spearheaded by Escoffier was inherently conservative and started to stagnate, defined as it was by rules and precise measurements that ensured his dishes could be replicated worldwide from Shanghai to San Francisco.

"No one revered the grand tradition more than Julia Child," writes historian Noël Riley Fitch.[21] Child's devotion to butter, cream, and the mother sauces can be traced directly back to Escoffier (her spiritual mentor). In this respect, *la cuisine classique* became the paradigm through which Child came to understand French cooking. Child lived in a world of butter and cream, and on her television show, she once remarked with a wink, "With enough butter, anything is good."[22] In case anyone had their doubts, she also said, "If you are afraid of butter, as many people are nowadays, just put in cream."[23] *Mastering the Art of French Cooking* is filled with recipes built on a foundation of butter and cream. If no butter or cream is mentioned in the recipe, they can often be found in the accompanying sauce (béchamel, hollandaise,

Fig. 6.3: Despite her formal bearing, Child had a wicked sense of humor and innately understood the recipe for a successful television cooking show: be fabulously entertaining. She laughed alongside her audience when she dropped a joint of lamb on the floor, remarking that no one would ever be the wiser. Child also enjoyed a tipple or two, and once quipped: "The best way to execute French cooking is to get good and loaded and whack the hell out of a chicken."[24] (*Courtesy of Lynn Gilbert, from* Women of Wisdom: Julia Child—in Particular Passions: Talks with Women who Have Shaped Our Times, *1981.*)

béarnaise, etc.). Flavored butters are also well represented: there are twelve different kinds, complementing several meat, fowl, and fish recipes. Every single *hors d'oeuvre* recipe includes butter or cream, but, rather portentously, not one contains an anchovy.

Granted, *Mastering the Art of French Cooking* is very much a product of 1950s French *haute cuisine*. It came out at a time when *hors d'oeuvres* with anchovies were by then few and far between in France, but were still found in some upscale American homes. In fact, it was only in southern French cooking that anchovies were used in *haute cuisine* during this period. Once again, this can be traced back to Escoffier and his codified mother sauces, which provided all the umami that was needed. Of the nine recipes that include anchovies in *Mastering the Art of French Cooking*, most are southern in origin, such as "Pissaladière," "Salad Niçoise," "Provençale style beef stew," and the intriguing "Épinards à la Basquaise" (a spinach, potato, and anchovy gratin from the Basque region of France). Aside from a couple of odds and ends, the only other recipes containing anchovies are the classics, anchovy sauce and anchovy butter.

By not including a single *hors d'oeuvre* with anchovies, Child presented a new way to approach nibbles at cocktail parties and pre-dinner drinks. Her *hors d'oeuvres* are little more than butter and dairy bombs residing on pastry dough: various turnovers with Roquefort and other cheeses, Camembert biscuits, and pastry shells filled with a variety of different cream, butter, and cheese combinations. For millions of Americans, Child's book and television show provided their only exposure to French cuisine. By omitting anchovies, she essentially wiped them from the world of French *hors d'oeuvres* in America.

Pizza: pride of place in American cuisine

Of all the contributions that Italian cuisine made to America, nothing comes close to that of pizza. But Italian-style pizza changed as it made its way across the Atlantic. Initially, Italians tried to replicate traditional pizzas from their homeland when they arrived in America, starting as early as the eighteenth century, but they were forced to work with new ingredients and techniques. In southern Italy, for example, *mozzarella fior di latte* was widely used on pizza. This is an extremely creamy cheese with a high water content and a short shelf life. There was not sufficient demand for fresh mozzarella at the turn of the century in America, so pizzas were topped with the more solid cheeses *scamorza* or *caciocavallo*, which came to be known as mozzarella. In Naples, mozzarella cheese would have been added to a pizza so sparingly that it would have looked like white paint drops splattered across a pale red sea. Likewise, in Naples tomato sauce was but a thin veneer spread across the dough. Americans, however, expected generous lashings of sauce and a pool of stretchy cheese, all part of their fantasy of Italian food being superabundant and over the top.

Perhaps the biggest change that pizza underwent in America concerned the toppings, and this had implications for the humble anchovy. Back in Naples, pizzas were usually topped with some greens or perhaps a small piece of cured pork or a salted anchovy. Vegetables were relatively cheap in Naples and could be piled on, but meat and anchovies were far more expensive, so they were added frugally. In New York, pizzas were piled high with meat as it was relatively cheap. Anchovies were affordable too, but they could be rather overwhelming in large quantities. Why buy a pizza with just a few imported anchovies when for the same price you could get one piled high with pepperoni or sausage? Even with the new-style pizza piled high with meats, prior to World War II very few Americans had even heard of it, let alone tried a slice. Still, once Americans finally registered pizza on their culinary radar, they took to it with a vengeance.

Scholars have debated what triggered Americans' sudden infatuation with pizza, but no clear consensus has emerged. One traditional explanation is that returning American troops from Italy brought their appreciation for pizza home with them. But more recent scholarship challenges this, as many profess to never having seen pizza while in Italy, let alone eaten it. Another problem: pizza was not widely available in the north of Italy until the 1960s. One obscure factor that may have indirectly contributed to pizza's acceptance in America was the ethnic food craze that swept through suburbia. Swiss fondue parties and backyard Hawaiian luaus were all the rage, and pizza was yet another "exotic" gastronomic experience. Culinary magazines and newspapers also began touting the fun new "finger food," at the very moment when millions of Americans found themselves singing along to Dean Martin's smash hit "That's Amore," which references a full moon and a "pizza-pie."

Whatever led to Americans embracing pizza, once the entrepreneurial spirit of franchising got in on the act, pizza was launched to worldwide fame. American technology, coupled with Americans' entrepreneurial drive, soon transformed Italy's humble export into a global, multibillion-dollar industry that stretched from the Empire State Building to Tiananmen Square. Incorporating standardized ingredients and cooked in electric ovens, American-style pizza conquered the world. Anchovies, however, were rarely invited to the party.

In 1958, two enterprising non-Italian brothers opened a pizza parlor and named it "Pizza Hut" in Wichita, Kansas. The name was determined by the size of the existing sign that hung in front of their shop: it could only accommodate eight letters. The name was a success, as was their franchising operation. Pizza Huts sprouted up all over the United States, eventually becoming the number-one pizza chain in the country. Over time, Pizza Hut became the world's largest restaurant chain, with over 34,000 locations. A year after Pizza Hut first opened, two more non-Italians, the husband-and-wife team of Mike and Marian Ilitch, opened the first "Little Caesars" restaurant in Garden City, Michigan. Within a few years, Little Caesars could be found in all fifty states, and it is currently the number-three pizza chain in the United States. Less than a year later, in 1960, another pair of non-Italian brothers started "Domino's Pizza" in Ypsilanti, Michigan. Franchising made them world-famous, and after decades of playing catch-up to Pizza Hut, in 2018 Domino's Pizza became the largest pizza chain in the world by sales. These three companies were all started by non-Italians living in the Midwest, far from any Italian American enclaves. Free from historical constraints, they formulated their recipes and ingredients to meet the needs of their standardized operations and the tastes of their Anglo-American customers.

But franchising had major downsides, and by standardizing and substituting ingredients, these major companies changed what pizza was perceived to be. Highly processed ingredients replaced fresh ones, and preservatives, stabilizers, emulsifiers, antioxidants, and sugar were all added to prolong shelf life or sweeten up the sauce. Pizza was piled high with cheap fatty meats, highly processed cheese (and an occasional frozen vegetable) that teenagers and the rest of America could not resist. The owners of the pizza franchises were not overly concerned with the quality of the ingredients used; they wanted to sell a dirt-cheap product full of fats that satiated their customers' cravings and tasted the same every time.

The other feature of franchised pizza that played a major role in its popularity was the speed of its delivery. In fact, speed—not flavor—was often the most important feature for famished kids sitting around messy dorm rooms. The speed of delivery nudged Domino's ahead of its competitors, with the company successfully running a series of promotions which offered your pizza free of charge if it took longer than thirty minutes to deliver. The campaign started in the 1970s and ran for years under the slogan "thirty minutes or less."[25] It was an enormous success, and Domino's market share improved dramatically, closing the gap on the industry leader, Pizza Hut. The promotion only ended when several franchisee drivers got into serious car accidents while trying to stay under the thirty-minute limit.

One thing that has vexed American pizza-eaters for generations is the fact that every pizzeria offers an "anchovy pizza," yet almost no one ever orders one. Americans' lack of interest in anchovy pizza was so pronounced that it even formed part of the storyline of the 1989 Hollywood movie *Loverboy*. Patrick Dempsey stars as a pizza deliveryman who moonlights as a gigolo. Given that no one ever orders an "anchovy pizza," it is used as a code for his sexual services. So why does every pizzeria squander valuable real estate on its menu if no one ever orders an anchovy pizza? The answer, according to journalist Brian Palmer, is simple enough: "They're traditional."[26] It's a way of recognizing that pizzas were historically often topped with anchovies in Naples, giving the establishment the mark of authenticity.

When one considers the poor quality of the anchovies used on pizzas, it is not surprising that no one wanted them. Most pizzerias purchased their anchovies in bulk, with a laser-like focus on price and little concern for quality. This resulted in some of the lowest grade anchovies—hastily cured and packed in cheap oil in Morocco—being served on top of pizzas. All too often, a bulk-sized tin of anchovies would sit in the kitchen for months on end, with many of the fillets becoming exposed to air and dying a slow death by oxidization. These degraded and bitter anchovies were then thrown carelessly onto pizzas, leaving diners with a decidedly unpleasant and bewildering experience.

A new interest in quality ingredients began to take hold in California in the 1960s and 1970s, and this had major implications for pizzas in general and anchovy pizzas in particular. Jeremiah Tower was reputedly one of the first to prepare a "gourmet" pizza in 1974 at a celebratory dinner at Alice Waters' Chez Panisse restaurant in Berkeley, California. Chez Panisse ushered in a new era of restaurant dining (including pizzas) with what became known as "California Cuisine." Waters determined that the key to great food—surprise, surprise—was seeking out the finest ingredients available. While this may seem absurdly obvious nowadays, at the time it helped to differentiate good food from great food. A few years after Tower's auspicious pizza, Waters installed a wood-fired oven in the backyard of Chez Panisse and proceeded to introduce a generation to the joys of gourmet pizza.

Across the bay in San Francisco, Ed LaDou was crafting beautiful wood-fired pizzas at Prego. In 1982, one of his creations (ricotta, pâté, red pepper, and mustard) caught the eye (and tastebuds) of famed chef Wolfgang Puck. Puck lured LaDou to join him in West Hollywood to become the *pizzaiolo* (pizza chef) of his new restaurant, Spago. Together they changed the game in Los Angeles, and their wood-fired pizzas were the talk of the town. One of their signature dishes was a "Smoked salmon pizza" topped with golden caviar, sour cream, and chives. Another version featured smoked salmon with caviar, red onions, and crème fraîche. In one fell swoop, they elevated the lowly pizza to the very highest rungs of gastronomy, and the fine-dining crowd took notice.

So did other restaurateurs. Pizza, regardless of what the big chains kept churning out, could now be fit for a king. "All of a sudden," writes John Mariani, "with the benediction of Alice Waters and the chutzpah of Wolfgang Puck, the food that Italian restaurateurs had thought they had put behind them—pizza— was threatening to come back with a glitzy vengeance."[27]

Artisanal, wood-fired pizzas went on to take the country by storm, and for the first time, anchovy pizzas started to get the respect they deserved. What had once been little more than a nod to tradition, was now enhancing pizzas in bold new ways. By the 1980s, high-quality anchovies were being paired with artichokes, beets, Brussels sprouts, goat cheese, and every other topping imaginable. Jim Lahey's New York City restaurant offered an "Anchovy and zucchini purée pizza" that was dotted with vibrant, orange zucchini blossoms, an instant classic that garnered rave reviews and nods of approval from the culinary *cognoscenti*. Gourmet pizzas had come of age, worthy of the most discriminating palate. At the other end of the market, standardized pizzas churned out by big chains had conquered the fast-food world, enjoyed by millions every day.

Anchovies in America: the time to shine

Sustainability and quality-focused "California cuisine" helped anchovies to proliferate beyond the cupboards and fridges of Italian American home kitchens. This new approach was less rule-bound than traditional French cuisine. A willingness to experiment with new ideas, ingredients, and ways of preparing dishes finally gave anchovies the opportunity to shine.

The 1980s was a watershed decade for anchovies in America, and for the first time they could be found in restaurants from coast to coast. For example, anchovies appeared on the menu of the Gramercy Park Hotel restaurant in New York City in August 1980, as a key ingredient in their coleslaw salad. And in 1984, anchovies, shallots, capers, and sun-dried tomatoes complemented thinly sliced raw beef fillet on the menu of Chez Panisse. Even the seemingly humdrum anchovy pasta received new attention. One of the signature dishes at Vanessa, an upscale Italian eatery on Bleecker Street in New York City, was "Angel hair pasta with walnuts, almonds, olive oil, anchovy, and currants." Writing for *The New York Times*, the influential restaurant critic Mimi Sheraton gave them a coveted two stars and singled out this dish. Anchovy dressings were also making their mark, and at Mr. William Shakespeare's restaurant in 1987, one of the most popular dishes was a "Seafood salad with an anchovy dressing," a seemingly novel dish with deep historical roots.

A wave of new northern Italian restaurants opened in the late 1970s, exploding into fame in the following decades. Tuscan, Bolognese, Piedmontese, Ligurian, and Venetian restaurants (among others) served an entirely different repertoire of dishes from those based on southern traditions, and anchovies often featured on their menus. If the restaurant was from Genoa, you might find fish served with a vegetable and green sauce comprised of parsley, olive oil, capers, pine nuts, garlic, and anchovies. If the restaurant hailed from the Piedmont region, you might start with the always popular "Bagna càuda." If the chef was from Lombardy, you might dine on lasagne prepared with anchovies and aromatics like sage, rosemary, and bay leaves. And if you were dining in a Tuscan-inspired restaurant, some crostini of chicken livers with anchovies, onions, celery, and carrots might be on offer.

As soon as northern Italian restaurants started to garner rave reviews and catch the public's attention, the pendulum swung in the other direction, and by the mid-1980s, a new crop of southern-style Italian restaurants appeared on the scene. They distanced themselves from traditional Italian American, southern-style cooking, featuring recipes such as "Artichokes stuffed with breadcrumbs and anchovies" and "Rice balls stuffed with anchovies" ("Arancini"). Even "Pasta c'anciova e muddica" (a Sicilian-style pasta with anchovy and breadcrumbs) became a hit, despite being nearly impossible to find in the United States just a decade earlier.

John Mariani pinpoints 1984 as a critical year for Italian restaurants in the United States, as they upped their game and started to utilize higher-quality ingredients, resulting in new levels of flavor. Anchovies happily tagged along for the ride. By 1986, Federal Express began direct flights to and from Italy, and for the first time, restaurant owners were able to fast-track imports of high-quality ingredients. It proved to be a game-changer: fresh truffles from Alba in Piedmont, artisanal pasta, Arborio rice, and real Parmigiano Reggiano could be procured within a day. This led to dishes of incredible simplicity but bursting with flavor. Equally important, after decades of buying sub-par Italian olive oil in 1-gallon tin cans, restaurants could now offer genuine extra virgin olive oil of such refined taste that it was served alongside bread at the beginning of a meal.

The rise of Italian restaurants, both northern and southern, coincided with a slow downward spiral for traditional French restaurants. For over 300 years, French food had been considered the very pinnacle of great food. But while high-end French restaurants were still in operation in the 1980s, their days were numbered as they buckled under the burden of their own traditions. According to Professor Paul Freedman, the end of French gastronomic dominance was "as significant in its own way as the fall of the Berlin Wall."[28] Elaborately folded napkins and an array of glassware did not make up for overly heavy sauces served in a stuffy atmosphere. Diners were fed up with imperious maître d's looking down their noses and snubbing anyone less than the old guard or glitterati. Getting shunted off to the back room, known as "Siberia," left many diners with a bad taste in their mouth before their meal had even begun.

While the gastronomic shift from French to Italian cuisine was underway, new voices in Italian American cooking helped to rejuvenate the cookbook world. Marcella Hazan's *The Classic Italian Cook Book* (1973) and her sequel, *More Classic Italian Cooking* (1978), introduced a new generation of Americans to the pleasures of traditional Italian cooking. Anchovies were not accorded any special attention in Hazan's recipes, but they were treated as a staple ingredient that had featured in Italian cooking for hundreds of years. Many of her recipes are practical dishes, and her "Beef patties baked with anchovies" was no doubt a workhorse in many Italian homes. Lidia Bastianich was another successful Italian American chef who parlayed her small Queens restaurant, Buonavia, into an empire. Her "Zucchini sauteed with anchovies" is a marvel of simplicity and flavor.

By the early 2000s, Italian restaurants had become so prevalent in every major American city that Robert Shoffner was prompted to title his dining article for the *Washingtonian*, "The Italians Won!"[29] Mariani goes even further, considering the 1990s to be the era when Italian food rose to global preeminence, even naming his book, *How Italian Food Conquered the World* (2011). Indeed, upscale Italian restaurants—northern, southern, and from the islands to the Alps—have since become ubiquitous around the world. And this has done wonders for anchovies.

The American anchovy fishery: plentiful supply, pitiful demand

The story of the American anchovy fishery largely mirrors that of anchovies in American cuisine, but after the 1950s took a decidedly different turn. At the beginning of the twentieth century, in Monterey Bay, California, vast schools of sardines swam in the nutrient-rich coastal waters. Starting with a single cannery in 1902, the sardine fishery in Monterey Bay developed into the largest fishery in the western hemisphere. It became a gold rush, where fishermen mined productive veins of sardines in what came to be known as the "silver harvest." Billions upon billions of sardines were harvested over the years. Yet what rarely gets mentioned in all the sardine hubbub are anchovies, which swam in the same waters and were equally as abundant.

Frank Booth opened the first sardine cannery in Monterey Bay, but he did not bother with anchovies as there was no market for them. To Booth's dismay, it turned out that Americans were not particularly interested in any kind of canned fish, especially small ones. If they did eat fish from a can, they preferred the imported French brands that carried more cachet. Booth tried to fool his consumers by marketing his sardines as "mackerel," which are larger and more valuable. But even this sleight of hand failed to ignite much interest in his product. Much to Booth's surprise, a more profitable product emerged, one which changed the very nature of the Monterey fishery industry: fish reduction. Fish reduction takes all the leftover scraps from the canning process and utilizes them to make oil, meal for animals, and fertilizer. With demand for fertilizer soaring, whole sardines (and the occasional anchovy that found itself swimming with the wrong crowd) were soon being processed for reduction, rather than human consumption.

The sardine fishery in Monterey Bay created a thriving economy in the first decades of the twentieth century, drawing many Sicilian families to California's central coast. Entire neighborhoods in Monterey changed demographically, and parts of the upper town became known as "Garlic Hill" and "Spaghetti Hill." A few years later, a second cannery opened, and the make-up of the town changed even further, as Portuguese, Spanish, Yugoslavian, Japanese, and Chinese families settled alongside the local Mexicans and Americans.

While demand for canned sardines for human consumption increased dramatically with the advent of World War I (as a convenient way to feed the troops), sales plummeted as soon as the war ended. Reduction of sardines for fertilizer once again became the name of the game, despite many Americans going to bed hungry each night. Yet sardines were increasingly recognized as a resource that was too valuable to be squandered for short-term economic gain through reduction, and the industry was regulated in the early 1920s. Countless loopholes, however, effectively negated the state's good intentions and rampant overfishing continued unabated. Combined with the impact of "regime shifts"—changes in water temperature that favor either sardines or anchovies—sardine stocks became seriously depleted.

Canneries in desperate need of alternative products introduced new lines of canned seafood, including squid, mackerel, and anchovies, despite a history of marketing failures with these fish in the past. Processing lines were re-engineered to accommodate anchovies, and fishermen swapped out their sardine nets for smaller-meshed anchovy nets. Canned anchovies were marketed during this period under several different brand names, such as "New Hope" and "Mesa Del Rey." But as a progress report for the California Department of Fish and Game noted in 1956, they encountered "sales resistance," a technical euphemism meaning Americans just were not buying them.[30]

Although anchovies were subsequently packaged and marketed to emphasize their similarity to sardines, sales remained sluggish. The anchovy label of the "La Sirena" brand of canned anchovies is revealing. For one thing, it associates anchovies with sardines, a common tactic that many canneries adopted in an attempt to sway consumers. In addition, packing them in "tomato sauce" instead of oil gave the impression of something fresh and low fat. It must have been a big selling point, as it is mentioned in three places on the label (Fig. 6.4).

But despite these persistent efforts, anchovies still encountered "sales resistance" in the domestic marketplace. Most sales were shipped to South America (hence the Spanish names "La Sirena" and "Mesa Del Rey") or Asia. By the early 1950s, competition from South African and Japanese processors forced Monterey's cannery row to abandon anchovies for human consumption. Not long after, they were reduced to selling anchovies as pet food, the ultimate indignity for any fish.

The California Department of Fish and Game introduced new legislation in the early 1950s capping the total number of ancho-

Fig. 6.4: Dated to 1947, this anchovy label tried its best to lure Americans towards anchovies. Alas, not even a topless mermaid could convince them to buy a can of them.

vies that could be taken in coastal waters. Additional measures safeguarded young, immature anchovies so that stocks could replenish seasonally. Without a viable local market, and with new catch limits in place, the processing of anchovies in the United States came to an end.

Nowadays, despite the resurgence of interest in anchovies, almost all commercially caught anchovies off the West Coast are used as bait for recreational fishing: only a few fresh-caught anchovies turn up at fishmongers' stalls. And so we have it: anchovies are still out there in coastal waters, schooling in their millions upon millions. With no American processors, however, and lots of international competition, particularly from Morocco, Spain, and Italy, the economics of harvesting simply do not add up.

Anchovies: the fish of the future?

While locally sourced, tinned anchovies failed to take hold in America, imported anchovies have surged in popularity in the last couple of decades. In many respects, the fate of anchovies in America mirrors attitudes towards them in Europe over the last 2,000 years. Loved and cherished by some—especially professional cooks—yet scorned by others, anchovies have fallen in and out of favor with shocking regularity. But the tide may have turned as more consumers and home cooks have come to recognize the incredible flavor-enhancing potential of the humble anchovy. Quite unlike any other fish, anchovies have the uncanny ability to improve the flavor of almost everything they cross paths with.

Looking to perk up a French vinaigrette dressing? Add half an anchovy to the dressing and watch the salad come alive with not a hint of fishiness. And anchovies pair perfectly with vegetables: Lidia Bastianich likes to cut her zucchini match-stick style and then sauté it with a little anchovy, garlic, and chili flakes. In fact, the golden trifecta of anchovy, garlic, and chili flakes improves almost every vegetable, from cauliflower to kale. Nothing in the fridge but leftovers and a forlorn bag of frozen spinach in the freezer? *Voilà!* Anchovies for the save. You now have a delicious side of spinach that elevates the entire meal.

Chicken and anchovies are best of friends and always have been. In the early eighteenth century, Vincent La Chapelle's recipe, "Roasted fowls, with anchovies," used anchovies two ways, first in the sauce, and then as whole fillets draped across the top of the fowl just before serving. Such a dish would have appealed to the eye *and* the palate. *New York Times* writer and cookbook author Melissa Clark simplifies things by sautéing her anchovies with garlic, capers, and chili flakes before adding the chicken to brown it in all the savory goodness. It is a simplified approach to chicken and anchovies in keeping with our contemporary lifestyles, but the bird nonetheless gets magically transformed until it is "impossible to stop eating."[31]

If you are thinking of fish, a few fresh herbs and a couple of anchovies will have you well on your way. Vincenzo Corrado, the eighteenth-century Italian chef, liked to top his fish with chopped onions, garlic, parsley, marjoram, capers, and anchovies, all dressed with a little salt, pepper, oil, and lemon juice. It is still a winner to this day. If basil, mint, and parsley are what you have on hand, why not make a salsa verde with anchovies, a combination that has been complementing fish for the last 500 years? Basil, tarragon, and chives are another good herby topping for fish. While there is a lot of leeway when it comes to the herbs, no matter what, do not forget the anchovy, which unites the herbs and fish in a delectable way.

If the recipes in this book have illustrated one thing, it is that anchovies pair perfectly with meat and ramp up the umami to a whole new level. Quite simply, anchovies make meat meatier, and who can resist that? Precisely for this reason, they are a chef's secret weapon, often surreptitiously added to beef, lamb, or pork.

And do not forget the all-time classic French *hors d'oeuvre* of anchovies on toast to start a meal. While Escoffier liked to fancy his up, a simple piece of crusty bread slathered in butter and topped with anchovies is the perfect appetizer ... a sure thing ... even if the rest of the meal (or your guests) are not!

Regarding which anchovies are best—a not uncommon conversation—anchovy aficionados agree that those from Spain's Cantabrian and Basque coastline are currently the reigning champions. But there are a lot of incredible options on supermarket shelves, and Italian anchovies never fail to impress. As processing anchovies has continued to improve around the world, do not be surprised if your next tasty tin comes from Argentina or Peru. Even Morocco, where anchovies have been known to be packed in sub-par olive oil, has upped its game in recent years, and now produces decent anchovies at an affordable price.

Not only have anchovies been steadily improving in quality, but they are also a nutrient-dense fish that is good for you. Full of heart-healthy omega-3 fatty acids, anchovies can potentially lower the risk of cardiovascular diseases. In addition, they are packed with protein and deliver loads of vitamins and minerals such as calcium, iron, niacin, and vitamin D, all of which are essential for good bone health. Unlike larger, slower-growing, and longer-lived fish that reside higher up the food chain and become repositories for mercury, anchovies are fast-growing, reside at the bottom of the food chain, and are largely free of heavy metals. Eat and enjoy.

If your intake of salt is a concern, give your anchovies a bath. Remove the anchovies from the tin and press dry in a paper towel to remove all the oil. Next, let them soak in warm water or milk for ten to fifteen minutes. Press dry again and repeat the process. While the fillets may lose some of their intoxicating deep red color, the decrease in their salt may be just what the doctor ordered. Thankfully, they will still be as flavorful as ever.

While anchovies are good for you—just watch the sodium in preserved ones—they are also the right fish to eat when sustainably harvested. Most of our oceans are dangerously over-fished (Atlantic salmon, Chilean sea bass, sturgeon, and some types of tuna all hover on the brink of collapse, or have already done so), and this leads many scientists to argue that we need to eat fewer big fish at the top of the food chain and more of the forage fish that occupy the bottom. Eating sustainably caught anchovies may help bring entire pockets of the marine ecosystem back into alignment.

It is how anchovies are harvested to which we must pay attention. Most commercially caught anchovies are purse seined, which involves encircling a school of anchovies with a large net that gets drawn tight at the bottom, trapping the fish within. While purse seining for some species results in large bycatches, anchovies fished in this manner generally have little bycatch and are more sustainable.

The anchovies caught by purse seining in the Bay of Biscay off the Cantabrian coastline currently carry the Marine Conservation

Society's highest rating, "Best choice." These stocks are well managed and sustainably harvested, making them an ideal choice for consumers. But further south off Portugal it is another story, as the status of that anchovy fishery carries the lowest rating, "Avoid." Caution also needs to be exercised when purchasing anchovies that originate in the Mediterranean Sea. Episodes of overfishing have plagued Mediterranean fisheries, but there are some bright spots. Anchovies caught in the Adriatic Sea off Italy are considered sustainably caught and a good choice by the Marine Conservation Society, but all others are currently rated "Avoid."

The depleted state of our fisheries around the world is leading many consumers to exercise the power of the pocketbook and to make more sustainable choices, which bodes well for anchovies as a fish of the future. As we move towards more plant-based diets with less red meat, anchovies will undoubtedly be called upon to do more of the culinary heavy-lifting. Writing his recipes in the nineteenth century, Father Delle Piane clearly understood the value of anchovies as a meat substitute, and they feature as the star attraction in his meat-free cookery book for exactly this reason. Cooked into a dish, the humble anchovy works behind the scenes to tantalize the taste buds without one even realizing it—an especially useful technique for the self-proclaimed anchovy-averse. The next time you are preparing a pot of lentils, follow Father Delle Piane's lead and toss an anchovy or two (or three) into the mix to add some immensely satisfying and guilt-free flavor, without the problematic environmental implications or inflammatory properties of red meat.

In looking to the future, we can draw upon the best of the past. As this tale comes a close, we would therefore be remiss not to pay tribute to one of the greatest anchovy aficionados of all time, Bartolomeo Stefani, the Italian royal cook who in 1662 published his masterpiece, *L'arte di ben cucinare*, in which our small friends play a prominent role. He concluded his work on such an elegant and simple note, that it bears repeating here: "*Vivete felici. Il fine*" (Go well. The End).[32]

NOTES

INTRODUCTION: TANGLED TASTES—DECIPHERING ANCHOVY PREFERENCES

1. An anonymous opinion in the comments section of a discontinued blog.
2. Maria Lucia De Nicolò, *Del mangiar pesce fresco, "salvato", "navigato" nel Mediterraneo: Alimentazione, mercato, pesche ancestrali (secc. XIV–XIX)* (Bologna-Pesaro: Museo della Marineria Washington Patrignani Pesaro, 2019), 127. Available online: https://www.academia.edu/42199641/Del_mangiar_pesce_fresco_salvato_navigato_nel_Mediterraneo_Alimentazione_mercato_pesche_ancestrali_secc_XIV_XIX_
3. Table abridged and adapted from Ole G. Mouritsen and Klavs Styrbæk, *Umami: Unlocking the Secrets of the Fifth Taste* (New York: Columbia University Press, 2014), 229.

1. THE ROMAN AND MEDIEVAL ANCHOVY: FROM SOUGHT-AFTER SAUCES TO A SCARCELY GLIMPSED FISH

1. Sally Grainger, *Cooking Apicius* (Totnes, Devon, UK: Prospect Books, 2006), 27.
2. Maguelonne Toussaint-Samat, *A History of Food*, trans. Anthea Bell (Oxford: Wiley-Blackwell, 2009), 338.
3. Artemidorus Daldianus, *Onirocriticon Libri V*, ed. R. A. Pack (Stuttgart: Teubner, 1963), 1.66. Pliny, *Historia naturalis* 31.93. As cited in Robert I. Curtis, "In Defense of Garum," *The Classical Journal* 78:3 (1983), 232.

4. Seneca, *Ep.* 95.25. As cited in Curtis, "In Defense of Garum," 232.

5. Horace, *Sat.* 2.4.66. As cited in Thomas H. Corcoran, "Roman Fish Sauces," *The Classical Journal* 58:5 (1963), 204.

6. Pliny, *Historia naturalis* 31.93. As cited in Corcoran, "Roman Fish Sauces," 204.

7. Horace, *Sat.* 2.4.66. As cited in Corcoran, "Roman Fish Sauces," 204.

8. Martial, *Epi.* 13.102.

9. Ugo Enrico Paoli, *Rome: Its People, Life and Customs*, trans. R. D. McNaughton (Florence, 1940; rpt. New York: David MacKay, 1963), 91.

10. M. F. K. Fisher, *Serve It Forth* (1937; New York: North Point Press, 2002), 39.

11. Mary Beard, *The Fires of Vesuvius* (Cambridge, MA: Harvard University Press, 2008), 21.

12. Martial, *Epi.* 13.102. As cited in Curtis, "In Defense of Garum," 234.

13. Jake Braun, "Marketing is Not New," Kapok Marketing, September 17, 2018. Available online: https://www.kapokmarketing.com/marketing-is-not-new-lessons-from-the-ancient-roman-city-of-pompeii/

14. Heather Pringle, "Mad Men—Roman Style," *Archaeology*, October 3, 2008. Available online: https://archive.archaeology.org/blog/mad-men-roman-style/

15. Joanne Berry, *The Complete Pompeii* (London: Thames & Hudson, 2014), 226; Mary Beard, *Pompeii: The Life of a Roman Town* (London: Profile Books, 2009), 186.

16. Beard, *Pompeii*, 186.

17. Beard, *Pompeii*, 186.

18. Berry, *The Complete Pompeii*, 228.

19. Berry, *The Complete Pompeii*, 65.

20. Alfredo Carannante, "The Last *Garum* of Pompeii: Archaeozoological Analyses on Fish Remains from the '*Garum* Shop' and Related Ecological Inferences," *International Journal of Osteoarchaeology* 29:3 (2019), 383.

21. Carannante, "The Last *Garum* of Pompeii," 385.

22. Robert I. Curtis, "A Personalized Floor Mosaic from Pompeii," *American Journal of Archaeology* 88:4 (1984), 564.

23. Christopher Grocock and Sally Grainger, *Apicius: A Critical Edition* (Totnes, Devon, UK: Prospect Books, 2006), 209.

24. Florence Dupont, "The Grammar of Roman Dining," in *Food: A Culinary History from Antiquity to the Present*, ed. Jean-Louis Flandrin and Massimo Montanari (New York: Columbia University Press, 2013), 118.

25. Grocock and Grainger, *Apicius*, 382.

26. Beard, *The Fires of Vesuvius*, 154.

27. Curtis, "A Personalized Floor Mosaic from Pompeii," 565.

28. Curtis, "A Personalized Floor Mosaic from Pompeii," 566.

29. Sally Grainger, *The Story of Garum* (Abingdon, Oxon: Routledge, 2021), 223.

30. Grainger, *The Story of Garum*, 224.

31. Petronius, *The Satyricon*, trans. J. P. Sullivan (London: Penguin Books, 1986), 223.

32. Joseph Dommers Vehling, ed. and trans., *Apicius: Cookery and Dining in Imperial Rome* (1936; New York: Dover Publications, 1977), 12.

33. Grocock and Grainger, *Apicius*, 301.

34. Grocock and Grainger, *Apicius*, 165.

35. Alberto Capatti and Massimo Montanari, *Italian Cuisine: A Cultural History*, trans. Aine O'Healy (New York: Columbia University Press, 2003), 88.

36. Alfredo Carannante, Claudio Giardino, and Umberto Savarese, "In Search of Garum: The 'Colatura d'alici' from the Amalfitan Coast (Campania, Italy): An Heir of the Ancient Mediterranean Fermented Fish Sauces," in *Proceedings of the 4th Italian Congress of Ethnoarchaeology, Rome, 17–19 May 2006*, ed. F. Lugli, A. A. Stoppiello, and S. Biagetti (Oxford: BAR International Series S2235, Archaeopress, 2011), 69–79.

37. Benedict of Nursia, "Saint Benedict's Rule," in *Western Asceticism*, ed. Owen Chadwick (Philadelphia: Westminster Press, 1958), 315–23. Cited in Ken Albala, ed., *The Food History Reader* (London: Bloomsbury, 2015), 214–20.

38. Benedict of Nursia, "Saint Benedict's Rule," 315–23. Cited in Albala, ed., *The Food History Reader*, 216, 220.

39. Capatti and Montanari, *Italian Cuisine*, 74.

40. Anthimus, *On the Observance of Foods*, ed. and trans. Mark Grant (Totnes, Devon, UK: Prospect Books, 1996), 47–59. Cited in Albala, ed., *The Food History Reader*, 223.

41. Robert-Henri Bautier and Gillette Labory, eds., *Helgaud de Fleury: Vie de Robert le Pieux: Epitoma vitae regis Rotberti PII* (1041) (Paris: Editions du Centre National de la Recherche Scientifique, 1965), 103.

42. Fulvio Basteris and Aldo Rodino, "Millennia of History," in *Alice o acciuga?*, ed. Irene Rizzoli and trans. Richard Sadleir (Milan: Mondadori Electa S.p.A., 2015), 20.

43. Académie de Mâcon, *Millénaire de Cluny: Congrès d'histoire et d'archéologie tenu à Cluny les 10, 11, 12 septembre 1910* (Mâcon: Protat Frères Imprimeurs, 1910), 273.

44. M. L'Abbé Migne, *Lexicon manuale ad scriptores mediae et infimae Latinitatis* (Paris: J.-P. Migne Editeur, 1858), 129.

45. James Barrett, Alison Locker, and Callum Roberts, "'Dark Age Economics' Revisited: The English Fish Bone Evidence AD 600–1600," *Antiquity* 78:301 (2004), 623.

46. C. Le Cornec, "Les Vertus diététiques attribuées aux poissons de mer," in *Monde Marins de Moyen Âge*, ed. C. Connochie-Bourgne (Aix-en-Provence: Presses Universitaires de Provence, 2006), 281.

47. Rachel Laudan, *Cuisine and Empire: Cooking in World History* (Los Angeles: University of California Press, 2013), 184.

48. Allen J. Grieco, "Food and Social Classes in Late Medieval and Renaissance Italy," in *Food: A Culinary History*, ed. Jean-Louis Flandrin and Massimo Montanari (New York: Columbia University Press, 1999), 305.

2. THE FRENCH ANCHOVY: A GLORIOUS RISE AND SAD DEMISE

1. Terence Scully, ed., *The Viandier of Taillevent: An Edition of All Extant Manuscripts* (Ottowa: University of Ottowa Press, 1988), Google Books version, 260. Retrieved from: https://play.google.com/books/reader?id=a8P7LvJEvUC&hl=de&printsec=frontcover&pg=GBS.PP1

2. Scully, ed., *The Viandier of Taillevent*, Google Books version, 216.

3. Ken Albala, "Introduction," in *A Cultural History of Food in the Renaissance*, ed. Ken Albala (London: Bloomsbury Academic, 2016), 11.

4. D. Eleanor Scully and Terence Scully, *Early French Cookery: Sources, History, Original Recipes, and Modern Adaptations*, with illuminations by J. David Scully (Ann Arbor: University of Michigan Press, 2002), 210.

5. Scully and Scully, *Early French Cookery*, 55.

6. Albala, ed., *The Food History Reader*, 292.

7. Stephen Mennell, *All Manners of Food* (Urbana: University of Illinois Press, 1996), 50.

8. Massimo Montanari, *Medieval Tastes: Food, Cooking, and the Table* (New York: Columbia University Press, 2018), 152.

9. Montanari, *Medieval Tastes*, 152.

10. Fernand Braudel, *La Méditerranée et le monde méditerranéen* (Paris: Armand Colin, 1949), 349.

11. François Rabelais, *Gargantua and Pantagruel*, ed. and trans. with an introduction and notes by M. A. Screech (London: Penguin Books, 2006), Kindle edition: location 3953.

12. Rabelais, *Gargantua and Pantagruel*, Kindle edition: location 4152.

13. Rabelais, *Gargantua and Pantagruel*, Kindle edition: location 15128.

14. Rabelais, *Gargantua and Pantagruel*, Kindle edition: location 15264.

15. Ken Albala and Robin Imhof, "Food," in *The Rabelais Encyclopedia*, ed. Elizabeth Chesney Zegura (Westport, CT: Greenwood Press, 2004), 79–81.

16. Personal communication.

17. Timothy J. Tomasik, "Fishes, Fowl, and *La Fleur de toute cuisine*: Gaster and Gastronomy in Rabelais's *Quart livre*," in *Renaissance Food from Rabelais to Shakespeare: Culinary Readings and Culinary Histories*, ed. J. Fitzpatrick (Abingdon, Oxon: Routledge, 2010), 29.

18. Tomasik, "Fishes, Fowl, and *La Fleur de toute cuisine*," 27.

19. Tomasik, "Fishes, Fowl, and *La Fleur de toute cuisine*," 34.

20. Rachel Laudan, "The Origin of the Modern Western Diet," *Scientific American*, June 2015. Retrieved May 3, 2019.

21. Susan Pinkard, *A Revolution in Taste: The Rise of French Cuisine, 1650–1800* (New York: Cambridge University Press, 2010).

22. Pinkard, *A Revolution in Taste*, 65.

23. Laudan, "The Origin of the Modern Western Diet."

24. Laudan, "The Origin of the Modern Western Diet."

25. Laudan, "The Origin of the Modern Western Diet."

26. Pinkard, *A Revolution in Taste*, 40.

27. François Pierre de La Varenne, *The French Cook* (London: Thomas Dring, 1673), 227.

28. T. Sarah Peterson, *Acquired Taste* (Ithaca, NY: Cornell University Press, 1994), 193.

29. François Massialot, *The Court and Country Cook*, trans. J. K. (London: Printed for A. and J. Churchill and M. Gillyflower, 1702), 193.

30. Vincent La Chapelle, *The Modern Cook*, Vol. I (London: Nicolas Prevost, 1733), 104.

31. La Chapelle, *The Modern Cook*, Vol. I, 82.

32. La Chapelle, *The Modern Cook*, Vol. I, 278.

33. Mennell, *All Manners of Food*, 80.

34. Nicolas de Bonnefons, *Les Délices de la campagne* (Paris: Chez Pierre Des-Hayes, 1654, 1662), 213–14. As cited in Mennell, *All Manners of Food*, 73.

35. Menon, *The Art of Modern Cookery Displayed*, Vol. I (London: R. Davis, 1767), 121.

36. Hans J. Teuteberg, "The Birth of the Modern Consumer Age," in *Food: The History of Taste*, ed. Paul Freedman (London: Thames & Hudson, 2007), 235.

37. Olwen H. Hufton, *The Poor of Eighteenth-Century France, 1750–1789* (Oxford: Oxford University Press, 1974). As cited in Pinkard, *A Revolution in Taste*, 200.

38. Ian Kelly, *Cooking for Kings: The Life of Antonin Carême* (London: Short Books, 2004), 79.

39. Marie-Antoine Carême, *Le Maître d'hôtel français*, 2 vols. (Paris: Firmin Didot, 1822), vol. I, 309. Recipe translated by Pauline Harlay (2020).

40. Sakhi Nair, "Food and International Relations: French Hegemony in Cuisine and Changing Trends," Culinary Institute of America, POLB631, 2012. Written for Culinary Institute of America.

41. Nathan Myhrvold, "The Art in Gastronomy," *Gastronomica: The Journal of Food and Culture* 11:1 (2011), 15.

42. Florence Fabricant, "Celebrating the Ringmaster of the Restaurant Circus," *The New York Times*, February 14, 2007. Available online: https://www.nytimes.com/2007/02/14/dining/14bocu.html

43. Daniel Boulud and Dorie Greenspan, *Daniel Boulud's Café Boulud Cookbook* (New York: Scribner, 1999), 232.

44. Boulud and Greenspan, *Daniel Boulud's Café Boulud Cookbook*, 232.

45. Nathan Myhrvold, "Nouvelle cuisine," in *Encyclopaedia Britannica*, May 3, 2018. Accessed September 1, 2020: https://www.britannica.com/topic/nouvelle-cuisine

46. Amanda Hesser, "A Little Fish, Much Maligned," *The New York Times*, February 18, 2004. Available online: https://www.nytimes.com/2004/02/18/dining/a-little-fish-much-maligned.html

3. THE BRITISH ANCHOVY: CURTAILED BY THE CONVENIENCE OF CONDIMENTS

1. William Shakespeare, *Henry IV, Part 1* (1596). Accessed online: http://shakespeare.mit.edu/1henryiv/full.html

2. Anonymous blog. Retrieved from: https://shakespearesenglish.tumblr.com/post/19719280454/anchovy

3. Thomas Dekker, *The Noble Spanish Soldier* (1622). Accessed online: https://www.gutenberg.org/ebooks/16753

4. Tobias Venner, *Via recta ad vitam longam* (1620). Accessed online: https://digitalcommons.andrews.edu/cgi/viewcontent.cgi?article=1000&context=library-books (1638 edition).

5. Kate Colquhoun, *Taste: The Story of Britain through its Cooking* (London: Bloomsbury, 2007), 175.

6. Samuel Pepys, *The Diary of Samuel Pepys* (London: George Bell & Sons; Cambridge: Deighton Bell & Co., 1893), entry dated October 4, 1660. Accessed online: https://www.pepysDiary.com/diary

7. Pepys, *The Diary of Samuel Pepys*, entry dated April 4, 1663.

8. Pepys, *The Diary of Samuel Pepys*, entry dated January 26, 1660.

9. Pepys, *The Diary of Samuel Pepys*, entry dated January 26, 1660.

10. Attributed to Alice Roosevelt Longworth: https://quoteinvestigator.com/2014/08/09/sit-by-me/

11. Pepys, *The Diary of Samuel Pepys*, entries dated June 6, 1661; July 19, 1660.

12. Pepys, *The Diary of Samuel Pepys*, entry dated August 27, 1660

13. Colquhoun, *Taste*, 170.

14. Hannah Woolley, *The Queen-like Closet; or, Rich Cabinet stored with all manner of rare receipts for preserving, candying and cookery. Very pleasant and beneficial to all ingenious persons of the female sex* (London: Printed for R. Lowndes, 1670). Accessed online at Apple Books, 1670, recipe 133.

15. Woolley, *The Queen-like Closet*, recipe 225.

16. B. E. Gent., *A New Dictionary of the Terms Ancient and Modern of the Canting Crew* (London: Printed for W. Hawes, P. Gilbourne, and W. Davis [circa 1698]). Accessed online: https://archive.org/details/newdictionaryoft00begeuoft/page/n77/mode/2up

17. Charles Lockyer, *An Account of the Trade in India* (London: Samuel Crouch, 1711), preface. Accessed online: https://play.google.com/books/reader?id=CdATAAAAQAAJ&pg=GBS.PA2&hl=en

18. Lockyer, *An Account of the Trade in India*, preface.

19. Eliza Smith, *The Compleat Housewife* (London: J. Pemberton, 1727), 77. Accessed online: https://www.loc.gov/item/48039324/

20. Mary Kettilby, *A Collection of Receipts* (London: W. Parker, 1734), 170. Accessed online: https://openlibrary.org/books/OL20560640M/A_Collection_of_Above_Three_Hundred_Receipts_in_Cookery_Physick_and_

21. Hannah Glasse, *The Art of Cookery Made Plain and Easy* (London: W. Wangford, 1747), i. The 1805 edition accessed online: https://www.loc.gov/item/05005034/

22. Glasse, *The Art of Cookery Made Plain and Easy*, i.

23. Glasse, *The Art of Cookery Made Plain and Easy*, iii.

24. Glasse, *The Art of Cookery Made Plain and Easy*, 9.

25. Clarissa Dickson Wright, *A History of English Food* (London: Arrow Books, 2012), 308.

26. Ann Blencowe, *The Receipt Book of Mrs. Ann Blencowe, A.D. 1694*, introduction by G. Saintsbury (Original collection undated; rpt. London: G. Chapman, 1925).

27. Patrick Lamb, *Royal Cookery, or, The Complete Court-Cook* (London: John Morphew, 1710), 108, Illustration 14. Accessed online: https://www.loc.gov/item/44025907/

28. R. Smith, *Court Cookery, or, The Compleat English Cook* (London: T. Wotton, 1725), preface. Accessed online: https://www.loc.gov/item/44028414/

29. Smith, *Court Cookery*, 4.

30. William Verral, *A Complete System of Cookery* (Lewes: Printed for the Author by Edward Verral and John Rivington, 1759), preface, xxx. Accessed online: https://www.loc.gov/item/73169877/

31. Verral, *A Complete System of Cookery*, 96.

32. Verral, *A Complete System of Cookery*, 219.

33. Verral, *A Complete System of Cookery*, 219.

34. Leonard N. Beck, *Two "Loaf Givers"* (Washington: Library of Congress, 1984), 117.

35. Elizabeth Raffald, *The Experienced English Housekeeper* (Manchester: J. Harrop, 1769), iii. Accessed online: https://catalog.hathitrust.org/Record/009706565

36. Mennell, *All Manners of Food*, 97.

37. Colquhoun, *Taste*, 220.

38. Charlotte Mason, *The Lady's Assistant* (London: J. Walter, 1777), 245. Accessed online: https://archive.org/details/ladysassistantf00masogoog

39. William Kitchiner, *Apicius Redivivus; or, The Cook's Oracle* (London: Samuel Bagster, 1817), preface. Accessed online: https://books.google.ch/books?id=X4gEAAAAYAAJ&printsec=frontcover&source=gbs_ge_summary_r&cad=0#v=onepage&q=On%20peacocks&f=false

40. Kitchiner, *Apicius Redivivus*, recipe 433.

41. Kitchiner, *Apicius Redivivus*, recipe 443.

42. Kitchiner, *Apicius Redivivus*, recipe 573.

43. Kitchiner, *Apicius Redivivus*, recipe 574.

44. William Hogarth, Shop card for Mrs. Holt's Italian Warehouse, Museum of Modern Art, NY. Accession # 59.600.271, Public Domain. Accessed online: https://www.metmuseum.org/art/collection/search/396784

45. David Newton, *Trademarked: A History of Well-known Brands, from*

Aertex to Wright's Coal Tar (Stroud, Glos., UK: Sutton Publishing, 2008), 184.

46. T. A. B. Corley, "The Celebrated Reading Sauce: Charles Cocks and Co. Ltd. 1789–1962," *Berkshire Archaeological Journal* 70 (1979), 101.

47. Adam Edwards, "The Height of Good Paste," *The Telegraph*, December 28, 2000. Accessed online: https://www.telegraph.co.uk/foodanddrink/4811559/The-height-of-good-paste.html

48. Brian Keogh, *The Secret Sauce: A History of Lea & Perrins* (Worcester, UK: Leaper Books, 1997), 28.

49. Keogh, *The Secret Sauce*, 29.

50. Kathryn Hughes, *The Short Life and Long Times of Mrs Beeton* (London: Fourth Estate, 2005), 189.

51. Ameer Kotecha, "The Very British History of HP Sauce," *The Spectator*, June 17, 2021. Accessed online: https://www.spectator.co.uk/article/the-very-british-history-of-hp-sauce

52. Colquhoun, *Taste*, 346.

53. Nigella Lawson, *Cook, Eat, Repeat* (London: Chatto & Windus, 2020), Kindle edition: 9.

54. Lawson, *Cook, Eat, Repeat*, Kindle edition: 14.

55. Lawson, *Cook, Eat, Repeat*, Kindle edition: 26.

56. Glasse, *The Art of Cookery Made Plain and Easy*, 91.

57. Advertisement: The Nation's Pantry. Accessed August 9, 2022 at https://www.alamy.com/stock-photo-bottle-of-anchovy-sauce-54227380.html?imageid=6D293485–0D55–4EE4–856C-D810C333A 430&p=30541&pn=1&searchId=5fc301fc828c3d02f4422f5e80804f4a &searchtype=0

4. THE SPANISH ANCHOVY: FROM NOSES UP TO FORKS DOWN

1. Carolyn Nadeau, *Food Matters: Alonso Quijano's Diet and the Discourse of Food in Early Modern Spain* (Toronto: University of Toronto Press, 2016), 62.

2. Ruperto de Nola, *Libre del coch* (Barcelona, 1520), recipe 219. Accessed online: https://www.florilegium.org/files/FOOD-MEATS/anchovies-msg.html

3. William Stirling, *The Cloister Life of the Emperor Charles the Fifth* (London: John Parker & Sons, 1853), 44.

4. Stirling, *The Cloister Life of the Emperor Charles the Fifth*, 61.

5. Robert Goodwin, *Spain: The Centre of the World, 1519–1682* (London: Bloomsbury, 2016), 123.

6. Lurdes Boix, *L'Alfolí i la Festa de la Sal a l'Escala*, Guies del Patrimoni 3 (L'Escala: Ajuntament de l'Escala, 2007), 189.

7. Francisco de Zamora (1789), referenced in Lurdes Boix, "La salaó de peix a l'antic port de l'Escala, segles XVI al XIX," in Museu d'Arqueologia de Catalunya Empúries, *La salaó de peix a Empúries i a l'Escala* (L'Escala: Ajuntament de l'Escala, 2014), 39.

8. H. D. Miller, "The Pleasures of Consumption," in *Food: The History of Taste*, ed. Freedman, 154.

9. Miller, "The Pleasures of Consumption," 156.

10. Charles Perry, "Through the Ages, a Fried Fish Triathlon," *Los Angeles Times*, October 27, 2004. Available online: https://www.latimes.com/archives/la-xpm-2004-oct-27-fo-fish27-story.html

11. Charles Perry, trans., "Manuscrito anónimo," ed. David Friedman and digitized by Edoardo Mori (2018), 124. Available online: https://www.mori.bz.it/gastronomia/Andalusian%20Cookbook.pdf

12. William H. Prescott, "History of the Reign of Ferdinand and Isabella, the Catholic, Volume II," Biblioteca Virtual Universal (2008), 222. Available online: https://biblioteca.org.ar/libros/167807.pdf

13. Manuel Andrino Hernández, *Victorianos: ¿Denominación jocosa o conventual? Málaga y sus boquerónes* (Madrid: De Buena Tinta, 2013), Kindle edition: location 2119.

14. Dionisio Pérez (Post-Thebussem), *Guía del buen comer español: Inventario y loa de la cocina clásica de España y sus regiones* (Madrid: Sucesores de Rivadeneyra, S.A., 1929), 110.

15. Luis Bellón, et al., *El boquerón y la sardina de Málaga* (1950; Sevilla: Junta de Andalucía. Consejería de Agricultura y Pesca, 2003), 37.

16. Bellón, et al., *El boquerón y la sardina de Málaga*, 109.

17. Juan Altamiras, *Nuevo arte de cocina, sacado de la escuela de la experiencia economica* (Madrid: Antonio Perez de Soto, 1760), 77. Available online at Pennell Collection (Washington: Library of Congress):

https://www.loc.gov/resource/rbc0001.2010pennell15433/?sp=5&st=image. For an English translation of his recipes, and much useful commentary and insight, see Vicky Hayward, *New Art of Cookery, by Juan Altamiras: A Spanish Friar's Kitchen Notebook* (Lanham, MD: Rowman & Littlefield, 2017).

18. Lara Anderson, *Cooking up the Nation: Spanish Culinary Texts and Culinary Nationalization in the Late Nineteenth and Early Twentieth Century* (Woodbridge, Suffolk, UK: Tamesis, 2013), 122, 121.

19. Angel Muro, *El practicón: Tratado completo de cocina* (Madrid: Librería de Miguel Guijarro, 1894), 187.

20. Muro, *El practicón*, 541.

21. María José Sevilla, *Life and Food in the Basque Country* (Lanham, MD: New Amsterdam Books, 1990), 54.

22. Luis Javier Escudero Domínguez, "Italianos en el Cantábrico: Identidades e historia de una migración particular," *Itsas Memoria: Revista de Estudios Marítimos del País Vasco* 7 (2012), 316.

23. Domínguez, "Italianos en el Cantábrico," 320.

24. Domínguez, "Italianos en el Cantábrico," 319.

25. Domínguez, "Italianos en el Cantábrico," 322.

26. Ernesto López Losa, "Escabeche, salazón y conserva: Una primera aproximación a la transformación del pescado en el País Vasco (1795–1975)," in *Las conservas de pescado en el País Vasco: Industria y patrimonio* (San Sebastián: Museo Naval, 1997), 94.

27. Miguel Ángel del Arco Blanco, "Hunger and the Consolidation of the Francoist Regime (1939–1951)," *European History Quarterly* 40:3 (2010), 476.

28. Maria Paz Moreno, "Food Fight: Survival and Ideology in Cookbooks from the Spanish Civil War," in *Food & Communication: Proceedings of the Oxford Symposium on Food & Cooking, 2015*, ed. Mark McWilliams (Oxford: Prospect Books, 2016), 280.

29. Moreno, "Food Fight," 280.

30. Del Arco Blanco, "Hunger and the Consolidation of the Francoist Regime (1939–1951)," 30.

31. Clifford A. Wright, "Tapas." Available online: http://www.cliffordawright.com/cookery

32. Maria Paz Moreno, *Madrid: A Culinary History* (Lanham, MD: Rowman & Littlefield, 2017), Kindle Edition: location 2719.

33. José Sarrau, *Tapas y aperitivos* (Mairena del Aljarafe, Sevilla: Extramuros, 1944), 42.

34. Sarrau, *Tapas y aperitivos*, 8.

35. Sarrau, *Tapas y aperitivos*, 62.

36. Sarrau, *Tapas y aperitivos*, 61.

37. Jessica Jones, "The Real Reason Why Spaniards Eat Late," *BBC Travel*, May 8, 2017. Available online: https://www.bbc.com/travel/article/20170504-the-strange-reason-spaniards-eat-late

38. Editorial: "Por qué en España comemos a las tres y no a la una, como los demás europeos," *El Confidencial*, January 5, 2015. Available online: https://www.elconfidencial.com/alma-corazon-vida/2015–01–05/por-que-en-espana-comemos-a-las-tres_615856/

39. Personal conversation with the author; Santoña, Spain, October 2017.

40. Eric Hobsbawm, "Introduction: Inventing Traditions," in *The Invention of Tradition*, ed. Eric Hobsbawm and Terence Ranger (Cambridge: Cambridge University Press, 2012), 8.

5. THE ITALIAN ANCHOVY: FOREVER A FAVORED, FLAVOR-FUL FISH

1. De Nicolò, *Del mangiar pesce fresco*, 127.

2. Toussaint-Samat, *A History of Food*, 287.

3. Wanessa Asfora Nadler, "Collecting and Interpreting Apicius in Fifteenth-Century Italy," *Food & History* 14:2/3 (2016), 190.

4. James Harvey Robinson, ed. and trans., *Petrarch: The First Modern Scholar and Man of Letters* (New York: G. P. Putnam, 1898), 61.

5. Sally Grainger, "The Myth of *Apicius*," *Gastronomica: The Journal of Food and Culture* 7:2 (2007), 71.

6. Grainger, "The Myth of *Apicius*," 71.

7. Grainger, "The Myth of *Apicius*," 75.

8. Grocock and Grainger, *Apicius*, 368.

9. Damiano Acciarino, "Antiquarian Studies on Ancient Banqueting during the Renaissance: The Role of the Antiquitatum Convivialium Libre

Tres by Johann Wilhelm Stucki (1542–1607)," *Reformation and Renaissance Review* 16:2 (2014), 107.

10. Pinkard, *A Revolution in Taste*, 40.

11. Luigi Ballerini, "Introduction," in *The Art of Cooking: The First Modern Cookery Book, The Eminent Maestro Martino of Como*, ed. Luigi Ballerini, trans. Jeremy Parzen (Berkeley: University of California Press, 2005), 14.

12. Ballerini, "Introduction," 23.

13. Cited in Basteris and Rodino, "Millennia of History," 26.

14. Gillian Riley, *The Oxford Companion to Italian Food* (New York: Oxford University Press, 2007), 325.

15. Montanari, *Medieval Tastes*, 115.

16. Riley, *The Oxford Companion to Italian Food*, 492.

17. Massimo Montanari, *Italian Identity in the Kitchen, or, Food and the Nation* (New York: Columbia University Press, 2013), 21.

18. Fabio Parasecoli, *Al Dente: A History of Food in Italy* (London: Reaktion Books, 2014), 100.

19. Bartolomeo Scappi, *The Opera of Bartolomeo Scappi (1570)*, trans. with commentary by Terence Scully (Toronto: University of Toronto Press, 2011), 517.

20. Scappi, *The Opera*, 351.

21. Scappi, *The Opera*, 353.

22. De Nicolò, *Del mangiar pesce fresco*, 39–46.

23. De Nicolò, *Del mangiar pesce fresco*, 127.

24. De Nicolò, *Del mangiar pesce fresco*, 127.

25. Alessandro Petronio, *Del viver delli romani et di conservar la sanità* (Roma: Appreffo Domenico Bafa, 1592), 192.

26. Ken Albala, *The Banquet* (Chicago: University of Illinois Press, 2007), 11.

27. Capatti and Montanari, *Italian Cuisine*, 112.

28. Antonio Latini, *The Modern Steward, or the Art of Preparing Banquets Well (1692–4)*, ed. and trans. Tommaso Astarita (Leeds: Arc Humanities Press, 2019), 205.

29. Barbara Santich, "A la recherche de la tomate perdue: The First French Tomato Recipe?" *Gastronomica* 2:2 (2002), 69.

30. David Gentilcore, *Pomodoro! A History of the Tomato in Italy* (New York: Columbia University Press, 2010), 61.

31. Giacomo Casanova, *The Story of My Life*, ed. Gilberto Pizzamiglio, trans. from the French by Stephen Sartelli and Sophie Hawkes (London: Penguin Classics, 2005), 212.

32. Casanova, *The Story of My Life*, 217.

33. John Dickie, *Delizia!* (London: Hodder & Stoughton, 2007), 191.

34. Francesco Leonardi, *L'Apicio moderno* (Rome: Giunchi, 1808), 82. Translated by Ilaria Edoardi, personal communication, October 2020.

35. David Gilmour, *The Pursuit of Italy* (London: Penguin Books, 2012), 234.

36. Gilmour, *The Pursuit of Italy*, 202.

37. Gaspare Delle Piane, *Cucina di strettissimo magro* (Genova: Marchese & Campore, 1931), 174.

38. Delle Piane, *Cucina di strettissimo magro*, 92.

39. Karima Moyer-Nocchi, *Chewing the Fat: An Oral History of Italian Foodways from Fascism to Dolce Vita* (Perrysburg, OH: Medea, 2015), xvi.

40. Carol Helstosky, "Recipe for the Nation: Reading Italian History through *La scienza in cucina* and *La cucina futurista*," *Food and Foodways* 11:2/3 (2003), 114.

41. Pellegrino Artusi, *Science in the Kitchen and the Art of Eating Well (1891)*, trans. Murtha Baca and Stephen Sartarelli (Toronto: University of Toronto Press, 2014), x.

42. Artusi, *Science in the Kitchen*, x.

43. Artusi, *Science in the Kitchen*, 117.

44. Artusi, *Science in the Kitchen*, 117.

45. Artusi, *Science in the Kitchen*, 118.

46. Filippo Tommaso Marinetti, *The Futurist Cookbook* (1932), trans. Suzanne Brill (London: Penguin, 1989), 84.

47. Marinetti, *The Futurist Cookbook*, 213.

48. Helstosky, "Recipe for the Nation," 134.

49. Gilmour, *The Pursuit of Italy*, 335.

50. Gentilcore, *Pomodoro!*, 176.

51. Capatti and Montanari, *Italian Cuisine*, 296.

52. Francesco Cipriani, "Temporal Trends in Wine and Food Consumption in Italy," *Contemporary Drug Problems* 34:2 (2007), 235.

53. Kenneth Silverman, *Lightning Man: The Accursed Life of Samuel F. B. Morse* (New York: Alfred A. Knopf, 2003), 102.

54. Capatti and Montanari, *Italian Cuisine*, 27

55. Karima Moyer-Nocchi, "Italians Avoided Pizza for Centuries—Tourism Changed Everything," Food 52, January 11, 2022. Accessed online, January 30, 2022: https://food52.com/blog/26979-neapolitan-pizza-history#:-:text=Pizza-,Italians%20Avoided%20Pizza%20for%20 Centuries%E2%80%94Tourism%20Changed%20Everything,as%20 the%20%E2%80%9Cpizza%20effect.%E2%80%9D

56. Agehananda Bharati, "The Hindu Renaissance and its Apologetic Patterns," *Journal of Asian Studies* 29:2 (1970), 273.

57. Moyer-Nocchi, *Chewing the Fat*, xiv.

58. Katie Parla quoted in https://edition.cnn.com/travel/article/italian-regional-food/index.html

6. THE AMERICAN ANCHOVY: INCHING TOWARDS ACCEPTANCE

1. Library of Congress, "America at the Turn of the Century: A Look at the Historical Context," April 5, 2020. Available online: https://www.loc.gov/collections/early-films-of-new-york-1898-to-1906/articles-and-essays/america-at-the-turn-of-the-century-a-look-at-the-historical-context/

2. Isabel Gordon Curtis, *Mrs. Curtis's Cook Book*, in Sidney Morse and Isabel Gordon Curtis, *Household Discoveries and Mrs. Curtis's Cook Book* (New York: Success Company, 1909).

3. Irma S. Rombauer, *The Joy of Cooking*, adapted for use in England by M. Baron Russell (1931; London: J. M. Dent & Sons, 1957), 27.

4. James Beard, *Hors D'Oeuvre and Canapés: With a Key to the Cocktail Party* (New York: M. Barrows & Co., 1940), 14.

5. Beard, *Hors D'Oeuvre and Canapés*, 19.

6. Earle R. MacAusland, "Introduction: Bon Appétit!" in *The Gourmet Cookbook*, Vol. I (New York: Gourmet, 1950), 8.

7. Emily Green, "The Age of Indulgence Gets its Own Gourmet," *Los Angeles Times*, October 6, 2004. Available online: https://www.latimes.com/archives/la-xpm-2004-oct-06-fo-watch6-story.html

8. Quoted in Dan Charles, "The Making of Meat-Eating America," *NPR*, June 26, 2012. Available online: https://www.npr.org/sections/the-salt/2012/06/26/155720538/the-making-of-meat-eating-america

9. Dan Jurafsky, *The Language of Food* (New York: W. W. Norton, 2014).

10. June Sohn, "History of Pasta and its Influence in the U.S.," blog: CHN/ITAL370W Noodle Narratives, August 10, 2019. Available online: https://scholarblogs.emory.edu/noodlenarratives/2019/08/10/history-of-pasta-and-its-influence-in-the-u-s-june-sohn/

11. Dan Myers, "15 Things You Didn't Know About Caesar Salad," *Daily Meal*, June 27, 2017. Available online: https://www.thedailymeal.com/eat/10-things-you-didn-t-know-about-caesar-americas-favorite-salad

12. John F. Mariani, *How Italian Food Conquered the World* (New York: St. Martin's Griffin, 2011), 51.

13. Quoted in Mariani, *How Italian Food Conquered the World*, 163.

14. Mariani, *How Italian Food Conquered the World*, 104.

15. Hilary Sargent, "Celery and Olives Dominated Thanksgiving for Nearly 100 Years—Until They Didn't," *Boston Globe*, November 24, 2014. Available online: https://www.boston.com/food/food/2014/11/24/celery-and-olives-dominated-thanksgiving-for-nearly-100-yearsuntil-they-didnt

16. Sargent, "Celery and Olives."

17. Jeffrey Miller, "An Ode to Mac and Cheese, the Poster Child for Processed Food," Colorado State University, May 29, 2020. Available online: https://source.colostate.edu/an-ode-to-mac-and-cheese-the-poster-child-for-processed-food/

18. Donna R. Gabaccia, "Food, Recipes, Cookbooks and Italian-American Life," *Italian Americana* 16:1 (1998), 16.

19. López Losa, "Escabeche, salazón y conserva,"

20. Rose L. Sorce, *The Complete Italian Cookbook* (New York: Grosset & Dunlap, 1953), vi.

21. Noël Riley Fitch, "Notre Dame de la Cuisine and the Prince des Gastronomes," *Gastronomica* 5:3 (2005), 73–8.

22. Sheela Prakash, "4 Things We Learned About Butter From Julia Child," *The Kitchn*, March 2016, updated August 27, 2020. Available online: https://www.thekitchn.com/4-things-we-learned-about-butter-from-julia-child-228696

23. López Losa, "Escabeche, salazón y conserva," 121.

24. Jon Tseng, "Fat: by Jennifer McLagan," blog: More Cookbooks Than Sense, November 24, 2012. Available online: http://morecookbooksthansense.blogspot.com/2012/11/fat-by-jennifer-mclagan-fat-of-land.html

25. Matt Blitz, "The Tragic End of the Domino's Noid," *Food & Wine* 2020, updated December 16, 2022. Available online: https://www.foodandwine.com/comfort-food/pizza-calzones/tragic-end-dominos-noid

26. Brian Palmer, "Why do Pizzerias Offer Anchovies? Almost No One Likes Them," *Slate*, March 15, 2012. Available online: https://slate.com/human-interest/2012/03/why-do-pizzerias-offer-anchovies.html

27. Mariani, *How Italian Food Conquered the World*, 172.

28. Paul Freedman, *Ten Restaurants That Changed America* (New York: W. W. Norton & Co., 2018), 409.

29. Robert Shoffner, "The Italians Won!" *Washingtonian*, March 1, 2006. Available online: https://www.washingtonian.com/2006/03/01/the-italians-won/

30. Daniel Miller, "Anchovy," in *California Marine Research, California Cooperative Oceanic Fisheries Investigations, Progress Report, April 1, 1955–June 20, 1956.* Available online: https://calcofi.org/downloads/publications/calcofireports/v05/CalCOFI_Rpt_Vol_05_1956.pdf

31. Melissa Clark, *Dinner: Changing the Game* (New York: Clarkson Potter, 2017), 46.

32. Riley, *The Oxford Companion to Italian Food*, 511.

LIST OF TABLES AND ILLUSTRATIONS

Tables

Illustrations

LIST OF TABLES AND ILLUSTRATIONS

INDEX

INDEX

INDEX

INDEX

INDEX

INDEX

INDEX

INDEX

INDEX

INDEX

INDEX

INDEX

San Francisco, California, 3, 322
San Sebastián, Basque Country, 229
Santoña, Spain, 209, 310
sardinals, 180
sardines, 48–9, 53, 68, 216, 235, 237, 253, 326–8
Sardinia, Kingdom of (1297–1861), 175, 178
Sargent, Hilary, 307
Sarrau, José, 221–4
Satyricon, The (Petronius), 30–31, 36
Sauce Shop, The (Rowlandson), *147*
sauces, 61–2, 63, 65–7, 77–9, 80, 82–3, 84, 92–5, 122*n*
  béchamel sauce, 92–3, 97, 315
  fish sauces, *see* fish sauces
  gravies, 122*n*, 134–5
  Industrial Revolution and, 145–53
  ketchup, 122–30, 138–42, 300–302
  reductions, 92–3, 122*n*, 124, 125, 133
  sorrel sauce, 100–101
'Sausages Affair' (1522), 78
savory taste, *see* umami
Savoy, London, 96
Saxons, 42
Scalco alla moderna, Lo (Latini), 261–4, *263*
*scalco*s, 257–64
Scania, Sweden, 51

Scappi, Bartolomeo, 174, 249–52
Scaurus, Aulus Umbricius, 20–22, 25–32
Science du maître d'hôtel cuisinier, La (Menon), 85
Scienza in cucina, La (Artusi), 201, 274–9, 283
Scott, Robert Falcon, 146
Scully, D. Eleanor, 64
Scully, Terence, 64
sea bass, 26, 197, 253, 332
sea bream, 26, 216
Secret Sauce, The (Keogh), 151
Seneca, 18, 37, 53
Senlis, France, 47
Sephardic Jews, 189
Sergent, 75
Setúbal, Portugal, 15, 245
Sevilla, María José, 203, 204
Seville, Spain, 219
Shake 'n Bake, 307
Shakespeare, William, 110–12, 119
shepherd's pie, 91
Shoffner, Robert, 326
Shouvaloff, Ivan Ivanovic, 268
Sicily, 175, 178, 183, 187, 204, 206, 207, 211, 235, 251, 276
Siena, Italy, 235
silphion, 36–7
Sirena, La, 328, *329*
skipjack tuna, 68
Slow Food movement, 290–91
Smith, Eliza, 87, 125, 126, 130, 162
Smith, Robert, 133–5

375

INDEX